GOOD BUSINESS

GOOD BUSINESS

AN ENTREPRENEUR'S GUIDE TO CREATING A BETTER WORLD

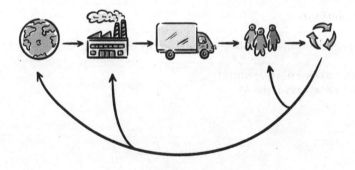

LILLY TENCH

RED ⚡ LIGHTNING BOOKS

This book is a publication of

RED ⚡ LIGHTNING BOOKS

1320 East 10th Street
Bloomington, Indiana 47405 USA

redlightningbooks.com

© 2024 by Lilly Tench

Manufactured in Canada

First Printing 2024

Cataloging information is available from the Library of Congress.

ISBN 978-1-68435-221-0 (paperback)
ISBN 978-1-68435-223-4 (ebook)

To my parents, who taught me to see the world with compassion and a sense of humor

CONTENTS

CONTENTS

GOOD BUSINESS

Introduction

Can business get us out of this mess?

Show up with fierce grace.
—ALABASTER DEPLUME

As a society, we've got a lot going on right now. We're facing a changing climate that is impacting how we grow food and increasing the magnitude and strength of dangerous storms. We're up against staggering inequalities, racial injustice, and global pandemics. This can all feel pretty overwhelming, but it's important to remember that there is hope; human beings are remarkable creatures. We've overcome major obstacles and achieved some incredible goals in our short history. We have created artificial intelligence, we have walked on the moon, we can travel across the earth in *a day*. Humans are powerful. Our innovation, problem-solving, and resourcefulness is powerful. And the world needs that ingenuity.

When we think of innovation, we tend to think of entrepreneurs. Much societal and cultural change has been shaped not by politicians, but by entrepreneurs. From Henry Ford and the car to the sharing economy pioneered by Airbnb and Uber, entrepreneurs have boldly re-envisioned and reshaped the way our society operates. Entrepreneurs are doers *and* dreamers; they see things not as they are, but as they could be. They drive new technological frontiers, create jobs, and reshape the way we meet our basic needs.

Entrepreneurs are arguably the most efficient and creative problem-solvers on earth. Today, it feels like we need problem-solvers more than ever. We already know that entrepreneurs can give us new apps, better headphones, and less smudgy lipstick. But can they help us solve the major problems that face our society? And can they do so with a business solution that also creates jobs?

The Need for Mission and Money

There is a Japanese concept called *ikigai* that basically translates to "purpose in life" or "reason to get up in the morning."[1] Ikigai is defined as the intersection among the following:

- What you're good at
- What you love
- What the world needs
- What you can be paid for

This concept resonates because of its honest depiction of human needs. It acknowledges the necessity of mission and money in the same breath.

Our society has traditionally separated the concepts of mission and profit. The two concepts use different parts of our brain, and it is hard to prioritize them both at the same time. While the two motivations sometimes sync up, they are often contradictory. Because of this uncomfortable contradiction, we tend to put mission and money safely into different compartments in our mind, our lives, and in our society. When we go home, we are generous to our family and friends, and we may even donate to charitable organizations. When we go to work, we often check our morals at the door. But separating the needs for mission and money is dangerous, not just for our own fulfillment and happiness, but for the world. This separation allows us to live a life where we are not our whole selves. It allows us to create businesses and organizations that do not reach their full potential. Finally, it allows the true pains of our society to be sidelined as our energy and innovation are poured into making new consumer goods rather than solving critical problems in the world.

Meanwhile, the critical problems are stacking up. We as a species must find a way to incentivize and focus human ingenuity on solving the core problems facing our society.

Social Entrepreneurship—A Win-Win?

In the last decade, a new mechanism for change has surfaced: the social enterprise. A social enterprise uses a market-driven approach to solve a social or environmental problem.[2] A social entrepreneur is someone who sees a real problem in the world such as poverty, environmental damage, or resource scarcity and introduces a solution that not only helps humanity but also makes a profitable business and creates jobs.

For generations, people have believed that you had to choose between making a good living for yourself and your family and making a difference in the world, but social entrepreneurship tells us otherwise. Since the concept of social entrepreneurship was introduced, our society has latched onto the idea with gusto. There are now at least eighty universities that teach courses on social enterprise and entrepreneurship. There are hundreds of social enterprise accelerators, support associations, summits, and conferences. A recent report by Deloitte described the social enterprise as "a profound shift facing business leaders worldwide."[3]

In theory, social enterprises make a lot of sense. Businesses are founded on discovering a problem and creating an innovative solution—why not focus on the major problems in our world and solve them with a business solution rather than a political or philanthropic one? Social entrepreneurship sounds like a win-win solution, so why aren't all businesses social enterprises? Because the reality of social entrepreneurship is more complicated.

The idea of entrepreneurship is often glorified, but being an entrepreneur is much more challenging. Entrepreneurship is hard, it is lonely, and truthfully, it rarely succeeds. Around the world, over one million new businesses start each year, but only 50 percent survive the first five years of business.[4] If being an entrepreneur is challenging, being a *social* entrepreneur is even more so. On top of all the ordinary challenges of being an entrepreneur, social entrepreneurship comes with its own unique batch of complications. Often, the people who directly benefit from a solution aren't the same ones that are willing and able to pay for the solution. How do you create a business model that serves both groups? Measuring impact is its own can of worms. How do you measure something as nebulous as impact? How do you select which environmental and social metrics are most crucial? How do you capture the important stuff without measuring your mission to death? And finally, what do you do when your impact goals conflict with your other priorities, such as your bottom line?

I wrote this book because I believe in social entrepreneurship. I believe it can deliver effective solutions to many of the most staggering problems our world faces today. But I also believe we need new tools. We can't keep doing business the way we always have and expect different results. We need new business models, new technologies, new strategies for measurement and motivation, and a new brand of leadership. We need bold and creative leaders with strong values who can prioritize both mission and profit within the same model. Are you this kind of leader? Or do you want to work for this kind of leader? If your answer to either of these questions is yes, then this book is for you. This book will introduce tools and models used by successful and innovative social entrepreneurs, with the goal of empowering the next group of leaders who will change how the world thinks about business.

What Makes an Enterprise a Social Enterprise?

So what is the difference between a social enterprise and a regular enterprise? Most businesses are fulfilling some sort of need, or they wouldn't have any customers. Where does a normal business cross the line into becoming a social enterprise?

There are certifications out there, such as B Corp, that label you as a social enterprise to the world. While this might be useful for communicating your impact goals to others, you don't have to have a certification to integrate environmental and social impact into your business model. To me, a social enterprise is defined by three things:

1. Function / Impact: The core function of your business must result in a positive social or environmental impact (even though the term is "social" enterprise, environmental impact counts too—all humans depend on the environment after all!). The "core function" aspect is key: this means that the primary operation of the business must result in positive impact in an ongoing way; a business cannot make a one-time contribution to a social cause and consider itself a social enterprise. However,

if a percentage of the profit from every product sale goes to a social cause, the business could potentially identify as a social enterprise because the impact is tied to the core, ongoing function of the business.

2. Intention: Intention matters, perhaps more than anything else. Is positive impact a fortunate by-product of running a profitable business? Or is it part of the core purpose of running the business in the first place? This may seem unfair—why would it matter if the business means to make a positive impact or not, as long as it does? It does matter, though, because mission and money will not always sync up. There will be forks in the road where a business leader must choose between their mission and short-term profit, and if the intention to better the world through the business is not a priority, mission will not drive the business in a long-term way.

3. Measurement: What a company measures shows what they truly prioritize. A CEO would never tell shareholders that they intend to increase profits by "the amount that feels right" in the next quarter; they measure and project profits to the cent because profit is a priority. Mission will never be held equivalent to profits until it is measured with equal precision. A business must determine which metrics truly matter to their success. For a social enterprise, these metrics must include their mission.

More Good, Not Just Less Bad

A term that has been commonly used to discuss environmental impact for many years is "sustainability." We might even have become so used to this term that we don't think much about the origins of the word and what it actually means. The definition of "sustainable" is "able to be used without being completely used up or destroyed." For our earth and species, this means to keep living without depleting our natural resources so much that our species can no longer endure. While this is important, it's not much in the way of goal-setting. "To sustain" is not the most aspirational choice of words. However, this term and way of thinking have aligned pretty well with how we've thought of environmental impact, particularly in business. The goal has not been to create *no* toxic waste—it's been to create *less* toxic waste. However, if we're really going to improve things, we need to think bigger than this. We must think of social enterprise as a model to create real solutions through business and actually make things better, rather than as a way to run businesses that aren't as bad as they could be. In short, we must strive for more good rather than less bad.

Social or Environmental Impact?

You'll notice that throughout this book I will talk about both social and environmental impact interchangeably. To me, they are the same. Environmental and social impact are inexorably linked. We live on the earth, so far with no alternative, so what happens to the earth happens to us. Toxins in the air mean more health problems, usually for our most vulnerable populations; water shortages and soil depletion mean food shortages for a growing population; rising sea water means thousands of destroyed homes and climate refugees. . . . I could go on, but I won't, because this book is about solutions! The point is that I focus on positive social and environmental impact in this book. I talk primarily about environmental impacts in some sections, and focus mainly on social impacts in others; but to me there is no real difference between the two.

This Is *Not* the Only Book You'll Ever Need to Read

I've seen some book jackets exclaim, "This is the only business book you'll ever need to read." That's not the case here. This is not, in fact, the only book you'll ever need to read. This book is not meant to teach you everything you'll ever need to know about social enterprises. It is meant to help you think strategically about how social and environmental impact fit into your unique business model and value proposition and to give you the tools to take the next steps and find the additional resources you need to implement strategies. It will not, unfortunately, teach you everything you need to know about any one topic, such as sustainable manufacturing. This would need to be a much bigger book for that, and then you wouldn't be able to read it on your commute or carry it in your bag, so really, you should thank me.

How to Use This Book

This book is meant to be an experience, not simply a book you read cover to cover. You *can* read it straight through, of course, but I'd rather you read it in the order and cadence that makes the most sense for you so that you get the advice and experience that is most relevant to your business or idea. If you skipped something that seems interesting, you can always go back and read the sections you missed.

In each section you will find examples of social entrepreneurs and businesses and the ways that they have integrated impact into their business models. To depict the business model of each company in a visual way, I have developed Business Model Maps that depict the various stakeholders and customers, the actions taken by each, and the flow of value, resources, and money. There are many tools to depict a business model. The Business Model Canvas, for instance, is a well known and useful tool that I have used often when working with entrepreneurs. However, what I like about the Business Model Map is that it shows movement throughout a business model and demonstrates, at a glance, the complexity or simplicity with which a business model functions. You will see that some models have money flowing to the business from multiple sources and depend on the involvement of many stakeholders, while others have a much simpler and straightforward model. As you read these examples, consider what these models tell you about the vulnerabilities, logistical complexity, and strengths of each business. See if you can determine opportunities for increasing positive impact or decreasing negative impact that the business has not yet identified or acted upon. Most of all, think about what you can learn from these businesses so that you can contribute to the next wave of social enterprises that will shape the world.

PART 1
Business Models for Social Impact

A few can touch the magic string,
And noisy Fame is proud to win them:—
Alas for those that never sing,
But die with all their music in them!
—OLIVER WENDELL HOLMES, SR.

If social enterprise was easy, everyone would be doing it! As demonstrated through the stories of the social enterprises shared throughout the book, the business model of a social enterprise is not always straightforward. Social enterprise business models may be complex and require more creativity, but that doesn't mean they need to be less profitable. In this section we will explore different business models to support social and environmental impact initiatives. To start off, we will use two tools to help a founder, prospective founder, or business leader think through their business model. First, answer the questions below and then move to the quiz on page 11.

When you are starting a business, there are three basic questions to answer:

1. **What value are you providing?** A business has to create value or there is no point in its existence. The product or service the business provides must either add a gain or help to alleviate a pain.

2. **To whom is the value being provided?** The first question cannot exist without this follow up question. In order for value to be real in a business sense, it must be valued by *someone*. This is where businesses with a social and environmental impact can get a little tricky because the primary value might be to the world at large (especially if we're talking about the environment), so we have to get a little more granular— who cares about that value? This will lead us to question 3.

3. **Who will pay for the value and how?** This part is just as important as the first two questions, but somehow gets forgotten— most likely because it can be a bummer to think about, because often the answer isn't clear. But don't let yourself be discouraged; the point of this book is to allow yourself to think creatively here. A business model does not have to be straightforward to be successful.

In this section, we will explore different ways that money and value can flow within a social enterprise. Take the quiz on page 11 to get you started with thinking through the ways that you can integrate impact into your business model and monetize the value you provide.

Social Impact Business Model Quiz

Take the quiz below to find the social enterprise business model that is the best fit for your business. Flip to the page numbers to learn more about each model

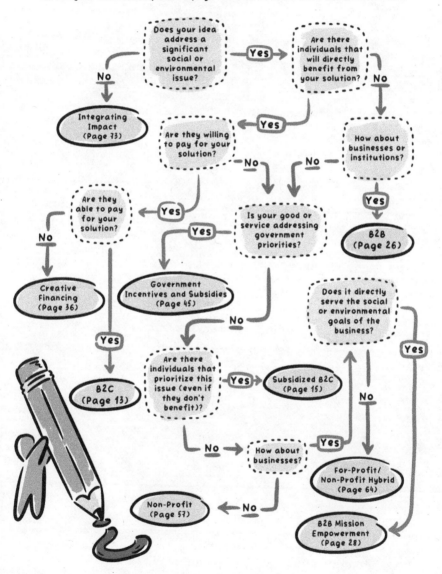

1

Business to Consumer (B2C) Model

Throughout this section, we'll look at a variety of different business models. We'll kick off with the business to consumer (B2C) model, because it is one of the most straightforward. In this model, the company is providing value directly to the customer that is benefiting from the product or service, and in most cases (except for in the subsidized B2C model described below), the customer is also paying the business directly for the value delivered. So how does social impact fit in? In a B2C social enterprise, the business model is generally structured in one of the following five ways:

B2C Model 1: Directly Serving an Essential Need to a Customer

In the simplest form of a B2C social enterprise, the business is able to deliver essential goods or services to a customer base that needs them, at a price the customer can afford, and still make a profit. An "essential" good or service is a subjective term, of course, but in this case, I am referring to B2C companies that provide fresh water, medicine, health care, internet, banking options for remote areas, food, agricultural solutions, renewable energy, and so on.

Some may feel that it is immoral to charge money for essential goods; however, others, such as C. K. Prahalad (discussed further on page 75), believe that businesses should—and even have an obligation to—focus on serving the billions of people living in poverty around the world. By treating this population as customers rather than charity cases, Prahalad argues, businesses are able to provide goods, services, and tools to help lift people out of poverty in the most efficient and sustainable way. The idea of creating sustainable businesses that serve the world's poorest populations also means that businesses' ingenuity and creativity is focused on developing goods and services to serve those most in need rather than trying to create new (often unnecessary) products to tempt the world's richest. This concept is discussed further in the Products and Services chapter.

An example in this category would be the social enterprise arm of Grow Appalachia, an initiative of Berea College in Berea, Kentucky. This organization works to empower sustainable food production and economic development across the central Appalachian region of the United States, one of the poorest regions in the country. The Grow Appalachia social enterprise sells growing supplies such as soil health kits and organic chicken litter fertilizer to farmers, and it will install agricultural infrastructure to improve production and increase efficiency such as high tunnels, rainwater catchment structures, and drip irrigation systems.[1] These goods and services are offered at an affordable price and sold directly to farmers.

B2C Model 2: Empowering an Underserved Population with Business Opportunities

A similar but slightly more complex model involves selling goods or services to underserved communities by means of providing training, supplies, and job opportunities to people in the community. In this model, the business benefits because the social enterprise is provided with better access to their target customer base by selling through people who are known and trusted within the community.

Solar Sister, for example, is a social enterprise that recruits and trains women across Africa to sell solar energy products and clean-burning cookstoves in their communities. The women earn income through selling the products, and the community benefits from access to clean energy solutions.[2]

B2C Model 3: Subsidized B2C
(Mixed Models & One-for-One)

A variation on the two models described above is a subsidized or mixed B2C model. In this business model a good or service is still provided directly to a customer, but the cost of the product may be subsidized by another group such as a foundation, a government entity, or even another group of customers.

- *Pay What You Can* is a model where some customers subsidize others. In this business model, the same good or service is provided to a wide variety of customers; those who are able to pay more do so in order that others, who have fewer resources, are able to pay little or nothing for the same good or service. Cafés are perhaps most known for this model, but other businesses such as medical clinics have utilized it as well.

  This model depends on two elements that are not commonly found in business transactions: generosity and trust. In order for the model to work, one customer segment must be willing to pay more so that others can pay less. Although many nonprofit organizations depend on generosity to operate, the human impulse of generosity is not often factored into business models. This model also depends on a certain amount of trust that people will not take advantage of the system and take goods for free when they have the ability to pay for them. The "pay what you can" model operates with the philosophy that if you expect the best from people, you are likely to get it. Although there are likely some that take advantage of the business model, and there are surely many that are not generous when they could be, the model has been proven to function in many cases, particularly in the food service industry. "Pay what you can" cafés have popped up around the country, often offering a suggested price and allowing people to pay above or below as needed, or to volunteer (by bussing tables, for example) to pay for their meal. Some cafés that practice this model include A Place at the Table in Raleigh, North Carolina, Gather 55 in Hartford, Connecticut, and Soul Kitchen, which operates in three different locations in New Jersey (fun fact: Soul Kitchen was started by Jon Bon Jovi).

• *One-for-One*: The one-for-one model was first pioneered by TOMS founder Blake Mycoskie. For every pair of TOMS shoes sold, a pair of shoes was donated to a person who needs them. When the model first launched, it was greeted with great enthusiasm. People loved the idea that not only were they getting a stylish new pair of shoes, but they were also helping someone in need. This form of giving is much more tangible than financial gifts; the idea of giving a person a pair of shoes is much easier to visualize and wrap your brain around than the idea of donating a percentage of funds toward advocacy or something more abstract. This model was soon replicated by other organizations giving away a wide variety of goods.

The problem with this model is that giving things is a surface-level solution that does not address the root causes of the issues at hand. "Poor people aren't poor because they lack stuff; they're poor because they lack the infrastructure to create wealth," said Michael Matheson Miller, director of PovertyCure.[3] Even worse, the one-for-one donation model can sometimes have the unintended consequence of undermining local economies, thus hurting the very infrastructure that would help create long-term solutions to poverty. TOMS received criticism for putting local shoemakers out of business—why would you buy a pair of shoes when you could get a free pair? TOMS has since adjusted their model, now donating one-third of their profits to charity.

The eyeglasses company Warby Parker has a similar but slightly altered "Buy a Pair, Give a Pair" model. Warby Parker works through partners such as VisionSpring to distribute discounted glasses to communities in need. These partners also train local community members to perform basic eye exams and sell and distribute the glasses. Through this model, Warby Parker captures some of the tangible appeal of the one-for-one model while also helping to stimulate economic opportunities (like B2C Model 2, described in this chapter).[4]

- *Other Subsidized B2C*: There are many other forms that subsidized B2C models can take, depending on your product or
  service and your customer base. Aravind Eye Care System,
  for example, located in India, offers free or reduced-rate eye
  care to 50 percent of its patients, yet it remains financially
  sustainable. The eye care provided to half of its customer base
  helps to subsidize the services for the other half.[5]

B2C Model 4: Enabling a Consumer to Do Something in a Way That Is More Sustainable or Impactful

This model differs from the business structures discussed in this chapter so far because rather than providing an essential good or service to
an underserved population, companies using this model help individuals who have disposable income to improve their own environmental
impact. Like the models described above, this model depends in part
on customers having the drive to improve their environmental impact;
this differs from traditional economic models that assume customers
are motivated by price and quality alone. However, according to a 2021
study, 78 percent of Americans are more likely to purchase a product
that is environmentally friendly, and 64 percent are willing to pay
more for it. Thus, many companies have been able to build successful
businesses by tapping into this market.[6]

A few companies that would fit into this business model category
are KnoxFill (company profile on page 152, and founder interview on
page 266), which provides household products such as shampoos and
cleaners in refillable containers so that consumers do not have to waste
packaging; Green Century Funds, which offers consumers more environmentally friendly investment options; and Dandelion Energy, a
company that installs geothermal heating and cooling in the houses
of customers, allowing them to tap into the heat of the earth to control
the temperature inside their homes.

B2C Model 5: B2C Company that Integrates Impact through Other Means

In B2C model 5, the final B2C model, a company sells products directly to consumers that *do not* necessarily fill an essential need, like

clean water or medicine, and also do not necessarily enable the consumer to improve their personal environmental footprint; however, these products may be particularly attractive to customers because of the companies' social or environmental mission and practices. These B2C companies integrate impact into their business models in ways other than the direct function of their product or service, such as through activism, community engagement, sustainable manufacturing, sourcing, and more. For a full analysis of the different ways a company can integrate impact into their business model, see part 2 of this book.

Some examples of companies in this category are Ben & Jerry's, which builds customer loyalty and engagement through their activism campaigns (company profile on page 218); Greyston Bakery, which uses an "Open Hiring" model to provide jobs and workforce development opportunities to underserved populations (company profile on page 168); and Patagonia, a company known for their sustainable practices as much as for their outdoor wear (company profile on page 190).

Tips for Success

Understand your customer

While knowing your customer is important for all businesses, it is particularly important for a social enterprise operating with a B2C business model. If you're selling to an underserved population (B2C models 1, 2, and 3), and you're not part of that population, you run the risk of misunderstanding the issues they face and the complexities of their circumstances. When this is the case, you run the risk of actually doing more harm than good. If you are attempting to do good in a community that is not your own, take more time than you think you need to understand the community and the potential unintentional impacts your work could have. The best way to make a positive impact in underserved communities is to work closely with local people and organizations that have been involved in that community for a long time and that have local people on their leadership team; or, even better, to hire a person from the community to serve on your leadership team.

Choose your pricing model carefully

Selling to an underserved population (again B2C models 1, 2, and 3) means that you must choose your pricing models very carefully. Pushing for the maximum price someone will pay (the standard pricing strategy) may not be moral when you are selling goods and services that meet essential needs. See chapter 17 for more details and advice on pricing for social enterprises.

Be realistic about your market size

If you are utilizing B2C models 3, 4, or 5, it is likely that part of your business model depends on your customer to be impact conscious, meaning that they will be more interested in your company because of the social and environmental impact you deliver, and may even be willing to pay more for it. While the percentage of people who express concern about environmental and social issues may be huge, keep in mind that there is often a barrier between people's beliefs and their pocketbooks. Just as we have learned to separate our values at home from our values at work, we have also learned to separate our theoretical values from our financial decisions. This means that businesses that depend on impact-conscious customers face an inherent challenge: they must put in extra effort to break down this mental barrier that society has enforced in their customers.

There also tends to be a discrepancy between what people say they will do and what customers actually do. People generally tend to be much more productive, proactive, and altruistic in their imagined behavior than they are in reality. So while people may tell you that they feel strongly about the cause you support, breaking through life's many distractions and the high competition for the customer's dollar to get them to the point where they actually make a purchase is another matter.

This doesn't mean that B2C models 3, 4, and 5, are impossible—quite the opposite. Many successful businesses operate with these exact models. It does mean, however, that businesses operating with these models need to be realistic about their market size and look not just at what customers *say* they will do, but at what they *actually* do. Businesses with these models should generally begin by targeting customers that they already know will pay extra to support their values, which means advertising to people who are already customers of other mission-driven businesses.

Build trust

As I mentioned earlier in this chapter, a 2021 study found that 78 percent of Americans are more likely to purchase a product that is environmentally friendly, and 64 percent are willing to pay more for these products. However, the study goes on to say that 74 percent of respondents don't know how to identify environmentally friendly products; on top of that, 53 percent say they are skeptical about companies' claims of their own environmental benefits.[7] So where does that leave mission-driven B2C companies? Customers want to purchase environmentally friendly products, but they are suspicious of you if you tell them your product is environmentally friendly. After years of widespread greenwashing (businesses that promote false or insincere environmental claims), years of public exposés about greenwashing, and endless streams of information through social media, it is more difficult—but also more important than ever—to build consumer trust. For a B2C social enterprise, the best methods for building customer trust are to:

- *Be transparent*: Tell your own story before someone else does. Be transparent about your achievements, your impact, and the things you're still working on. Both Patagonia and Ben & Jerry's share extensive information about their environmental and social impact practices on their websites. They share the advances they've made right alongside the goals they have not met. Read more about strategies and benefits of business transparency in the Operations chapter on page 187.

- *Make your impact tangible*: If you can let your customer touch and feel the impact of your business, there is less room for doubt about your social and environmental claims. Better yet, allowing customers to experience the positive impact of your business can help break through the wall between values and pocketbooks and make them feel more open to paying for products and services that benefit the earth and society. Customers of KnoxFill (company profile on page 152, and founder interview on page 266), for example, have a hands-on experience with the positive impact of the company because they are involved in returning and refilling bottles and can't help but notice the lack of containers in their recycling and trash bins. Customers of Sealed (company profile on page 41) see and feel the difference of energy saved in their own homes and, of course, take note of the difference on their electric bills.

- *Engage your customer*: If the positive impact of your company isn't tangible (let's face it, sometimes it's just not), you can find other ways to engage customers in your mission. Ben & Jerry's shares petitions on their website and social media around direct actions for causes they are supporting. Equal Exchange (a social enterprise that sells Fair Trade goods) holds monthly member meetings for their "citizen-consumers" to engage in discussions about topics such as food politics and climate justice. They also invite members to engage with their mission through committing to purchasing over one hundred dollars' worth of products per year, participating in their advocacy campaigns, or facilitating the distribution of Equal Exchange products in their community.[8]

- *Speak up:* Speaking out about social and environmental issues that align with the mission of your company can be a great way to make a difference, grab customer attention, build consumer trust, and generate earned media. See the Voice chapter on page 210 for more information on the strategies, benefits, and risks of business activism.

- *Find the right pricing strategy and payment structure*: As with most businesses, figuring out the right pricing strategy is essential. Not only do you have to find the right amount to charge (so that your business can survive and so that your customer will buy), but you also must determine the *way* that your customer wants to pay you. Using the wrong model can kill a customer relationship. Imagine if Zoom tried to charge you for every virtual meeting you hosted rather than using a subscription model, or if you had to purchase every component of your car separately. Check out chapter 17 on pricing for social enterprises.

Company Profile: Kreyòl Essence

Where the company integrates impact

- Material sourcing
- Labor
- Voice

Founders: Yve-Car Momperousse & Stéphane Jean-Baptiste

Yve-Car is a Brooklyn-born Haitian woman who grew up using black castor oil on her hair and skin. One day, when living in Philadelphia, she went to the salon to get her hair straightened, and, after an unfortunate run-in with a too-hot iron, her damaged hair began falling out. She looked for the black castor oil in natural and West Indian stores but couldn't find it anywhere. The idea for Kreyòl Essence was born. Yve-Car officially started the company alongside her business and life partner Stéphane Jean-Baptiste in 2014. The founders are driven not only by the mission of delivering good hair products, but also by the goal of providing sustainable jobs and economic growth to women in Haiti.

What they do

Kreyòl Essence sells natural and ethical beauty products sourced from Haiti. Their signature product is Haitian Black Castor Oil. On the Kreyòl Essence website, the company describes itself as "maniacal about creating sustainable jobs, protecting and conserving the island's environment and empowering women." The company specifically focuses on providing jobs, not handouts. After the 2010 earthquake in Haiti, Yve-Car considered changing her direction and diving into relief work. It was her Haitian mother who urged her to stay her path with natural beauty products, saying, "Now more than ever, our people will need jobs and a way to be self-sufficient. When the donations stop, how will the country survive?"[9] The company gained a boost after appearing on Shark Tank in 2020, and it brought in an estimated $4 million in revenue in 2022.[10] Kreyòl Essence has been featured in *Cosmopolitan*, *Elle*, and *Goop* and counts celebrities such as Cardi B within its fanbase.

Business model

The company was founded in 2014 and initially operated with a B2B model, operating as a bulk supplier to other businesses. In 2016 it pivoted to selling directly to consumers, now operating with a vertically integrated B2C model. The company owns farms in Haiti, directly sourcing their own materials and controlling the impact of their supply chain. They sell directly to their customers through e-commerce as well as distributing through retailers such as Ulta Beauty, Whole Foods, JCPenney, Urban Outfitters, and Sprouts Farmers Market.

In terms of marketing and sales tactics, Kreyòl Beauty knows all the tricks. They offer customized yet scalable customer service through a Hair and Skin Health Quiz on their website and Hair Prescriptions based on your hair type. They incentivize customers to continue purchasing from them through their subscription option and their Kreyòl Essence Tribe Rewards program, and to bring in new customers through the Refer a Friend program. They have a strong brand identity, describing their community as "fun, smart, determined" as well as "globally and socially minded."[11] They also regularly engage their customers through a blog and newsletter with beauty tips and advice.

Kreyòl Essence's unique positioning and strong vision have enabled them to raise funding from a diverse variety of sources ranging from traditional venture capital funding to social-impact–oriented loans to foundation funding. Examples of funders include Shark Tank, RSF Social Finance, and the Clinton Foundation. They selectively partner with nonprofits that embrace their vision of social business over charity and jobs over handouts, such as Hope for Haiti, Complete Caribbean, Yunus Social Business, and Kiva.[12]

Impact

MATERIAL SOURCING

Kreyòl Essence creates beauty products with materials imported from Haiti with a goal of providing sustainable jobs and economic empowerment to Haitian women, and helping Haiti decrease its trade deficit by increasing exports. Kreyòl Essence also has an environmental mission, providing natural and organic products that are plant-based with no parabens, sulfates, or synthetic dyes. Castor plants are generally seen as a sustainable crop because they are resource-efficient, naturally tolerant to pests and droughts, and able to grow in ground that is unsuitable for growing food and other crops.[13]

LABOR

Kreyòl Essence believes that poverty and unemployment lie at the heart of most social issues, and that long-term change will come from jobs, not donations. "Sassy, funny and exuding with confidence, our hard-working and uncompromising Haitian employees and team do not request charity, but rather jobs," the website proudly states. Although economically driven, the company pays their workers above market rate to help them to thrive.[14] The company specifically has a goal of empowering women, whom it describes as the backbone of Haiti, but also as at risk of suffering from high unemployment and gender-based violence. Kreyòl Essence is a woman-led company and to date they have provided jobs for 350 people, 90 percent of whom are women.

VOICE

Kreyòl Essence's message of women's empowerment is ingrained within their marketing, newsletters, and blogs. They have specifically engaged in social campaigns around wellness for women of color. They have also leveraged their position to promote diversity and inclusion through their retail partnerships, particularly through a collaboration with Ulta Beauty.

What I like about it

Kreyòl Essence seamlessly weaves together savvy business strategy with compassion, embodying my personal belief that sustainable business can be more impactful than charity as a way of helping to solve critical social and environmental issues. They are also a good example of a US-based company that integrates international development into their business model in a mindful way, looking to further sustainable economic development and empowerment. Most importantly, their leadership embodies their mission: the company is led by a Haitian woman who personally cares for and has a deep understanding of the complex issues faced by Haitian people.

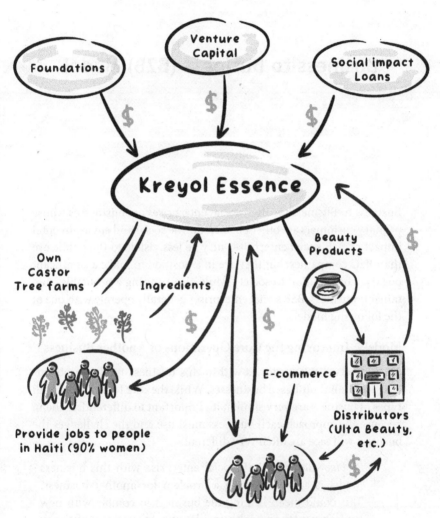

Outside funding to build out supply chain and operations

Foundations

Venture Capital

Social impact Loans

Kreyol Essence

Own Castor Tree farms

Ingredients

Beauty Products

Provide jobs to people in Haiti (90% women)

E-commerce

Distributors (Ulta Beauty, etc.)

Engagement with blogs, beauty quizzes and wellness campaigns for women of color

2

Business to Business (B2B) Model

Business to Business (or B2B) social enterprises are businesses whose primary customers are other businesses. The social and environmental impact of B2B social enterprises may be less visible to the public eye than B2C companies, but they are in a position to make a significant positive contribution to society while also running a profitable, sustainable business. B2B social enterprises generally operate with one of the following models:

Model 1: Improving the Core Operations of Another Business

There are two subcategories within this business model: problem-based and solution-based businesses. While the core functions of both types of business are very similar, it's important to differentiate them, because the approach each business must use and the challenges the business will face are often very different.

- *Problem-Based:* A B2B social enterprise with this business model is actively solving a problem for another business. This could mean helping the business to comply with new environmental or health regulations, to increase efficiency to a level where a process becomes profitable, or to improve their image after a public relations catastrophe. Problem-based B2B social enterprises are offering a solution that helps their customer and is also better for the world. The advantage that businesses operating with this model have is that their customer is *looking* for a solution. Problem-based businesses have to convince their customer that they are better than other solutions out there, but they don't have to convince their customer that they have a problem.

Often, businesses in this category have developed new technologies that allow a company to eliminate toxins in their product or manufacturing process, deal with a problematic waste stream, or improve operational efficiencies enough to make a major profitability difference. The biggest challenges these companies face are getting their customers' attention, convincing their customers that their technology works (because the nature of a new business means that it has generally not been proven on a large scale), and persuading them that it is better than other solutions out there. If the business is based on developing a new technology, this also costs money and takes time, which means that the inventor generally needs to find someone (either a future customer, an investor, or potentially the government) who believes in the potential of the solution enough to make an early investment in it.

An example of a company that operates with this model is Phinite (company profile on page 79 and interview on page 258). Phinite helps farmers deal with large quantities of animal waste that was previously an environmental liability. The new technology that Phinite developed to deal with this waste in a way that was profitable both for the farmer and for Phinite required early investment from venture capitalists, as well as buy-in from farmers who were willing to test the model and technology along with Phinite before it was perfected.

- *Solution-Based:* Companies in this category help other businesses to improve their core operations through improved efficiency, decreasing resource use, reducing toxins, and so on. The difference between solution-based and problem-based B2B companies is that solution-based companies are offering an improvement to their customer's current operations rather than a solution to a burning problem. This doesn't mean that there can't still be successful businesses in this category, but it does mean that they may have more of an uphill battle convincing their customers to make changes to their current operations. Companies in this category may face an added challenge of having to explain a new technology or offering while also convincing the customer they need to solve a problem that the company may not have thought they had.

For companies that operate with a solution-based B2B business model, clearly understanding the needs and priorities of your customer and being able to articulate your value proposition is crucial. Will your solution save the customer money in energy savings? How much? Will it allow them to qualify for new certifications that could give them a competitive edge? Which of their competitors have this certification? How do you know their customers will care about the certification? Solution-based companies must really do their homework before they pitch a customer if they want to get the customer's attention.

Examples of social enterprises with a solution-based B2B structure include Amperon, a data and AI company that provides real-time electricity demand forecasts for energy suppliers and utility companies, allowing them to operate more efficiently and profitably, and Stony Creek Colors (discussed in more detail on page 123), which supplies the first 100 percent plant-based indigo dyes to denim and textile companies.

Model 2: Mission Empowerment

B2Bs that serve the social and environmental missions of other organizations fall into this category. Unlike traditional capitalism, this model depends on other businesses having a mission to do good in the world (rather than solely existing to make a profit). There are two subcategories within this model: (1) Business Empowerment: Social enterprises that serve the business operations of other mission-based organizations, and (2) Impact Empowerment: Social enterprises that specifically serve the Corporate Social Responsibility (CSR) and Environmental, Social, and Governance (ESG) goals of another company (not necessarily a social enterprise).

- *Business Empowerment:* Social enterprises that operate in this category specifically serve other mission-based companies to empower their work and amplify their success. Companies in this category provide tools, services, and connections specifically designed to serve mission-driven initiatives and organizations. An important differentiation from impact empowerment companies is that business empowerment companies support the core operations of another company; they may help other mission-driven companies with services such as accounting, access to funds, graphic design, technological solutions, and so on.

  Examples of companies that use this model include StartSomeGood, a crowdfunding platform for social impact initiatives; Plank, a digital design studio that specifically serves arts and culture and nonprofit organizations; and eCAMION, a company that provides technology, services, and design for electric vehicle charging systems.

- *Impact Empowerment:* Companies in this category help other companies, not necessarily social enterprises, achieve their CSR and ESG goals. It is becoming more and more common for companies (even those that do not consider themselves social enterprises) to set goals around diversity, community impact, decarbonization, waste and water use reduction, and toxin elimination. As consumer demands around CSR increase, many large corporations have begun to voluntarily release public reports detailing the advancements they have made in sustainability and social impact. These companies will often work with other B2B social enterprises to help them achieve these goals.

  Examples of companies in the impact empowerment B2B category would be companies that facilitate and sell carbon credits, such as Nori, which sells carbon credits to businesses like Rarible and Shopify and then pays farmers to adopt environmentally friendly agricultural practices.[1] Companies that purchase these carbon credits can then share that they have offset a portion of their carbon footprint. Another example is

Revivn (company profile on page 205), which allows companies to safely repurpose and refurbish their used electronics rather than sending them to a landfill or unsafe recycling site overseas. Companies in this category may also be consultants like ReadySet, a consulting firm that helps companies with their diversity, equity, and inclusion (DEI) strategies. CariClub offers another variation on this model. The digital platform helps to pair a company's employees with opportunities to serve on associate boards of leading nonprofit organizations to help improve employee satisfaction, fulfillment, and retention.

Model 3: Businesses that Incorporate Impact through Other Means

Finally, there are B2B companies that integrate impact through means other than their core product or service, such as through their hiring strategies, their manufacturing practices, or giving back to their communities. Turn to part 2 on page 73 for strategies and examples of the many ways to integrate impact into a business model. An example of a company in this category would be Sama (described in more detail on page 159), an artificial intelligence company with a job training program to provide employment to young people in Nairobi, Kenya. Interface (company profile on page 93) would also be an example of a company that falls in this category. On the surface, there's nothing particularly inspiring about selling carpet, but Interface has been an innovative pioneer in sustainable design and manufacturing practices.

Tips for Success

There can, of course, be crossover between the models described in this chapter. A B2B social enterprise may be able to help their customer to both advance their CSR goals and save money on their operations simultaneously (this is ideal!). But it's important to know where your business falls on this spectrum of B2B social enterprise models because it will answer some key questions that will help to shape your approach, such as:

- *Are you saving your customer money or costing them money?* Some B2B businesses will provide solutions that show swift monetary returns, such as an energy-saving technology. Others, like implementing an employee volunteer program, may not show instant financial returns, but will enrich the company culture, impact company satisfaction, and improve public image. Knowing the key value you bring to your customer will tell you what approach you should use. Will you be appealing to their desire for more efficient operations, an improved bottom line, or their potential to boost their marketing and employee relations by being seen as a leader on social and environmental change? Knowing what approach you should be taking will also impact whether you should be contacting the HR, Marketing, Operations, or Finance department.

- *Are they seeking a solution? Or is your product a "nice-to-have"?* Spend time talking to your customers and understanding their needs. Remember to quantify what you learn whenever possible. It's not enough to know that your customer cares about improving energy efficiency—find out what percent increase is enough to turn their heads.

- *Selling a vision:* If you are developing a technology product, you most likely face the challenge of having to sell someone on the idea of your technology before you actually have a finished product, so that you can raise money to fund the technology development. This requires passion and vision from the founder and the ability to clearly articulate your value proposition, your technology, and an understanding of your customer and market. Turn to Chapter 20 on page 293 to read more about funding sources.

Company Profile: Re-Nuble

Turn to page 278 to read the founder interview.

Where the company integrates impact

- Product and service
- Material sourcing
- Manufacturing
- Community

Founder: Tinia Pina

Tinia became inspired to go into food production when she was volunteering as an SAT prep teacher in Harlem in 2012. She was struck by all the processed food she saw students eating in school and couldn't help noticing the effects it had on their attention spans and ability to concentrate. This realization made Tinia wonder why processed food was so much more accessible than fresh, healthy food in the first place. It was this exploration that initially led her to indoor agriculture, because indoor produce farms can be more easily located within cities to provide healthy sources of food from inside the city itself.[2] In 2015, Tinia started Re-Nuble. She put $140,000 into the company, maxing out her credit cards and taking out personal loans. After participating in the Food-X accelerator, she began to attract outside venture capital investment that allowed her to scale her business to where it is today.[3]

What they do

Re-Nuble uses a proprietary process to create nutrients and fertilizers for indoor farming (or Controlled Environment Agriculture, also known as CEA) made from recycled food waste. These nutrients serve as replacements for synthetic mineral salts and result in a growing operation that is more environmentally friendly, decreases greenhouse gas emissions, and can even make growing operations more profitable.[4]

Business model

Re-Nuble describes their business model as B2B2C. The New York–based startup collects food waste from wholesale produce distributors, manufacturers, and processors. The company then pasteurizes it, uses a proprietary process to make nutrients water soluble, packages the product, and sells it to indoor farms, which, in turn, sell their produce to consumers. Re-Nuble also offers a closed-loop system that can be installed onsite to allow an indoor farm to recycle its own waste products into plant nutrients. Finally, the company has partnered with the city government in Glens Falls, New York, to create an experimental, indoor micro-farm in an abandoned building downtown to provide greens and produce to restaurants and consumers within walking distance of the facility.

Impact

PRODUCT AND SERVICE

Synthetic fertilizers are skyrocketing in price due to volatile supply chains and depleting natural resources, leaving food producers scrambling to finance their fertilizer needs. However, in addition to being expensive and volatile, synthetic fertilizers can also have a damaging effect on the environment. Meanwhile, cities are paying millions of dollars to dispose of nutrient-dense food waste. In 2012, when Tinia began to envision Re-Nuble, she learned that New York City was paying $77 million to dispose of all the food waste generated in the city. Re-Nuble uses food waste as a source of value and creates products that replace synthetic mineral salts for indoor growers, providing them with more stable, reliable, and sustainable nutrient options for their farms.[5]

While food waste has been composted and used to fertilize traditional, soil-based farms for a long time, using food waste in sterile, controlled environments like indoor hydroponic growing systems has been more of a challenge; this is part of what makes the Re-Nuble solution unique.

MATERIAL SOURCING

Re-Nuble uses my favorite sustainable sourcing strategy—sourcing from waste! Food waste is unfortunately a plentiful resource. In the United States alone, nearly forty million tons of food is thrown away each year (approximately 219 pounds per person!). Food takes up more space in US landfills than anything else; yet, we know that food is full of valuable nutrients that need to be captured in order to fertilize crops and keep feeding our population.[6] A linear waste system will not sustain us in the long run in a world with finite natural resources. That's why companies like Re-Nuble that find innovative ways to capture and recycle nutrients from waste are so essential.

MANUFACTURING

Re-Nuble aims to make zero or minimal carbon footprint products. They are mindful of this goal not just through the sourcing and function of their products, but through the manufacturing process as well.

Tinia estimates that they currently have less than one percent of waste in their manufacturing process that cannot be recycled or reclaimed. The water they use in the creation of their product is all either utilized in the product directly or reincorporated through reverse osmosis. Re-Nuble is currently in the process of conducting a life cycle assessment where they will look beyond their manufacturing process into the emissions generated from the transportation of their raw material, the shipping of their product, and so on, and allow them to continue to refine and improve the full environmental impact of their company.

COMMUNITY

As the number of farms and farmers falls rapidly in the United States, it is important for our future that young people learn about food production and become interested in entering the industry. Meanwhile, we have a growing global population demanding an increasing amount of food production in the face of diminishing natural resources and a changing climate. It is equally important for the next generation to learn about new (and old) agricultural solutions and growing methods that could help us reach a more sustainable future. Re-Nuble plays a part in this journey not only by developing new agricultural solutions, but also by providing mentorship and experiential educational experiences for young people through partnerships with organizations such as Teens for Food Justice and NY Sun Works to help kids to become interested in food and agtech.[7]

What I like about it

I love a business that can create a positive impact at both ends of their business through the materials they are sourcing and the products they are producing. Although agriculture is something we all participate in by eating food, the industry can feel a bit daunting, and many innovators are scared away from pursuing much-needed innovation within those arenas. Tinia is an example of an entrepreneur who was not born into agriculture but was drawn to the cause because of the stark needs she saw to provide people with stable sources of healthy, sustainable food.

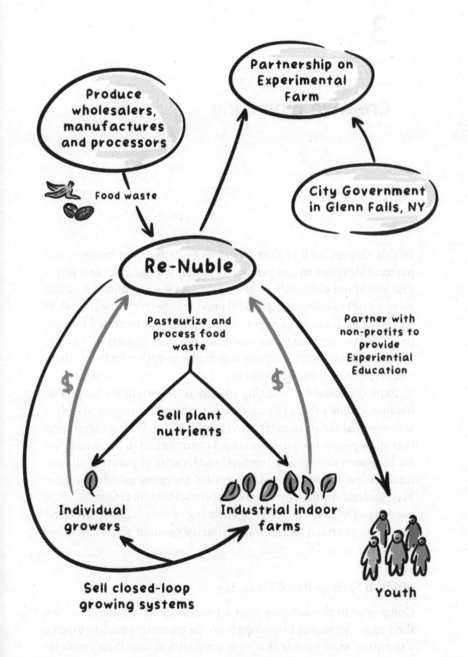

3

Creative Financing

In this chapter, we'll explore strategies to design your business and payment structure so that people can pay for your product or solution that would not ordinarily be able to do so. Often, companies in this category offer a solution that would provide long-term benefits to their customer, such as cost savings or opportunities for increased income, but if the targeted customer base does not have disposable income, investing in long-term solutions may not be an option for them. That's where creative financing comes in.

Exploring creative financing models is important for businesses because it allows them to access an entirely new customer base. It is also essential for sustainable poverty alleviation. Without structures that allow people from disadvantaged communities to think and plan for long-term savings and improvements, cycles of poverty will continue. Below I have outlined six creative financing models that have been successfully used by social enterprises. Please note that this list is not exhaustive; there are existing financing models not listed here, and there is ample room for innovation and the creation of new financing structures.

Model 1: Savings-Based Financing

Companies in this category offer a product or service that will save their customer money in the long term. To utilize this model properly, a company must be *sure* that their product will save their customer money; a business cannot operate with this model if savings is just a possibility and not a certainty. Instead of requiring that the customer pay the full amount of the product or service outright, the business receives their payment over time through the savings gained by the customer. This eliminates the barrier of up-front costs for the customer and also eliminates the risk for the customer—if they do not save money, they will not be charged.

A company that successfully utilizes this model is Sealed, a New York-based company that offers home improvements that allow homeowners to save money on their energy bills (company profile on page 41). Sealed works through vetted contractors to provide services such as heat pump installation, weatherization (adding insulation, sealing windows and cracks around the house, etc.), and smart thermostat and LED light installation. Sealed covers up to one hundred percent of the up-front costs and enters into a payment plan with customers that charges them based on the savings on their actual energy bill—if they do not save money on their energy bill in a particular month, Sealed does not get paid that month.

The Sealed business structure successfully makes energy-efficient home investments accessible to people who may not ordinarily be able to afford them. From a business perspective, the Sealed business model is strong, but it requires upfront capital from outside sources to help with cash flow because customers repay the cost of the services they receive over time.

Model 2: Revenue-Based Financing

Revenue-based financing is a similar model to the savings-based financing, but instead of being repaid through the savings your customer achieves, you are repaid through a percentage of the additional revenue your customer receives as a result of your product or service. This structure is most commonly utilized by investors that are investing money in an enterprise, allowing the company to purchase necessary equipment or make hires that would enable them to scale their revenue. Rather than requiring the customer to leverage assets to receive a loan, as in traditional debt financing, or providing money in exchange for an ownership stake in the company, as in traditional venture capital financing, revenue-based financing means that the investor gets a percentage of the company's revenue moving forward. This structure is used as a financing vehicle championed by companies such as Lighter Capital as well as social enterprise accelerators such as Flywheel in Cincinnati, Ohio. However, it could theoretically be utilized by other B2B businesses that enable revenue growth of another business, or by B2C companies that provide education and job training programs that allow individuals to access a higher-paying salary.

Model 3: Payment Plan

This one may seem obvious since payment plans are offered on everything from cars to furniture, but it's worth mentioning here because companies that are willing to wait for their cash and receive small payments over time, rather than the full payment up front can access a whole new customer base. Payment plans can allow low-income customers to budget for larger investments that might otherwise be out of reach for them. As with most payment models, it should be noted that payment plans can also be used as a predatory financing strategy, encouraging people to make purchases that they cannot afford. However, many other businesses use payment plans with good intentions. ÉCHALE, for example, is a social enterprise based in Mexico City that promotes home ownership through a combination of affordable housing and accessible payment plans (profile on page 66).[1] Airfordable is a tech company that aims to make travel accessible to everyone by offering payment plans for airline tickets. The company was founded by a woman named Ama Mafro who was inspired by her own difficulties trying to travel as a college student to Ghana to see her family.

Model 4: Shared Infrastructure / Timeshare Model

Although "social impact" is likely not what leaps to your mind when you hear the word "timeshare," a similar model can be utilized effectively by social enterprises for positive community impact. While an investment in equipment, infrastructure, or facilities may be out of reach for one individual, family, or business, if there are many families, individuals, or businesses that could benefit from the same thing, a business can provide an impact and make a profit by providing a resource that can be shared between many. An example of this is the social enterprise Real Good Kitchen in Knoxville, Tennessee. The business provides shared commercial kitchen space and facilities for early-stage food entrepreneurs. Many types of food are required to be prepared in a commercial facility with the proper permits; this is a limiting factor for many food entrepreneurs who cannot afford access to such facilities or to the equipment to make, scale, and package food to sell commercially. However, at Real Good Kitchen, entrepreneurs can buy a membership to access shared facilities and have the opportunity to network and collaborate with other food entrepreneurs. This model can be used for other shared resources that are out of reach financially for individuals, yet valuable for a large enough group of people.

Model 5: Subsidized Financing

A subsidized financing model can be used in a situation where a customer finds value in a product or service but is simply not able to pay a high enough price to make providing the good or service financially viable for a business. In this case, the social enterprise can seek supplemental funding to offset or subsidize the cost to the consumer from outside sources, such as the government (see chap. 4), foundations (see chap. 5), or even another customer base (see subsidized B2C on page 15).

A business may choose to subsidize prices only for a subset of their customers. For example, many arts and culture organizations invite local community members to attend events for a free or discounted price but charge tourists and out-of-town guests the full admission price. A B2B company may offer discounted prices to small businesses, nonprofits, or educational organizations, whereas a B2C company may offer more affordable pricing to people under a certain income bracket.

Model 6: Supported Financing

This model is similar to the subsidized model, except that, instead of the social enterprise acquiring outside funding to bring the price down for the customer, the business charges the full price, but helps the *customer* to access outside funds to help them pay.

Community Development Partners, a for-profit company based in Nashville, Tennessee, is a good example of this model. Community Development Partners provides urban planning and project management services for community development projects in rural areas.

They also offer a third, very important service to their customers: grant writing. This means that the company is able to offer a full suite of community development services to small towns and municipalities that might not otherwise be able to afford them. Community Development Partners helps their customers plan and obtain funding for the project (and also to pay Community Development Partners), and then helps manage and implement the project. Utilizing this model, Community Development Partners has worked with communities to implement greenways, parks, infrastructure, and economic development plans.[2]

Tips for Success

Keep an open mind

We are taught that business works a certain way and, because of this, we sometimes forget that we're allowed to think creatively about it. In truth, the payment structure of your business is as much of an opportunity for creativity as any other aspect. Financial structures are mechanisms for exchanging one form of value for another form of value and moving value from one place to another. The way the value is exchanged is up to you. Allow yourself to think creatively and build upon the models described in this chapter.

Identify and articulate your value proposition for all parties

If you have multiple customer bases or multiple key stakeholders within your business (for example, your end customer and a foundation that subsidizes the cost of your product), these stakeholders will have different interests and needs. Your business must clearly define the value proposition it offers to each customer and stakeholder and be sure that your business continues to communicate, measure, and deliver this value. No one said social enterprise was easy!

Finding funding for your business

If you came to this chapter thinking you were going to learn about creative ways to *obtain* startup funding for your business, don't worry, you're still reading the right book! Turn to the Opportunities chapter on page 293.

Company Profile: Sealed

Where the company integrates impact

- Product and services

Founder: Lauren Salz and Andy Frank

Lauren Salz joined Andy Frank as a co-founder of Sealed when she was in her twenties, after working as an investment analyst at Mc-Kinsey & Company. Lauren was raised by a frugal immigrant family that taught her to hate wastefulness. This influenced her desire to join Andy and start Sealed. The two founders came together with a mission to make electrification and efficiency easier for all homeowners to access. Andy was experienced in the energy industry and had previously started a software company for utility companies. The two founders met on AngelList. Andy serves as president of the company and Lauren as CEO.[3]

What they do

Sealed provides electrification and energy efficiency retrofits to homeowners, allowing customers to finance these retrofits through future energy savings. The company works with contractors to assess a home's potential for energy saving upgrades such as heat pump installation, air sealing, insulating, and installing the latest in cooling and heating technology. If it is determined that retrofits could make a significant difference on the homeowner's energy bill, Sealed works with contractors to make the retrofits, charging the homeowner no money up front.

Sealed uses an artificial intelligence technology to create an "energy profile" for a home, taking into account the time of year, house structure, and how many people live there. They then use this profile to assess the customer's previous energy bills and compare past bills to the current energy bills after the retrofit. Sealed charges customers only when the customer has experienced savings on their energy bill that month. So if the customer did not save money, they are not charged. This means that Sealed takes on both the risk and up-front costs of electrification, energy efficiency, and home comfort retrofits for customers, making these services accessible to a broader customer base.

Business model

Sealed operates with a savings-based B2C model. Sealed originally used a B2B model, working directly with utility companies, but pivoted to B2C when a key partnership was delayed, threatening their revenue plan and outside investment partnerships. Now Sealed sells directly to individual homeowners, making revenue from the money that customers save from their services, with contracts that last up to twenty years. Sealed is able to take on up-front costs for retrofits in exchange for the promise of future cash flows through backing from the New York Green Bank and an energy savings insurance policy from Munich RE. Sealed also partners with utility companies to bring their services to homeowners.

Impact

PRODUCT AND SERVICES

The positive impact of Sealed is two-fold:

1. Environmental: Sealed's services and innovative financing model accelerate the transition to more energy-efficient homes. According to a study by the Sierra Club, transitioning from a gas furnace and water heater to an electric heat pump will reduce heating and cooling emissions on the average house by over 45 percent over the next ten years.[4]

2. Accessibility: Building electrification and weatherization is one of those wonderful things that makes sense both financially and environmentally. In addition to decreasing household climate emissions, home energy efficiency retrofits save homeowners money on electricity bills in the long term, while also improving comfort and air quality in the home. The only problem is that home retrofits usually require a large amount of cash up front in order to benefit from future savings down the road. Like many investments for the future, this requirement of up-front cash automatically makes home retrofits inaccessible to a large percentage of the population. The Sealed model helps to solve this problem by allowing homeowners to finance retrofits through their future energy savings rather than through up-front cash.

This means that a new segment of the population is provided the opportunity to invest in their future and their assets, while also taking actions that improve their environmental impact—an option that is usually reserved only for those with substantial disposable income.

What I like about it

The savings-based financing model of Sealed closes a gap between those that can access clean energy retrofits for their homes and those that cannot, effectively using a for-profit business model to expand the group of homeowners that are able to invest in their own futures and the future of the planet. The innovative financing model can also be used as inspiration for other businesses that enable investments for the future.

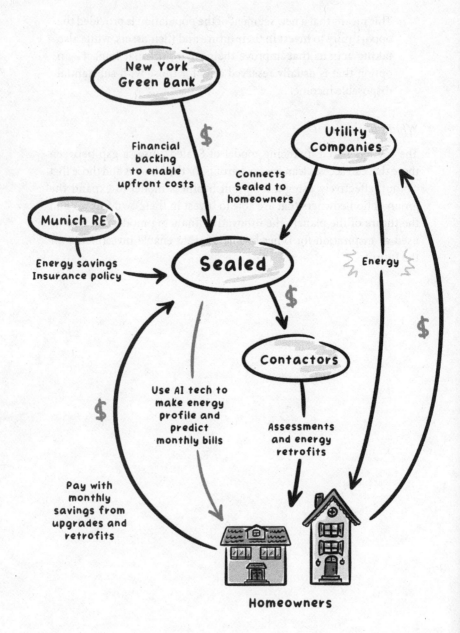

New York Green Bank

Utility Companies

Financial backing to enable upfront costs

Connects Sealed to homeowners

$

Munich RE

Energy savings Insurance policy

Sealed

$

Energy

Contactors

Use AI tech to make energy profile and predict monthly bills

Assessments and energy retrofits

$

Pay with monthly savings from upgrades and retrofits

$

Homeowners

4

Government

You knew this one was coming ... there is another very large potential source for funding and revenue for social and environmental causes. You guessed it—it's the government! Most of us have a general sense that there is a lot of funding available through our government, possibly funding that is set aside for goals that align with the work you are doing. However, knowing how to navigate and access this funding is another story. Government resources can feel very opaque and difficult to access, and it is often hard to understand how to integrate funding from the government into your business model.

Unfortunately, government funding feels opaque for a reason—it *can* be very difficult to navigate! There's also no one right answer that will work for every business. However, I am going to walk through seven primary ways that businesses integrate government funding into their business models (but as always, feel free to mix and match!):

Model 1: Government as a Customer

The first model is to actually sell to the government as your customer. This means that you are providing a product or service that the government would like to purchase and use. There are different levels and branches of government, and selling to each level and division works differently.

Selling to local city and state governments is generally an easier first step than going right for a federal agency such as the Department of Agriculture or Department of Education. There is often a preference from local governments to keep tax dollars local and purchase from local businesses when possible. Community Development Partners, described in the previous chapter on page 39, is an example of a company in this category. They offer urban planning, grant writing, and project management services to city governments for community development projects.

If you are eventually looking for a federal contract, the US General Services Administration (GSA) offers resources and guidance for selling to federal agencies, including how to register and search for contract opportunities on SAM.gov and take advantage of special opportunities for small and disadvantaged businesses coordinated through the Office of Small and Disadvantaged Business Utilization, and government efforts to support goods manufactured in the United States through the Made in America program.[1] Generally, if a business wants to take this route, they should be fairly established; they should have been in business for at least two years and be financially stable.

If the product is an early-stage technology that the government is interested in, this model can also be mixed with the Government Kickstart Model described in more detail below, in which the government will provide funding to support the development of an early-stage technology with the hope that they will eventually be able to purchase and use it. An example of a company in this category is Cosmic Eats, a North Carolina-based startup focused on providing closed-loop food supply chains in remote areas. The invention began in response to a challenge from NASA about how to provide nutrition to astronauts in space. After the startup won the NASA challenge, they were approached by a representative from a government agency, the Defense Advanced Research Projects Agency (DARPA) inviting them to apply for a Small Business Innovation Research (SBIR) grant, which they were eventually awarded, to support the initial research necessary to make their invention a reality. It's important to note that although the Cosmic Eats story is a good example of alternate ways to get your foot in the door with the government, stories like this are definitely the exception, not the rule.

Model 2: Government Supported

Government Supported business models are similar to Government as a Customer, but instead of selling directly to the government, a

Government Supported business model is dependent in part on money from the government that flows to other sources. TruePani is a good example of a company in this category (profile on page 53). TruePani is an interdisciplinary team of engineers and consultants that specialize in water quality and cleantech solutions. Among other services, the TruePani team has tested for lead in drinking water in over 2,500 schools and childcare facilities, funded at least in part through the Environmental Protection Agency (EPA) via the Water Infrastructure Improvements for the Nation (WIIN) Act, which provides funding to states, territories, and tribes to assist with drinking water testing, infrastructure improvement, and accessibility, and includes a voluntary testing program for schools and childcare facilities.[2]

Government-Supported businesses depend, at least in part, on government funding to support their business model. Like Government as a Customer models, businesses in this category also have to stay on top of the fluctuating funding opportunities available through the government. However, the Government Supported strategy is not to apply directly to government contracts, but to know who has received government funding as a means of anticipating who will soon be looking to purchase the product or services you offer and who will have money to spend.

Model 3: Regulation Driven

Businesses that operate with a Regulation Driven model look for new business opportunities that arise as a result of new government regulations. These opportunities can take one of two forms: 1) helping businesses to comply with new regulations, or 2) reacting to shifted regulations that make room for new business opportunities.

An example of a business that helps other businesses to comply with regulations is the Cotocon Group, based in New York City. The Cotocon Group is an engineering firm that works with real estate owners as well as building managers and developers to increase energy-efficiency initiatives and comply with regulations, such as Local Law 87. Local Law 87 mandates that New York City buildings larger than fifty thousand feet conduct energy audits every ten years and make necessary adjustments and repairs to existing building infrastructure such as HVAC systems. Businesses like the Cotocon Group recognize this law as a business opportunity, knowing that every ten years a set of buildings will be seeking firms to conduct energy audits in order to comply with this regulation.[3]

Shifts in regulation can also open up new business opportunities. For example, policies such as "net metering" that put a value on excess energy generated from solar panels have led to new opportunities for businesses such as WeSolar (company profile on page 81 and founder interview on page 249), a business based in Baltimore that enables customers to purchase solar energy generated from solar arrays that are not located on their own roofs.[4]

Model 4: Government Kickstart

A company that takes advantage of the Government Kickstart model is likely a technology-based startup that requires substantial research, development, and testing before it is close to having a product it can sell to customers. Government agencies offer grants to support companies through this research and development stage called Small Business Innovation Research (SBIR) or Small Business Technology Transfer (STTR) grants.[5] These grants are issued to provide funding for a particular scope of work to complete technical objectives or testing. Different government agencies provide unique grant opportunities, generally seeking solutions for problems the agency would like to solve. US agencies such as the Department of Agriculture, the Department of Energy, the Department of Defense, and the Department of Health and Human Services offer these grant opportunities around specific solicitations. The National Science Foundation accepts submissions on any topic as long as the proposed project is technologically innovative, has commercial potential, and will have a positive impact on society.[6]

SBIR and STTR grants can provide critical and non-dilutive funding that enables startups to get past technical hurdles. These government grants can provide an essential kickstart to a company when they are at too early a stage to receive money from traditional investors such as angel investors, banks, or venture capital investors.

Model 5: Government Boost

Like the Government Kickstart, companies that take advantage of the "Government Boost" must utilize another business model as well (such as B2C or B2B), because receiving a "boost" or "kickstart" through the government can be of great benefit but is not, on its own, a viable business model. I am using "Government Boost" here to describe companies that take advantage of grants and loans from the government to purchase new equipment, install new technology, or implement other "boosts" that will help take their business to the next step. For example, the Value-Added Producer Grant, offered through the US Department of Agriculture, provides funding to help farmers generate new products that could add value to their farming enterprise through purchasing processing equipment and expanding marketing.[7] Serenity Acres Farm, a goat dairy located in Pinetta, Florida, used the Value-Added Producer Grant to design and brand products such as its goat milk soap.[8] See more examples of opportunities in this category in the Opportunities chapter on page 293.

Model 6: Government Subsidies and Incentives

One role the government plays in steering economic activity is to provide subsidies. This means that the government agrees to offset the market price of certain goods or services in industries they would like to support and see growth in, such as the energy and agriculture sectors. The goal of government subsidies is generally to support economic growth and stimulate demand until the industry is strong enough to stand on its own. While there is much controversy around whether or not government subsidies are the right way to stimulate economic activity, there is no denying that many businesses use government subsidies to support business models that may not be viable otherwise.

For example, the state of California has introduced a number of incentives to support the electric vehicle industry, including rebates to consumers who purchase electric cars as well as grants and low-cost leasing options. There are also federal tax credits available to those who install electric vehicle fueling infrastructure.[9] These government programs have helped to stoke the flames on electric vehicle production and purchasing. The incentive programs have helped to increase consumer demand for electric vehicles which in turn has caused major car manufacturers from Ford to BMW, as well as startups such as Canoo and ChargePoint, to jump into the electric vehicle fray.

The question to consider with a business model based on government incentives is whether or not the incentives will help support the industry in the long term. In other words, what will happen to the industry when the incentives go away? Will consumer demand decrease as well? Or will the industry have increased to a significant enough scale that the price will remain low without the incentives? Will the products have become sufficiently integrated into society that consumers will continue to purchase them even if the prices increase? Economists can help make bets on the answers to these questions, but often, only time will tell. This means that basing a long-term business strategy on government incentives can be a gamble.

Model 7: Public-Private Partnership

Finally, there are public-private partnership models, which are a collaboration between private, for-profit businesses and a government agency. These initiatives are often large-scale projects that offer some public benefit as well as economic benefits such as tax or operating revenue for the for-profit entity. When these initiatives work well, they can benefit from the perks of both private and public backing, but they can also receive criticism for blurring the line between public and private and using tax dollars for private gain.[10] However, these partnerships often enable capital-intensive projects (meaning that they require a lot of money and/ or infrastructure up front) that may not otherwise be possible.

Newlab, a collaborative workspace for deep tech startups located in the Brooklyn Navy Yard in Brooklyn, New York, is an example of a public-private partnership. Newlab is a for-profit entity that provides space and access to equipment to help technology startups to grow, resulting in economic benefit for the city. However, the rehabilitation of a former ship building facility into a collaborative workspace and shared labs for startups required partnering with city and state governments and would not have been possible without public investment.[11]

In ideal circumstances, public-private partnerships enable initiatives that benefit the public and are economically sustainable but require partnerships between public and private entities in order to get off the ground.

Tips for Success

Know your market

As with any business engagement, take the time to know your market and research your stakeholders and customers. If you are hoping to sell to or partner with a government agency, find out what agencies are spending money on and where you might fit in. The website USA spending.gov is a good place to start for learning how government money is being spent and who is winning grants and contracts.

Consider partnering

As we've discussed, the government is a tough nut to crack, and it helps to have established relationships and an existing track record. To get your foot in the door, you may want to consider being a subcontractor or partnering with another organization that has already won government grants or contracts.

Government moves slowly

No matter what approach you take, businesses that are looking to incorporate the government into their business model in a significant way should remember that in general, governments move very slowly, and businesses that depend on them must be mindful of their cash flow. A late payment may be no big deal for a large company, but it can mean death for a startup that is struggling to make payroll and pay rent each month. Have a contingency plan in place in case the money you expect doesn't come through or takes longer than anticipated.

Be ready for paperwork and headaches

I won't sugarcoat it: partnering with the government can mean a lot of tedious paperwork and a lot of hoops to jump through, which can be very daunting for a startup that likely operates completely differently than a large government agency. However, for those with the patience and persistence to see these opportunities through, there can be huge payoffs. If you have the money to do so, it can often be worth it to hire a consultant to help you navigate the process and paperwork.

Plentiful, but inconsistent

There is a lot of money out there for businesses to take advantage of through government partnerships. However, the downside of these partnerships is that government funding is often inconsistent. As leadership and political tides change, so too do government incentives, grants, and the appetite to make purchases. Businesses that decide to incorporate government opportunities into their business model in a significant way should be aware that this is often a gamble, and, ideally, they should not rely solely on their government partners. That said, business is full of calculated risks, no matter what route you take.

Government officials and employees are more accessible than you think

Government can seem remote and untouchable, but there are actually thousands of employees that work for the government, many of whom have been hired specifically to help small businesses access opportunities. If you find yourself falling into a wormhole of online resources and programs and really just need a human to speak to, it's often easier than you think to access one. Check websites for a contact number, and if you can't find one, look for employees of your local government agencies—you can often find contact information provided publicly. They might not be the right person to talk to, but they will likely be able to quickly point you to that person.

Find the front doors within your community

Building on the point above, there are many "front door" organizations to help entrepreneurs access and navigate government resources. You don't have to do it all alone! Search for your local small business development center, chamber of commerce, or entrepreneur center. The Small Business Administration (SBA) also runs a Community Navigator program, which provides funding to organizations tasked with doing outreach and providing resources to businesses in underserved communities.

You can pay people to help you

Finally, as I mentioned previously, if you have the resources to do so, it may be worth it to you to pay a consultant to help you navigate, apply for, and access opportunities. For those who are living and breathing in the world of grants and contracts, government opportunities may seem straightforward and accessible. For those that are new to the processes and lingo, accessing government resources can feel nearly impossible. I stand by the fact that anyone can do it if they put the time and energy into it and lean on the resources available to them.

However, if a business is able to pay a consultant to assist them, it may be worth it.

Company Profile: TruePani

Where the company integrates impact

- Product and services

Founders: Samantha Becker and Shannon Evanchec

Samantha and Shannon met during college at Georgia Tech University. Samantha, who studied civil engineering, and Shannon, who studied environmental engineering, worked together on a summer research project that took them to India. During this trip, the founders witnessed the water quality issues that many households struggled with. Shannon and Samantha were inspired to join CREATE-X, an entrepreneurial support program at Georgia Tech. The students developed a thin copper cup and copper lotus flower that could be used to drink from directly or be submerged in a water tank to kill common bacteria like E. coli.[12] Shannon and Samantha won $5,000 through the People's Choice Award at the InVenture Competition at Georgia Tech and headed back to India to run a pilot test in a rural Indian village. The two founders discovered that, while their device worked, there wasn't a clear path to market. The water quality market was crowded with nonprofits giving away free devices that weren't being utilized. This experience taught Shannon and Samantha a valuable lesson about entrepreneurship and the importance of learning from your customers. Meanwhile, in Flint, Michigan, it was discovered that an estimated 18 million Americans were drinking water that was contaminated with lead. Samantha and Shannon were inspired to focus on water quality issues closer to home.[13] After experimenting with a few different products, they eventually realized that the most pressing need was not necessarily a new product, but proper tracking, testing, and implementation of existing technology. This realization brought Shannon and Samantha to the consulting and communications model that TruePani uses today.

What they do

TruePani is an engineering consulting firm specializing in water quality and cleantech that provides solutions for environmental and public health. Their primary business is helping schools, childcare facilities, and other organizations test for lead in drinking water and providing remediation solutions. TruePani offers the tools and training to test for lead, along with sophisticated data tracking systems, project management, and platforms for communicating to all affected parties what happens if lead is found in drinking water. Along these same lines, TruePani also assists with compliance with changing rules and regulations around building new water systems or refurbishing plumbing. TruePani will even help to identify funding sources for completing the necessary testing and remediation work.

Finally, TruePani also uses this same suite of consulting services, including engineering, data collection and management, project management, and communications, to provide other cleantech and public health services, such as optimizing zero-emission vehicle fleets through route and rate modeling.

Business model

In addition to the services they offer to their customers, another key area that TruePani has excelled at is identifying and accessing government funding opportunities. This allows TruePani to provide services to customers such as schools and childcare facilities that may not independently be able to pay for them. TruePani utilizes a Government Supported B2B model. Much of their work is paid for through government funding, such as the Water Infrastructure Improvements for the Nation (WIIN) Act that provides grant funding to test and remediate water infrastructure in schools, childcare facilities, and disadvantaged communities. Once states receive the grant funding, they can hire TruePani to do the legwork. The small business has worked with local and state agencies to develop and manage drinking water sampling programs for over twenty-five hundred school and childcare facilities.[14]

TruePani provides water sampling services through three different routes: traditional, digital, and hybrid. Through the traditional approach, TruePani sends trained field technicians onsite to perform the testing and documentation. In the digital approach, TruePani provides training and testing materials to enable people in the community to complete the appropriate testing themselves. The hybrid option offers a combination of these two services. These flexible models allow TruePani to scale up or down as needed to expand capacity as necessary to meet project demands.

Impact

PRODUCT AND SERVICES

TruePani is one of those important social enterprises whose core service offering addresses a significant environmental and societal need. Testing for and removing lead from drinking water is an essential service. Lead contamination is generally caused by city water lines or in-house plumbing fixtures that were soldered with lead.[15] Proper data collection, identification of the source of lead, and mapping of possible exposure points is crucial. If children are exposed to lead, it can result in damage to the brain and nervous system, leading to slowed growth and development, learning and behavioral issues, and hearing and speech problems.[16]

What I like about it

There are two primary reasons I love the TruePani business model:

1. *Iteration on product and business model while sticking to the core mission:* From inception to final product, TruePani changed their offering drastically. What began as a business that offered a product in an international market evolved to a business that provided a service in the domestic market. What did not change was the mission of providing clean water and contributing to the health of society and the environment. Shannon and Samantha's ability and willingness to pivot both their offering and their market based on what they learned about the needs of their customers, while staying true to their mission, demonstrates the markings of effective social entrepreneurs.

2. *Innovative Business Model:* TruePani demonstrates a complex and innovative business model - the kind that is often required of social enterprises. The company provides a crucial service to a customer base (schools and childcare facilities) that would ordinarily not have the funds to pay for it. In order to provide the service to the target customer and still run a profitable business, TruePani has located external funding sources, such as Environmental Protection Agency funding, to complete their business model.

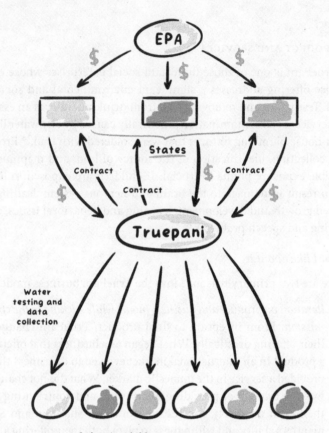

EPA

$ $ $

States

Contract   Contract
        Contract
$ $

Truepani

Water
testing and
data
collection

Schools within contracted states

5

Nonprofits

This chapter is necessary, even in a book about social enterprise, because even with all the models and tips in this book, sometimes a nonprofit is the only viable model for a particular organization or cause. In many ways, a nonprofit organization still operates like a business; however, the business model is generally based on grants, foundations, and donors, rather than on customers. While there are many reasons why I do not recommend a nonprofit model as the first choice if there are other models available to you, there are many nonprofit organizations utilizing innovative models to make their organizations operate efficiently and effectively with a sustainable financial model.

What Is a Nonprofit?

Nonprofits are organizations that have been granted a tax-exempt status by the IRS because they are designated as an organization that provides a public benefit or furthers a social cause. Nonprofits are most commonly designated as a 501(c)(3) organization, but they can also have other 501 designations such as a 501(c)(4) (an organization that promotes social welfare, and is more likely to be involved in political activism and lobbying) or a 501(c)(6) (a business league or chamber of commerce)[1]. In general, nonprofit organizations are not charged taxes by the federal government on income they earn or donations they receive.

Benefits of Nonprofit Organizations

There are many reasons that a nonprofit organization is often the first thought for mission-driven organizations. The primary reason is that our culture still tends to separate the ideas of making a positive impact and the idea of making a profit, assuming that if an organization's purpose is to make a positive social or environmental impact that it *must* be a nonprofit. The objective of this book is to prove that this is not the case. However, while an organization should not select a nonprofit structure by default, there are still many attractive benefits of operating as a nonprofit:

- **Tax exemption:** The first benefit that comes to mind is also the most compelling. Although, like a business, nonprofits must bring in money to support their operations, unlike a business, they do not have to pay taxes on this income (unless the income is unrelated to their mission). Taxes can be a very significant expense for a business. We've all heard the stories of businesses going to great lengths (only some of them legal) to dodge tax expenses, so for the tax exemption alone a nonprofit structure can be appealing to a mission-driven organization.

- **A variety of funding sources available to you:** Because a nonprofit's core operations can, but often do not, generate enough income to cover their expenses, they often seek other outside funding sources. The good news is that there are many different kinds of entities willing to contribute to nonprofit organizations. The bad news is that for every funding opportunity out there, there are generally dozens if not hundreds of other nonprofits competing for the same funding source. A few of the most common funding sources include grant-making foundations, government grants, individual donors, corporate donors, and earned income. It is a common misconception that nonprofits cannot bring in income through their operations, but this is not true. Nonprofits can earn income, but they cannot exist for the sole purpose of earning profit, and there are some rules surrounding this strategy that they need to be careful of so that they do not lose their nonprofit status. A nonprofit should run their plan by a lawyer before pursuing this funding option.

- **Volunteers:** Another benefit that nonprofit organizations enjoy over businesses is the ability to utilize volunteers. Volunteers are individuals who are willing to contribute their time and energy to a cause they support for no monetary compensation. It is generally frowned upon, and in some cases illegal, for a for-profit business to accept unpaid labor. Nonprofit organizations on the other hand often utilize volunteer labor, especially in the United States where there is a strong culture of volunteering.

  Volunteers can be of huge benefit to an organization with a small budget; however, there are also some downsides to depending heavily on volunteer labor. While there are certainly superstar volunteers out there who are as effective as employees (or even multiple employees!), volunteers in general tend to be less dependable than paid employees, for obvious reasons. Volunteers also take a large amount of staff time to recruit, motivate, and manage, and are generally not held to the same standards as paid employees.

  For organizations that are looking to utilize volunteer labor, make sure you have fully thought out your volunteer strategy. (Don't look to lean on volunteers just because you are short-staffed! Effectively managing volunteers will take more time than you think.) Make sure you have carefully thought through tasks that can benefit the organization and will also leave volunteers feeling satisfied, so that they will continue to come back. Remember, volunteers are not compensated financially for their work; they are paid through the feelings of satisfaction and fulfillment they get by contributing to a cause they believe in. So remember to set them up for success and a rewarding experience. Also make sure to select tasks that will be helpful to the organization but will not leave you in a bad spot if they are not completed in a timely manner.

- **Ability to provide services that there is no other viable model for:** The most compelling reason for utilizing a nonprofit structure is that there are some activities and causes for which there is no other viable option. Save the Children, for example, is a nonprofit organization that provides humanitarian aid to children around the world. The children that are the primary recipient of their services certainly could not pay for them, and in most cases, neither could their parents. As Save the Children works in many different countries around the world, many of them war-torn or suffering from natural disasters, the organization cannot rely exclusively on government funding either. While Save the Children could likely benefit from some social enterprise techniques and strategies to diversify their funding, they would have a hard time finding a fully sustainable for-profit model. There are some organizations that do vital work for which a nonprofit is the most logical structure. If an organization is freed from having to make money from their operations, they are then able to take on work and challenges that other organizations are not able to.

Downsides of Nonprofit Organizations

With the benefits of a nonprofit structure fully acknowledged, there is a reason this book is written to encourage social enterprises rather than nonprofit entities. The nonprofit structure also comes with its own unique batch of challenges and difficulties, some of which include:

- **Inefficiencies:** Although this certainly does not apply to *all* nonprofit organizations, nonprofits are often known for struggling with inefficiencies. Inefficiencies in nonprofits occur for two reasons: first, funding and operations are not inherently linked. For businesses, the core operations of the business generate income, meaning that the more efficient the business is and the faster and the more effectively it can deliver its value proposition, the more money it will make. This means that inefficient and ineffective parts of the business are likely to be noted and eliminated or changed relatively quickly. This is not the case with nonprofits. Second, fundraising is separate from service delivery. This means that it is possible for a nonprofit organization to be very good at fundraising but not very good at service delivery, or very good at service delivery but bad at fundraising. And because a nonprofit must be simultaneously doing these interdependent but separate activities, inefficiencies can often result.

- **More restrictions on how you can use your funding:** Nonprofit organizations that are grant-funded generally face a much higher level of restriction on what they can use their funding for. Whereas a business can generally use the money they earn however they see fit (as long as it's legal!). A nonprofit is often held to restrictions put in place by the grant-making body, especially if that grant-making body is the government. This limits a nonprofit's flexibility to save for the future and to deal with unexpected circumstances.

- **Lack of funding for overhead and fundraising:** Like any organization, nonprofits have significant costs for keeping the lights on, paying the rent on an office, paying administrative staff, and so on. Unfortunately, there aren't many donors or foundations that get excited about paying for these things. Donors want to pay for the meal that goes to a hungry child, not the hands that prepared it or the facilities required, or the outreach and coordination time it took for the meal to reach its recipient.

- **Mission creep:** The other thing that donors like to fund are *new* initiatives. Many foundations aren't as keen on contributing to the same program that's been going on for twenty years, even if it's very successful. They'd prefer to fund a new program or initiative with specific parameters. While this may be a natural inclination, it causes difficulties for nonprofits. Organizations can end up running so many new initiatives in order to secure funding that they become spread too thin, overwork their staff, and decrease in effectiveness.
  Another common problem that results from this predicament is called "mission creep." Mission creep occurs

when nonprofits chase funding opportunities that diverge from their original mission and expertise. For example, if a nonprofit that offered services to the homeless got a grant to plant trees and fight deforestation, this would be an example of mission creep. As with a business, diverging from a nonprofit's core competencies and brand identities without a strategic plan can be deadly for the organization.

- **Difficulty with investment and planning:** Because of the restrictions around the use of grant funding, and the uncertainty of future funding cycles, nonprofits are often at a disadvantage in terms of investing in their operations and planning for the future. Restrictions on the use of grant funding often mandate that grant funds have to be used within a certain amount of time, and for certain purposes, which means nonprofits are less able to save money for the future, weather unexpected lean periods, and respond to unanticipated needs. Lack of funding for overhead and operations can result in more uncertainty for nonprofit organizations, less ability to plan strategically, and ultimately less effectiveness.

    The blame for these circumstances lies more heavily on the funders and the ideology around nonprofit funding than it does on the nonprofits themselves. However, the funders' perspective is also understandable, as they have a mandate to ensure that charitable funding is used responsibly. This situation is one of the reasons why I would encourage any nonprofit or social enterprise to generate as much of their funding through earned revenue as they are able to, as long as it doesn't hurt their mission.

- **Burnout:** These factors unfortunately result in the fact that nonprofit organizations must be a two-sided business, running an organization and delivering services on one side, and raising funds from donors and foundations on the other. This is not inherently bad, but funding limitations mean that nonprofit organizations are often short-staffed, and the same staff that is delivering the programming is often also responsible for raising the money to fund the programming. Couple this situation with the fact that employees of nonprofits are often working on emotionally taxing issues and paid lower than market rate for their skills, and the result is high rates of burnout. A survey by Opportunity Knox, a nonprofit human resources organization, found that half of employees in the nonprofit sector were either burned out or in danger of burnout.[2]

Tips for Success

When possible, I support a social enterprise model over a nonprofit structure. However, as I have described in this chapter, a for-profit model is not always an option for mission-driven organizations. However, I would encourage mission-driven organizations to think carefully and strategically about their business model before committing to a structure. Do not automatically assume you must be a nonprofit organization if you have a social or environmental mission. If you do decide to pursue a nonprofit structure, here are a few strategies to help you along your way.

- **Fundraising is constant:** Fundraising cycles can be long. That means that nonprofits can't wait until they *need* money to begin applying for grants or courting donors. Fundraising is a constant part of the business.

- **Explore different models:** Nonprofits can be just as clever, innovative, and resourceful as a startup. Many leading nonprofits have found creative funding models to help finance their operations. A few of these include:

  ○ *Earned income:* As mentioned previously in this chapter, nonprofits can earn revenue for the services they deliver, as long as they are careful about following regulations and maintaining their nonprofit status. There's a common misconception that nonprofits need to give all of the value they provide away for free, but if they have an audience that is able and willing to pay for some of this value, the nonprofit can, and should, charge for it. The Great Smoky

Mountains Institute at Tremont is a great example of this model. Tremont delivers outdoor, experiential learning programs, helping to develop strong leaders, a curiosity and wonder for the natural world, and good stewards of the earth. Tremont offers many free or low-cost programs and trail access, as well as paid programming that aligns with their mission, such as retreats, group hikes, naturalist trainings, and nature photography classes. These classes do not cover all of their expenses, but they do help create a steady and reliable stream of income for the organization.

o *For-profit/nonprofit hybrid:* Another model many mission-driven organizations have utilized is a for-profit/nonprofit hybrid. This means that one arm of the organization operates as a nonprofit organization and the other operates as a for-profit. Generally, in this model, the nonprofit either owns the for-profit entity, or the nonprofit branch and the for-profit branch operate as two separate legal entities that complement each other. While this can get a little complicated behind the scenes, it can be a great structure for organizations that need to serve different purposes with different sides of their business. Likewise Coffee in Knoxville, Tennessee, for example, is a for-profit coffee shop wholly owned by Raising a Voice, a nonprofit that works to fight human trafficking and support victims. The coffee shop helps fund the nonprofit's efforts and creates a physical gathering place for the community.[3]

o *Recurring revenue:* Recurring revenue models aren't only for for-profits; enterprising nonprofits can achieve this goal, too. Through memberships, earned income, ongoing partnerships with businesses, or even multi-year grants, nonprofit organizations can give themselves more room to breathe, plan strategically, and grow sustainably.

- **Don't put all your eggs in one basket:** As much as possible, nonprofits should try to differentiate their funding sources and strategies. If a nonprofit relies too heavily on a single donor with whom a relationship could go sour, or on a foundation that could adjust its funding strategy, they are left vulnerable in the face of unexpected changes. A nonprofit with a strong, durable strategy will have a variety of different funding streams made up of some combination of grants, donors, earned income, memberships, and corporate sponsors.

- **Pay well:** There is an unfortunate mindset that prevails in the nonprofit industry that nonprofit workers don't need to make a competitive wage because they are so fulfilled by the work they are doing—or, even worse, that nonprofit workers *shouldn't* make a competitive wage because it is unethical to pay workers well when more money could be contributed to the cause they are serving. While there are limits to what wages might be considered ethical, it is not wrong to invest in your employees. No one does their best work when they are overworked and underpaid. Many nonprofits lose talented workers to for-profit industries because employees could earn substantially more by using their skills for a for-profit business. While it may not be possible for a nonprofit to compete on wages with a Fortune 500 company, nonprofits should aim high and fundraise with the goal of paying their employees a salary that will help them thrive and support their families.

- **Avoid mission creep:** Keep your eye on the ball. Establish what you want to achieve and seek funding that supports that goal and the steps you need to take to get there. You can build on and reframe your existing programs and necessary steps, but you should be careful not to let your head be turned by shiny new funding opportunities. Don't let the mission of your organization be spread too thin or be diluted by trying to do everything at once, and even more importantly, don't add more deliverables to an already overburdened staff. New funding opportunities should support the steps and expansion you are already working toward. Be sure to assess growth and capacity before signing up for a new set of deliverables. In other words, don't agree to a funding opportunity that requires the addition of a new program that will take existing staff, already working at 100 percent capacity, to 120 percent capacity.

- **Seek funding sources that fit:** Along the same lines as avoiding mission creep, seek funding sources that fit your organization—don't try to shape your organization to fit funding opportunities. First of all, you are less likely to be successful if the opportunity is not a natural fit for your work. Secondly, if you are successful, you might get stuck doing work that doesn't serve your mission or does not make the best use of your team's expertise and talents. There are thousands of funding opportunities out there, but going after every one that comes your way is a quick road to burnout. Instead, spend time finding the 15 percent of opportunities that are a true fit for where you are going and crafting your strategy to make sure that when you do pursue a funding opportunity, you are strong, polished, and deliberate.

Company Profile: ÉCHALE

Where the company integrates impact
- Product and services
- Material sourcing
- Labor
- Community

Founder: Francesco Piazzesi

Francesco, the son of a civil engineer, was born in Mexico. Growing up he learned about the family construction business, Ital Mexicana. When Francesco was twelve years old, his father took him and his brother to a brick factory where he saw the hard and dangerous conditions of laborers. This visit made a lasting impression on the young Francesco and guided him as he developed his future career. When he was seventeen, Francesco began to work for Ital Mexicana, specializing in cement mixers and machinery. Ital Mexicana was originally responsible for developing the machine that made Ecoblocks (explained in more detail below), and after spending years training communities to use the machines, Francesco decided to form a foundation (while still working full-time at Ital Mexicana) to help further the community development work and to rebuild homes after hurricane Paulina. After five years of this work Francesco grew frustrated about the lack of financing options for families and decided to get his PhD to study microcredit opportunities for sustainable housing. After he graduated, he left his job at Ital Mexicana to focus on the foundation full-time. He created two separate for-profit entities to manage the Ecoblock initiative and to provide accessible financial solutions to families. Francesco also received a social enterprise fellowship with Ashoka that has helped him build ÉCHALE into what it is today. "The workers, the people who build the houses, the housing, the hospitals, the buildings, the cities; paradoxically it is the people who are homeless," said Francesco. "So, we said, we have to do something. And that's how ÉCHALE was born."

What they do

ÉCHALE provides affordable housing solutions and sustainable community development for vulnerable families in Mexico through a multi-pronged approach that includes the construction of affordable housing, accessible financing and financial education, technology training, and employment opportunities. To date they have built 250,000 housing solutions (either new houses or improved houses) and provided employment opportunities for 450,000 people across twenty-eight states in Mexico. Their programs have benefited over 1,000,000 individuals. ÉCHALE is a social enterprise that operates in three complementary but separate arms:

- ÉCHALE a social enterprise that runs housing projects, Eco-Block, and other community programs (initiatives described in more detail in the following sections)

- ÉCHALE Fundación, a nonprofit arm which accepts grants and donations, provides training, and manages volunteers

- ÉCHALE Financiera which provides accessible credit, savings facilities, financial education, and one-on-one advice.

Together, ÉCHALE provides service in the following key areas:

- **Housing:** ÉCHALE helps families to access housing and build wealth by constructing or repairing homes for families that would otherwise not be able to afford them. The housing solutions are designed to be simple, affordable, and sturdy. One of the programs they run is called Hogar Semilla (Seed Home) because it is designed to grow as a family saves money for new additions.[4]

- **Training and education:** ÉCHALE provides education and training in the following areas in order to help families and communities thrive, and to provide economic opportunity and workforce development: Savings, credit, financial literacy, use of technology, housing construction and repair, and the creation of Ecoblocks.

- **Financing:** Through ÉCHALE Financiera, ÉCHALE provides credit, savings accounts, and accessible financing and loans for housing construction, as well as coaching and education on finances.[5]

Business model

The ÉCHALE business model operates in three complementary parts:

- **Housing construction:** When ÉCHALE constructs new homes or repairs old ones, they take a small commission that goes back to fund the organization. Rather than sending in a construction crew, building a house, and leaving, ÉCHALE involves the family and community in the process so that the housing construction can have positive workforce development and economic impacts for the community. ÉCHALE's primary building material is the Ecoblock (described in more detail under "material sourcing"). One of the benefits of the Ecoblock as a building material is that it can be made onsite in the community where the house is being built. ÉCHALE brings the hydraulic machine used to make Ecoblocks to each community and trains local people on how to make and use the building material. In addition to providing a sustainable building material, this method can bring wealth to a community.

- **Housing financing:** When a family is interested in acquiring an ÉCHALE home, the first step is a financial education workshop focused on savings. When a family has saved enough for the down payment, construction can begin. ÉCHALE helps families finance homes through an innovative mix of funds consisting of the family's savings plus a government subsidy negotiated by ÉCHALE plus low interest credit provided by ÉCHALE Financiera, from which a small profit margin goes back to ÉCHALE to keep the organization sustainable.[6]

- **Nonprofit grants and donations:** Finally, ÉCHALE Fundación, the nonprofit arm of the organization, receives grants and donations from outside sources to fund education, workshops, and sustainable community development initiatives.[7]

Impact

PRODUCTS AND SERVICES

There are approximately nine million people in Mexico who do not have access to adequate housing. About one-third of these are eligible for government housing, leaving about six million people who fall through the cracks. Poor construction and overcrowding within existing structures can exacerbate problems of poverty, health issues, and abuse. Those living without homes in rural areas lack the proper materials and technical knowledge to build new housing. Furthermore, high-interest loans available for low-income individuals to build houses can drive families that do pursue housing construction into crippling debt. ÉCHALE fills a gap by offering housing materials, training, and accessible financing.

MATERIAL SOURCING

The primary material used in ÉCHALE houses is the Ecoblock, a concrete replacement that is made of 90 percent adobe (local soil); the remaining 10 percent is a mixture of lime, sand, cement, and water. An Ecoblock produces 30 percent less carbon dixoide than concrete to create, can be made onsite, utilizes local material, employs local people, and is recyclable. It also provides increased thermal and acoustic insulation when compared to concrete.[8]

LABOR

ÉCHALE uses the needs for building materials and housing as opportunities to employ local people and provide training and skills that they can use for future employment. The hydraulic machine used to make Ecoblocks often stays in a community and is managed by local people who are trained on the machine and go on to offer the ÉCHALE products and services to new families.

COMMUNITY

ÉCHALE aims to empower communities from within. Individual families pay for their own houses; but a community committee oversees the design and makes sure workers are paid fairly.[9]

What I like about it

A lack of adequate and sustainable housing is a complex and multifaceted problem that organizations and governments around the world have struggled to address. Often, organizations offer simple, Band-Aid solutions that do not address the underlying issues and thus do not offer long-term relief. Francesco Piazzesi and the ÉCHALE staff have put in the time, energy, and knowledge to develop complex and socially integrated solutions to address the unique challenges and opportunities faced in Mexican communities.

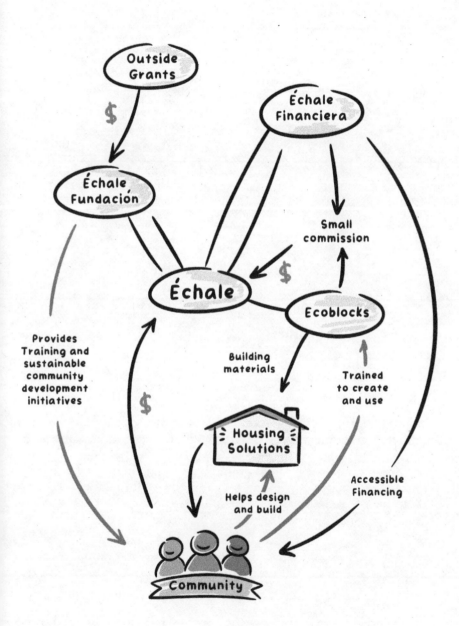

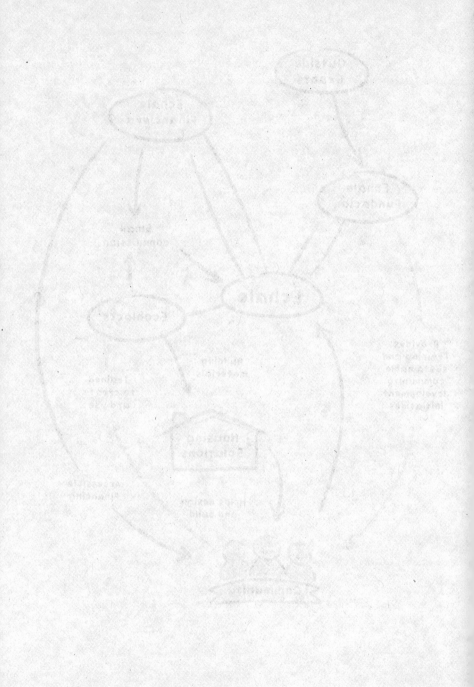

PART 2

Twelve Opportunities to Integrate Social and Environmental Impact into Your Business Model

We are called to be architects of the future, not its victims.
—R. BUCKMINSTER FULLER

There are endless ways for a company to integrate social and environmental impact into their business model. I would encourage all companies to think creatively and incorporate impact in a way that feels authentic to the mission and personality of your company. Mission should strengthen and reinforce your business model. In other words, it shouldn't feel like it has been tacked on as an afterthought. In this section, I have identified twelve core ways to weave impact into the daily functions and operations of your business. In the coming chapters I will discuss each of these twelve possibilities in more depth and provide at least one example of a company that has utilized this model in an authentic and impactful way. However, don't limit yourself to one of these models. I encourage you to blend them or even come up with an entirely new model for impact!

You will note in the following section that all twelve models of impact fall into two primary categories: amplifying positive impact (such as supporting local economies and regenerating soil health) and decreasing negative impact (such as decreasing pollution or waste).

Increasing positive impact is the ideal, and I encourage businesses to find ways to integrate positive impact into their core service or product offerings. However, the reality is that running a business, particularly if you are creating physical goods, often comes with an environmental price tag, and finding creative and responsible ways to mitigate this negative cost is just as important. While, as I mentioned in the introduction, I subscribe to the philosophy that we should aim high in business and seek "more good" rather than just "less bad," we still have a ways to go before we can completely stop thinking about the bad.

6

Products and Services

This chapter describes the simplest and most straightforward way of integrating positive impact into your business model: through the core function and operation of your business. This means that the service or product the business provides helps to mitigate a problem such as hunger or pollution, or that it adds tangible value to the world such as providing education or sequestering carbon, and that the business is able to generate a profit from providing that value.

In his book *The Fortune at the Bottom of the Pyramid*, C.K. Prahalad argues that the best way to address global poverty is not through charity, but through business solutions targeted at the billions of people living in poverty around the world today. Prahalad argues that instead of competing for the attention and dollars of the world's richest, companies should be turning their energy and ingenuity towards business solutions that uplift those in poverty. Although the world's poorest may not have as much disposable income, there are billions of people in this category, and together, they make up a sizable market. If a business can provide solutions that address a crucial need for these people, and if it can create the potential for them to improve their spending power, the business opportunity is huge. Prahalad cites solutions such as drip irrigation systems and banking services for the unbanked.[1]

When it works, the Products/Services social enterprise business model is probably my favorite. It is a straightforward way of both helping the world and making a good income. However, if this model was as simple as it sounds, this would be the only necessary chapter in this book. The complications with this business model lie not in the lack of problems to address, or in the lack of valuable products and services that could help address these problems; the challenge lies in the complex business models that are often required to make these businesses financially viable. There is a reason that people usually associate making a positive impact in the world with nonprofit organizations. Doing good is not always a straightforward route to making a profit. There are two primary reasons that this is true:

1. The people who are most in need are often unable to pay for solutions. Take food, for instance. We do not have a food shortage in this world—we actually have plenty to go around. In fact, approximately 931 million tons of food is wasted around the world each year.[2] If we have that much excess food, why are so many people starving? The people who are starving do not have the money to pay for food directly, or to finance the collection and transport of the food that is going to waste.

2. Many global problems fall into the territory of the "collective commons." This means that damage is being done to natural resources that we all depend on, but that are not owned directly by individuals or governments. Take air for example. Clean air is incredibly valuable—we all depend on it to survive. However, air cannot be divided into portions and owned by individuals; we all collectively share it. Although customers may be willing to spend money on air filters and purifiers inside their own houses, people cannot pay to clean their individual air source outside their house. The responsibility to clean this air lies jointly on all our shoulders, which means that no one takes responsibility. It is much easier to point fingers at others for polluting than to take real action when you know others are not. Even governments, which are theoretically responsible for the health and safety of their citizens, are reluctant to take action on climate change until they know that other countries are doing the same.

This does not mean that it is impossible to make an impact through directly providing a good or service. It simply means that socially driven entrepreneurs must often incorporate more creativity and ingenuity into both their products and their business models. Product/Service social entrepreneurs usually find business opportunities in one of the following ways:

1. First-to-market: Addressing a need that no one else has introduced a solution for

2. New market: Bringing an existing solution to a new population

3. Product innovation: Introducing a new product, often a technology, that solves a social or environmental problem that people are willing and able to pay for

4. Business innovation: Introducing a new business model that makes solving an environmental or social problem profitable when it wasn't previously (see Part 1: Business Models for Social Impact for examples.) The company Profile of Phinite on page 79 demonstrates both product and business model innovation.

5. Improvement and refinement of current solutions: Addressing a social or environmental problem or solution for which solutions already exist, but doing it better than the other available options.

What to Look Out for

There are a few stumbling blocks to be careful of when operating with this business model:

1. **Uncertainties of competition within social enterprise:** As noted above, "improvement and refinement" or, in other words, improving upon the product, service, or business model of a solution that already exists, is a perfectly viable business model in this category. The problem is that in social enterprise, competition can feel strange. Is it okay to try to take business from another company that is also trying to help the world? The short answer is yes. Competition between social enterprises can feel weird, but if you are truly addressing a social or environmental problem, and you find a better solution, or a stronger business

model for offering the solution, then your business *should* do better. This allows you to reach more people.

Should social enterprises compete against other social enterprises? Absolutely. Competition is not dirty, and nonprofits compete for funding all the time, even if they don't refer to it as competition. Competition is healthy, because it keeps businesses sharp and attentive to the needs of the population they are serving. Running smear campaigns against other social enterprises? Entering predatory price wars? Not so much. Be careful not to enter into competitive practices that make the industry as a whole unhealthy. But offering a superior product or service in a way that is *better* than your competitors? That is not only acceptable, it should be celebrated.

2. **How you run your business still matters:** If your business has found a cure for cancer or a way to stop climate change, it can understandably be pretty easy to forget about every other section of this book, such as the waste created when you manufacture your product or the wages you pay your workers. However, all of these things still matter, and as your business scales they will matter even more. Every section of this book discusses factors that contribute to the impact your business has on the world and the ethos of your company.

   Should you wait to stop climate change until you've found a way to do so without producing any waste? No. By all means, hurry up and get your solution to market! But don't ignore the waste. Monitor it, set goals to reduce the waste, and work toward them just like any other impact-driven company. And of course, make sure the negative impacts of your work do not outweigh the positive. When you're working in innovation, remember Peter Senge's principle that "today's problems were yesterday's solutions."

3. **Getting paid may not be straightforward:** If your only competitors are nonprofit organizations, there is probably a reason. The business model is most likely not a clear-cut one. The people paying for the solution you offer may not be the same people who are directly benefiting from the solution. Don't be afraid to think outside the box, and don't be deterred by complexity.

Some of the most successful social enterprises also have the most complex business models.

Businesses that solve a social or environmental problem through their core activities or offerings are some of the strongest social enterprise models out there. This model has the potential to offer solutions efficiently and to pay yourself and others a good wage while making a difference in the world. Be bold and innovative with the structure of your business model, and don't let yourself off the hook when it comes to social and environmental impact in other areas of your business. Just because you're providing positive solutions in one area doesn't mean it's okay to ignore the negative impacts created by other aspects of your business, such as manufacturing or labor.

Company Profile: Phinite
Founder interview on page 258.

Where the company integrates impact

- Products and services

Founder: Jordan Phasey

Jordan Phasey is an engineer originally from Darwin, Australia, where he was working to improve water supply for indigenous communities. Jordan was growing increasingly concerned about our ability to feed the world's growing population and the impact that shortages in natural resources would have on the world's poorest communities. In 2016, Jordan heard about a challenge for nutrient recycling hosted by the Environmental Protection Agency in the United States. Jordan applied to the competition with an idea to turn animal waste into renewable fertilizer—and won! Jordan was honored at the White House and invited by one of the country's largest livestock farmers to come to the United States and make his vision a reality. After several years of traveling back and forth between his wife and children in Australia and farms in the eastern US, Jordan and his family made the jump across the pond to turn Phinite into a reality. Today, the Phinite technology is commercially available on livestock farms, and their first batches of fertilizer are being sold to farmers.

What they do

Phinite is an early-stage company that has developed a technology to produce phosphorus-rich fertilizer from manure. The company uses technical ingenuity and a creative business plan to turn a waste stream and environmental liability into a renewable fertilizer and profit stream.

Phinite has created a technology to tackle two massive problems:

1. *Treating pollution caused by animal waste.* Currently, large-scale livestock farming results in massive amounts of animal waste that can be detrimental to the environment.[3]

2. *Creating a regenerative fertilizer supply.* Phosphorus is a key fertilizer ingredient used in food production, essential for feeding the global population. But our current phosphorus supply is running low. Much of the global phosphorus supply is currently mined from geological deposits; however, this supply is finite (or "phinite"—see what Phinite did there?) and is declining in quality. The good news is that phosphorus is readily available in human waste, food waste, and animal waste, so connecting this supply and demand can be really big for sustainability.[4] The tricky part is collecting, processing, transporting, and applying this waste as fertilizer in a cost-effective way.

The fact that phosphorus can be found in waste is not news—farmers have been using animal waste (particularly from cows, pigs, and chickens) as fertilizer for thousands of years. The problem is that it's difficult to collect and ship animal waste to other locations to be used as fertilizer, such as to farms that don't have animals. With their onsite robotic drying solution, Phinite has developed a solution for this problem. The Phinite team builds what looks like an outdoor greenhouse onsite at the livestock farm. An excavator collects the waste and pours it onto the concrete floor of the greenhouse, where a robot then spreads, turns, and stirs the waste until it is processed into a dry, odorless fertilizer.

Business model

While groundbreaking technology is an integral part of the Phinite business, finding the right business model is just as important. The

Phinite business model is a two-sided B2B model. On one side of their business, the company must sell their automated drying systems to farmers. The drying systems are housed and operated on the farmers' property and are designed to process the farms' animal waste onsite. The farmers will buy the drying unit because it has two benefits for them: it treats and processes the waste that has previously been an environmental liability, and they receive a cut of the profits when the fertilizer from the farm is sold.

On the other side of the Phinite business model, Phinite must sell the fertilizer they make to other farmers, fertilizer distributors, or plant nurseries. They also must manage the collection and shipping of their fertilizer to their end users. The Phinite business model is complex, and Jordan would be the first to tell you that they still have a lot to figure out. However, as of the spring of 2022, they have already gained the confidence of many farmers and investors and have sold every pound of fertilizer they have produced so far.

Impact

Phinite creates a positive impact on each side of its business model. On one side, Phinite processes animal waste, effectively solving a growing environmental problem in a way that profits farmers rather than penalizes them. On the other side, the company creates a renewable source of phosphorus, a crucial ingredient for fertilizer that, in the face of growing fertilizer prices and an increasing number of mouths to feed, is more important than ever.

What I like about it

Phinite is a perfect example of the fact that profitable mission-based business models can be found, but they may be complicated, and their founders will often have to bring as much ingenuity to their business model as they do to their product. The Phinite business model is not simple, but it effectively seeks a win/win solution for both farmers and the environment. A simple, yet ineffective solution to the environmental problem of excess animal waste would be to penalize the farmer without offering a better solution. What an entrepreneur can bring to this problem is the ability to seek a win/win solution for farmers, our food system, and the earth.

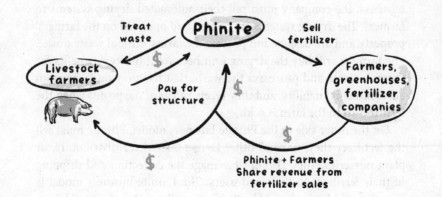

7

Design

When it comes to the sustainability of a product, few factors are as important as how it is designed. Impactful design means thinking beyond what will make the product sell—it means mindfully considering the role the product will have in the world after it is purchased by the customer and its impact through creation, use, and end of life.

While sustainable design driven by advanced technology might sound the sexiest, like Interface finding a way to integrate carbon directly into its carpeting (see company profile on page 93), small product tweaks can also make a huge difference. In 2010, Kimberly-Clark introduced the first "coreless toilet paper," simply meaning that they created a toilet paper roll without the cardboard tube in the middle. The toilet paper roll still holds its shape until you get down to the last few sheets. This is a small, simple product innovation that could make a big difference when scaled: if all toilet paper was coreless, it would save approximately 160 million pounds of waste per year, just in the US.[1]

As you develop the design of your product, consider three primary rules of sustainable design:

1. Design with Nature

Learning lessons from nature is a powerful tool for design. Nature has been refining its designs for thousands of years, and by observing some of the best practices in natural design, we can take huge leaps forward in efficiency, sustainability, and elegance. There are two primary fields of natural design: design inspired by nature, also called biomimicry, and integrating nature into design, also called bioutilization.

Biomimicry

Biomimicry is the practice of designing products that emulate and are inspired by nature. Unlike biomorphism, which borrows inspiration from the *appearance* of nature (such as a dress inspired by the texture of a leaf), biomimicry imitates the *function* of nature.[2] Biomimicry looks at how nature solves problems and emulates the process through design. Some examples of biomimicry at work include the following:

- **Structural design:** Although termites are known for being destructive to human-made structures, they are ironically very skilled architects. Even in well-insulated human-made structures, we generally spend thousands of dollars each year on heating and air conditioning to regulate temperature, not to mention staggering energy use and carbon dioxide emissions. Termite mounds, however, are able to naturally maintain an almost constant internal temperature using no electricity or gas. Architect Mick Pearce drew inspiration from the architecture of termite mounds to build a two-building office complex and shopping mall in Harare, Zimbabwe. By mimicking the design and ventilation system of a termite mound, the structure used approximately 65 percent less energy than comparable buildings in the same city and saved $3.5 million in energy costs in the first five years.[3]

- **Color:** Synthetic dyes are commonly used on a large scale to add color to paints, inks, resins, textiles, and food, often containing a whole slew of toxins and chemicals. The creation and use of these dyes can result in considerable health hazards and environmental pollution.[4] However, we live in a colorful world. How does nature create such vibrant colors without using harmful chemicals? The company Cypris Materials set out to emulate nature's strategies for color creation. Instead of using toxic pigments and dyes, paint created by Cypris Materials uses *structural* color, a method inspired by the wings of a butterfly. The blue morpho Butterfly has wings that appear to be a brilliant blue color. However, if you look closely at the wings, you will see that they are actually translucent and have no blue pigment. The nanostructure of the wings reflects blue light and makes the wings appear to be a vibrant blue. This effect is called structural color and is the basis for the paints and coatings created by Cypris Materials.[5]

Bioutilization

While biomimicry emulates design and methodology found in nature, some may say that bioutilization takes a shortcut by directly integrating nature and natural systems into design. Bioutilization is the practice of directly using nature in design. One of my favorite practitioners of bioutilization is an architecture, design, and research group called Terreform ONE. Co-founders Mitchell Joachim and Maria Aiolova co-authored a book called *Design with Life: Biotech Architecture and Resilient Cities*, the title of which is a good descriptor of their approach. Some examples of their work include Home Alive, a house made from living trees and plants, and Mycoform, pollution-free furniture grown from living mycelia (mushrooms) that can be fully composted and introduced back into nature at the end of its usable life.[6]

A more well-known example of bioutilization is the use of microorganisms for fermentation of food or alcohol or the anaerobic digestion of sewage. We enjoy many fermented foods and drinks such as alcohol, kombucha, miso, and kimchi that would not be possible without the participation of yeast and microorganisms. Similarly, most of our sewage and wastewater is treated at least in part through anaerobic digestion, a process that uses bacteria to break down organic matter and results in digestate, which can be used for fertilizer, and biogas, which can be used as a fuel.[7]

Biomimicry and bioutilization both focus on the *function* of nature. This type of design can often be confused for design in which the *aesthetics* of the design are inspired by nature. Although I have nothing against bio-inspired aesthetic design, it is important to remember that this is not the same as echoing the function of natural design. Aesthetic design inspired by nature does not necessarily have any real tangible benefit for the environment. So, while flower-printed fabric may be lovely, unless the fabric biodegrades like a flower and uses the natural nontoxic pigments of a flower, it doesn't belong in this section.

Often, the most efficient and elegant designs can be found in nature. By taking design lessons directly from nature, or integrating natural systems into design, we can save ourselves years of trial and error and create designs that will better serve our customers and the planet. When faced with a design problem, try to think of something similar that occurs in nature, observe the process, and learn about how nature solves the problem. For ideas and examples, check out AskNature, a virtual site run by the Biomimicry Institute that highlights dozens of biological strategies and innovations.[8]

2. Design for Use

When thinking about sustainable design, most people think of integrating sustainable materials into products (see the Material Sourcing chapter on page 101) or designing for sustainable breakdown of materials at the end of the product's usable life (see Design for End of Life on page 88). However, Leyla Acaroglu, designer and social scientist, advocates for design-led systems change, meaning that design can play a large part in influencing the workings of larger systems. Leyla argues that the most important aspect of design for sustainability is designing for *use*. This means that when a designer is creating a product for a consumer and is trying to be mindful of the social and environmental impact of this product, the best thing they can do is put themselves in the shoes of the consumer and consider how the consumer is likely to use the product and how design can be used as a tool to encourage sustainable behavior. Leyla cites two examples of simple design problems that, at a large scale, have a huge impact on our society and environment.[9]

1. <u>Refrigerator Design</u>: In the United States, refrigerators have steadily increased in size over time. This may seem like an increase in convenience so that we can store more food in our homes and decrease the need for regular trips to the grocery store. However, the unintended consequence of larger refrigerators is that more food ends up forgotten and ultimately wasted. Who can't identify with finding something disgusting and long

forgotten in the back of their refrigerator? As of 2013, 40 percent of fresh food purchased for the home in the United States was ultimately wasted. What impact could a mindful designer have on this number if their intention when designing a new refrigerator model was to not only increase convenience but also to decrease food waste?

2. Teakettles: Teakettles are generally either heated directly on the stove or heated electrically and often hold around two liters of water (about four-and-a-half cups). However, most people who use a teakettle are not making four-and-a-half cups of tea at a time. If you intend to make just one or two cups of tea, you have to take a guess at the appropriate amount of water to use, because most teakettles do not have easy-to-use markings showing you how much water to add to make one, two, or three cups of tea.

I know my teakettle doesn't include measurements, and as a result, I consistently heat more water than I need, because the thought of having to wait for more water to heat up to fill up the rest of my single cup of tea is too irritating. It turns out I'm not alone. Sixty-five percent of tea drinkers in the United Kingdom admit to overfilling their teakettles. This may not seem like a big deal when you think of your own one-off teakettle usage, but it is estimated that the amount of excess energy used in only *one day* from heating the extra, ultimately unused, hot water in a teakettle is enough to power all the streetlights in England for one night. Just think what an impact the designer of a teakettle could have simply by etching the appropriate fill lines for different amounts of tea on the side of the kettle. Not all impactful solutions require advanced technology; some just require a little mindfulness and forethought.

While design iterations on the product examples I used in this section (refrigerators and teakettles) could significantly decrease the inadvertent negative environmental impact of each product, it's also worth noting that at the end of the day, these examples are for consumer goods, and whether we really need to be using our collective design ingenuity to create more consumer goods is up for debate. Personally,

I believe that the greatest use of design is to focus on creating new solutions to our most pressing problems.

When designing for positive impact, think not only of the materials inside the product, where they came from, and where they will go, but also how you as a designer can shape the behavior of the user. Designers have an incredible opportunity to make a positive impact. Designers lay the tracks on which our daily lives and large-scale systems run. By considering how a product will be used once it reaches the customer's hands from a sustainability and social impact perspective, designers can make a huge impact even with the smallest of design tweaks.

3. Design for End of Life

As a continuation of the section above, a designer must not only think of how the product they create will be used, but also what will happen to the product when the customer is finished with it. Can the resources in the product be reclaimed or reused to add value elsewhere? Or will the product break down and add toxins to the soils and waterways? That answer will partly depend on the behavior of the customer, but the designer or business owner can also play a large part in influencing the final fate of a used product. There are two primary factors to consider when designing for end of life:

Materials in the product

What happens to the product when the customer is finished with it depends in large part on what materials were used in the creation of the product. There are a few key questions to ask yourself when designing a product with end-of-life in mind. Can the materials in the product . . .

BE REUSED?

Can you design a product so that the materials retain value or functionality after it has been used? Can the materials be reused or refilled? A good example of this is the CO_2 containers that come with a Soda-Stream machine. Instead of throwing away the CO_2 canister when it's empty, a customer can bring the canister back to the store that sells the product and have it refilled with CO_2 so that it can be used again.

Check out the KnoxFill profile on page 152 and founder interview on page 266 for a good example of a company that facilitates reuse.

BE RECYCLED?

Is your product made of materials that can easily be recycled? The easiest way to increase the likelihood that your product will wind up being recycled is to use materials that are able to be recycled through common curbside recycling programs. The tricky thing is that what can be recycled through municipal recycling changes from city to city. If your customer base is concentrated in one area, check with your local recycling program to see what is accepted through the curbside recycling program. If your customers are spread out across the country or world, the best bet is to use materials that are commonly accepted by curbside recycling, such as paper, aluminum, and certain kinds of plastic such as PET or PETE (Polyethylene terephthalate) and HDPE (High density polyethylene).[10]

One thing to note about plastics recycling is that the triangular recycling symbol on the bottom of the plastic does not necessarily mean that the material is recyclable (confusing, I know!). What matters is the number inside the triangular symbol. This tells you what kind of plastic is used in the product so that you can theoretically check with your local recycling program to see what kind of plastics they accept. The most commonly recycled plastics, PET and HDPE, are labeled 1 and 2, respectively.[11]

If you have a product that is more complicated, but you want to make sure it can be recycled, you could set up a special program with the company TerraCycle that specializes in recycling materials that are not easily recycled or with an electronics recycling organization such as Revivn (see company profile on page 205), or you could arrange your own mail-in or collection program for used products so that you can reuse the materials yourself, like Interface (company profile on page 93).

BE COMPOSTED?

Can the materials in your product be composted? This means that if your product was put in a backyard compost pile, would the material eventually compost and go back to the soil to provide nourishment to plants? Generally, this is true of biologically based materials such as food, paper, cardboard, untreated wood, and natural fibers such as cotton.[12] If you want to be sure, you can seek certification from organizations like the Biodegradable Products Institute.[13]

One thing to be careful of here is bioplastics. Bioplastics are made, at least in part, from plants and can be designed to mimic traditional plastics or to degrade in some way. Some bioplastics claim to be compostable, however, most "compostable plastics" can only be composted in an industrial composting facility where temperatures and conditions can be highly controlled and monitored. This means that if a compostable plastic cup is put in a backyard compost pile, it will likely remain a cup. If you are using compostable plastics in a controlled environment, such as a café where you collect the compostable plastic and have a plan for delivering the material to a composting facility, that would probably work just fine (although at that point you might as well use reusable dishes). However, if you are sending compostable plastic out into the world, most individual consumers don't have the slightest idea how to get the material to an industrial composting facility, which means the material will likely wind up in a landfill or contaminate the plastics recycling stream.[14]

BE SEPARATED?

Here's the tricky part. Most products aren't made out of just one material. If your product is made of a mixture of plastic and aluminum, for example, and the materials are combined in an inseparable way, the product most likely cannot be recycled, even though both materials could likely be recycled individually. If you design the product so that the materials can be easily separated (*and include instructions for doing so*), this increases the likelihood that at least part of the product will be recyclable.

Pathway of the product

The most important element of designing for end of life is designing a pathway for the used product to find its way to whatever destination you have planned for it. As I described in the previous section, it hardly matters what the material is made of if it's going to end up in the landfill anyway. Landfills are actually designed to contain trash and prevent materials from biodegrading and returning to the soil (although, of course, leaks do happen).[15] Unless you design an alternative pathway for your product at the end of its usable life, chances are that the product will end up in a landfill. It's worth mentioning here that landfills are not a sustainable system; they are part of a linear system that must ultimately change because we are running out of the space and resources required to keep a linear system going. Here are a few examples of how you can design a sustainable end-of-life pathway for your product:

REPAIR

This is the first and most important question to ask—is your product ready for its end-of-life journey? Or can it be repaired? And have you given your customers the tools and information necessary to repair it? Here's how you can help facilitate repairs:

- **Sell modular parts:** Have you ever had a simple but essential part of a product, like a knob or a latch, break in a way that could theoretically be easily repaired if you had the right part, but instead you had to throw the item away and buy a new one? I know I have. Companies can prevent this by selling modular parts to their customers. Allow customers to purchase new batteries, knobs, buttons, and so on from you directly so that your product doesn't land in the grave before its time. This also means that a customer will continue to make purchases from you on an ongoing basis, whereas if they bought one product from you that broke, you may lose them as a customer forever.

- **Offer repair services:** Consider allowing your customer to bring their product into a physical location for a repair (like Apple does) or mail it in (like Patagonia does). This service is an added value to your product that can bump it into the "premium" category and allow you to charge more for it if necessary.

- **Provide information:** If a product can be easily repaired at home, provide information on how to do so. Patagonia has a series of videos and articles on its website showing customers how to repair a zipper or patch insulation on a jacket (see Patagonia profile on page 190).

COLLECTION

The safest way to know what happens to your product at the end of its life is to collect it yourself. There are several common ways to orchestrate this:

- **Leasing Model:** A leasing model has been common for premium products such as large pieces of equipment for years. If properly designed, a leasing model can be a win for everyone. The business has a recurring revenue stream from a product and is able to reuse valuable parts and materials when the product is no longer usable; the customer is prevented from getting stuck with outdated models; and the earth ultimately gets saddled with less trash.

  In recent years, leasing or rental models have been set up for a more diverse range of products, such as clothing or tools (see the Shared Economy section on page 310).

- **Reuse:** Some companies design a unique pathway for their product to help it avoid the landfill. This can be done in partnership with another company or can be designed and facilitated internally. Patagonia manages a Worn Wear program for customers to mail in old Patagonia merchandise in exchange for store credit (see Patagonia company profile on page 190), and Interface will directly collect its used carpet (see Interface profile on page 93).

- **Information:** Whether you want your customer to recycle your product, toss it in a compost pile, drop it in a donation bin, or mail it back to you, the most important thing is that you *tell* them. Even the most well-intentioned customer will probably dispose of your product incorrectly unless they are provided with clear instructions on the best way to do so. This also provides you with an additional opportunity to communicate with your customer and reinforce sustainability, conscientiousness, and intentional design as part of your brand.

Designing for end of life completes the cycle of impact for your product and allows you to gain additional control of the environmental and social impact of your product and company. A well-designed end-of-life pathway can help you improve your brand and your relationship with your customer and can potentially give you the opportunity to save money by reclaiming and reusing valuable resources.

Remember, the two parts of this section must go together. No matter how carefully you design your product to be compostable, recyclable, or reusable, none of it will matter if your product ends up in the landfill alongside the banana peels and plastic packaging. Designing for end of life must include both careful product design and a thoughtful and creative pathway design for your product when your customer is finished with it. Finally, this design element also means communication with your customer so they will understand the role their behavior plays in the sustainability of your product.

Designing for end of life is a huge opportunity to be innovative and impactful in your product design. However, if you feel overwhelmed by the prospect, there are outside organizations that can help you with this process. Look for consultants with Cradle to Cradle or Life Cycle Assessment certifications to help you improve the end-of-life journey of your product.

Company Profile: Interface

Where the company integrates impact

- Design
- Material sourcing
- Manufacturing
- Community
- Voice

Founder: Ray C. Anderson

Ray founded Interface in the 1970s. He didn't start the company with an environmental mission—that came later. He started it because he thought carpet tiles were an excellent business opportunity (and it turns out he was right). Around twenty years later, he was asked by a customer what Interface was doing for the environment and was dismayed when he didn't have an answer. He read *The Ecology of Commerce* by Paul Hawken and described it as his "spear in the chest moment" that changed his view on business and sustainability.[16]

What they do

Interface makes carpet— that's the short answer. They sell carpet tiles and flooring to commercial spaces, such as offices, hotels, and schools. The longer answer is that they are one of the forefront business leaders in sustainable design and innovation as well as one of the leading carpet companies in the world.

Business model

Interface uses a straightforward B2B model to sell commercial flooring and carpeting to businesses, schools, offices, commercial spaces, and so on. They design, manufacture, and sell their own carpet. What is fascinating about Interface is that they have been able to achieve such notable advancements in sustainable design, manufacturing, and process within a fairly standard business model and product offering.

Impact

DESIGN

- **Floor tiles:** One of Interface's simplest but most impactful designs is integrating biomimicry into designing products, such as their i2 carpet tiles. In this case, the biomimicry element of the design is simple. The design of i2 carpet tiles is inspired by the random but cohesive look of leaves on the forest floor, the colored tops of trees in the fall, or the spread of wildflowers across a field. The design is meant to be cohesive without having a distinct or repeating pattern. This means that if red wine is spilled on one portion of the carpet, instead of replacing the entire carpet, only one or two carpet tiles need to be pulled up and replaced. The aesthetic of the carpet is designed to be varied enough that new additions to the carpet at a later time will not look out of place.[17]

- **Carbon-negative carpet:** Remember what I said in the introduction of this book about "sustainability" often meaning "less bad" instead of "more good"? Interface's Carbon Negative carpet lines are an excellent example of striving for "more good." Rather than aiming only to decrease the negative impact they make on the environment through the production of their carpet, they actually use the design, materials, and production of some of their carpet lines to make a net-positive environmental impact. Although all their flooring is "carbon-neutral," some of their carpet lines are actually "carbon-negative," which means that making the product takes more greenhouse gases from the atmosphere than it releases.[18] How did they do this? It wasn't easy. The process took four years to develop and incorporated recycled vinyl, processed vegetation, salvaged nylon, and a plastic made partially from smokestack exhaust (you read that correctly). Interface estimates that the carpet tiles have a carbon footprint of at least negative 300 grams per square meter.[19]

- **ReEntry Program:** As described on page 90, designing a recyclable product is a two-step process: 1) make sure the materials in your product can be technically recycled, and 2) design a collection system so that when the product reaches the end of its usable life, it can be collected and transported back to a place where it can actually be recycled (or find a way to integrate with existing recycling systems). Step 2 is the one that often gets forgotten in sustainable product design. If a product is technically recyclable but is going to end up in the landfill anyway, you might as well not have bothered.

  Interface uses a program called ReEntry to collect and recycle Interface carpet tile in the United States. If a customer wants to participate in the ReEntry program, they must specify upon carpet installation that they would like their carpeting to be recycled. The installation team will then install the carpet with a releasable installation system so that it can be easily removed and recycled later. When they're ready to recycle the carpet, customers can fill out a ReEntry request form on the Interface website. The customer is responsible for removing and packing the carpet according to Interface's specifications, and then an Interface driver will pick up the carpet. It will either be donated to a charity (if the carpet is still in good shape), or the materials will be dismantled and recycled into new carpeting.[20]

MATERIAL SOURCING

- **Unique materials:** The materials in an Interface carbon-negative product are not like those found in your standard carpeting. Interface states a goal of "Learning to Love Carbon" and thinking of carbon as an ally rather than an enemy. Indeed, carbon has a very important role to play in our world, our atmosphere, and even our bodies—the only problem is that we have too much of it in the atmosphere. Interface's CQuest carpet backings are made from unique materials including industrial waste, renewable organic materials, and concentrated carbon.[21]

- **Recycled content:** In addition to incorporating recycled materials from their own carpeting when a customer is finished with it, Interface also incorporates recycled materials from other industries, such as using discarded fishing nets to create the recycled nylon used in their products.[22]

MANUFACTURING

- **"Factory as a forest":** Interface utilizes biomimicry and looks to nature for inspiration for much of its design and its innovations in sustainability. The company takes biomimicry one step further by attempting to design a factory that "functions as a forest." The intention is to create structures and systems that function as an ecosystem, looking beyond the goal of decreasing negative impact, instead creating factories that cycle nutrients and replenish the community and environment in the way that natural systems in a forest do. This vision is a goal and "north star" for their facility, process, and product design.[23]

- **Sustainability measurement and accounting:** Not all aspects of operating sustainably are glamorous; a lot of it is

simply numbers and tracking. In their manufacturing facilities, Interface meticulously tracks their energy use, water use, renewable energy sources, direct emissions, supply
chain emissions, and waste streams.

- **Efficient machinery:** As Interface progressed in their sustainability journey, they retrofitted the machinery in their
manufacturing facilities to operate as efficiently as possible.
For example, rather than transferring yarn that is delivered
on twelve-inch cardboard "cones" to a twelve-foot beam before tufting it into carpet, Interface developed a "portable
creel" system to connect the tufting machines directly to the
cones, making it easy to return partial cones to inventory
and saving millions of dollars in yarn waste every year.

- **Recycling:** In addition to sourcing much of their material
from recycled sources, Interface also recycles much of the
scrap materials and waste created from their manufacturing processes. Within their manufacturing facilities, Interface runs a large recycling center designed to turn trim waste
from edges of finished carpet into new carpet tile backing
(combined with reclaimed post-consumer materials from
ReEntry).[24]

- **Carbon offsets:** Despite tremendous efforts toward sustainability and groundbreaking innovative design, Interface is
not perfect. They have not yet found ways to eliminate all
negative environmental impacts from their supply chain,
product design, manufacturing, use, and products' end of
life. To counteract the negative impact they do create, they
purchase carbon offsets to fund clean energy, sustainable
forestry, and ecological rehabilitation projects around the
world. Their offset program is so comprehensive that they are
a certified Carbon Neutral Enterprise, even as they strive to
become Carbon Negative without offsets by 2040.[25]

COMMUNITY

Interface operates factories around the world. As a company scales
and operates within different communities, it is important to be

conscious of how the company's presence impacts that community. Interface has two notable programs that positively impact communities in which they operate. The first program is a partnership with the Net-Works program that pays community members to collect used fishing nets and helps to develop a restorative supply chain and positive economic development in villages in Cameroon, Indonesia, and the Philippines. The second program is their employee-led Weaving a Better Life program in Thailand. Through this program, leftover yarn is given to local Chonburi and Surin villagers and then woven into new products such as hammocks and sandals. This system successfully turns a waste stream into much needed income for people in the local community.[26]

VOICE

In 2017, Interface lobbied for a California recycling bill mandating that carpet manufacturers in California implement a system that sets a goal of recycling 24 percent of carpet by 2020. If no approved collection plan was in place by this time, the carpet manufacturers would be banned from selling carpet within the state. As can be expected, this law was not popular with all carpet manufacturers, but Interface lobbied for the bill, joining with a coalition of organizers and legislators pushing for the bill. The CEO of Interface, Jay Gould, called the law "a positive step forward in driving a truly circular economy in our industry."[27] For opposing the industry on this and other state carpet recycling bills, Interface was forced to leave the membership of the carpet industry association, which opposes all non-voluntary carpet recycling. Interface has also supported legislation that sets limits on purchasing high carbon-footprint products by the state of California.

What I like about it

There are several things that stand out to me about Interface's business model that make their story particularly worth sharing:

1. <u>Striving for "more good"</u>: The Interface commitment to sustainability is undeniable. What I particularly like about their approach is that they don't stop at aiming for a decrease in their negative environmental impact. Instead, they strive for creating products, factories, and systems that are a net contributor to the

planet and aim to regenerate communities and natural systems in the same way that nature does. It's okay that they haven't figured this all out yet; the fact that they are aiming high and looking at the big vision for positive impact makes them worth talking about.

2. Pioneering spirit: Interface has developed some truly remarkable sustainable innovations and successfully taken them to scale. Their carbon-negative flooring, made from smokestack exhaust, biological materials, and carbon, isn't sitting in a lab somewhere—it is being walked on all over the world. Interface must be commended for not only having radical sustainable design ideas, but also turning them into reality.

3. Standard business model: Another thing I like about Interface is the fact that, despite all of their groundbreaking innovation, their business is built on a very standard business model for a very standard product—they make and sell carpet. Can you change the world through carpet? I wouldn't have thought so— I'm a fan of hardwood personally—but by using their nature-inspired innovation, production, and recycling practices as models for other businesses, Interface might do just that. As Ray Anderson said, "If we can become sustainable, maybe any company can."

4. Late entry into sustainability: Finally, another important note about Interface is that they operated as a company for twenty years before developing a commitment to sustainability. A company does not have to be founded with positive impact as a core goal in order to become a leader in the space. The Interface journey should serve as an inspiration for other companies. No matter what your product, service, or business model is, with the right commitment, vision, and willingness to experiment and explore, any company can be a sustainability pioneer—there is a lot of territory yet to be discovered.

Interface

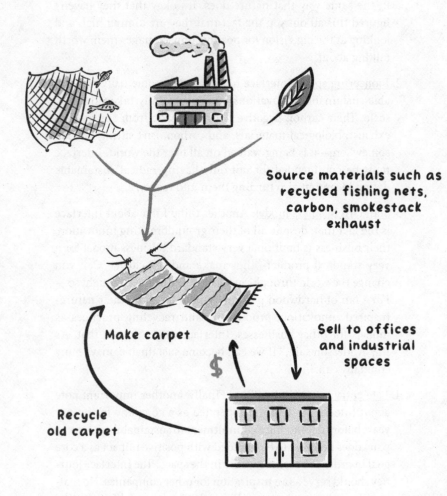

Source materials such as
recycled fishing nets,
carbon, smokestack
exhaust

Make carpet

Sell to offices
and industrial
spaces

Recycle
old carpet

$

8

Material Sourcing

If you sell a physical product, you must source your materials from somewhere, and this offers an excellent opportunity for integrating social and environmental impact into the core of your business model. Sourcing ethically means that you know where your materials come from and that you have gone out of your way to ensure that the materials that go into your product are coming from socially and environmentally responsible sources. Better yet, the materials you purchase can support sustainable economic and community development so that by purchasing the materials you need for your product, you are supporting positive job creation and good environmental stewardship. There are many ways to ensure that you are sourcing materials ethically. A few key methods for doing so are:

Looking for Relevant Certifications

One way to know that your materials are being purchased from ethical sources is to look for certifications and labels that verify that a material was produced ethically. Depending on what you are creating, the relevant certifications could vary widely. If you are sourcing wood or paper, for example, you may look for the Forest Stewardship Council (FSC) certification verifying that the wood was harvested in a sustainable manner.[1] If your product includes leather, you can search for certification from the Leather Working Group.[2] If you are sourcing food or an agricultural product, you may look for Fair Trade, Rainforest

Alliance, or Organic certifications. No matter what product you are sourcing, you could look to purchase materials from a certified B Corp. Businesses that are labeled as a B Corp are certified by an organization called B Lab, which verifies that these businesses create benefit for all their stakeholders, including local communities and the environment, not only for their shareholders, and that they monitor and report on the social and environmental metrics of their business.[3]

I have not covered an exhaustive list of certifications by any means. There are hundreds of social and environmental certifications for all industries. Certifications can serve as a great guide to finding ethical materials to source for your business. Certification bodies do the work that you don't have time to do by looking into the businesses you purchase from and confirming that their practices honor your values. Certifications are also a helpful way to communicate your ethical sourcing practices to your customers in a clear and concise way.

The downside of this method is that there are *a lot* of certifications out there, and no certification, no matter how thorough, can cover all the intricacies of ethical practices. If you choose a certification to trust, be prepared to hear from someone else that another different, but very similar, certification is really the way to go. Furthermore, certifications can be expensive. Not only does this generally mean that purchasing from certified businesses will likely be more costly for customers, but it also means that many businesses that are very socially and environmentally responsible with their practices may not have the extra cash to pay for certifications.

Tips for Success

1. **Do your research.** Look for the relevant social and ethically responsible certifications for your industry. Do the research to make sure that the certification agency is reputable and that the certification standards align with your vision and the values that really matter to you and your company. You may consider looking at another company whose values align with yours and checking which certifications they use.

2. **Determine which certifications your customers care about.** Often (though not always), certified materials will come at a

slightly higher price point. However, sometimes this can be off-set by the fact that customers may be willing to pay slightly more for a material that was sourced in an ethical manner. Sourcing ethically and being able to claim certifications may even help you reach new or broader customer bases.

3. **Remember that not all ethical businesses are certified.** As I mentioned, certifications are helpful because they provide the research that you may not have time to do and bring in relevant expertise that you may not have in-house. Certifications also allow you to quickly communicate standards and ethical practices to others. However, some of the most ethically run businesses may have no certifications at all, especially if the businesses are small. They may not be able to afford the cost of certifications or be willing to deal with the hassle. If your core motivation is to find suppliers that align with your vision and mission, nothing can beat actually knowing your suppliers and being familiar with their principles and practices.

Use Recycled Materials

We were born into a completely circular system—nature doesn't create waste! That fact always boggles my mind to think about, but it's true. Over time, everything in nature is reused or recycled for another purpose. Human beings more or less invented waste when we converted these intricate, circular, natural processes into a linear system. Our current system takes materials from the ground, makes them into new goods, and then, when they break, wear out, or go out of style, we bury them in a hole in the ground and try not to think about them again. Sounds a bit primitive, doesn't it? Not our best work. And unfortunately, this linear process is catching up with us. The holes in the ground are getting more and more full and we are sourcing materials from nature faster than it can replenish itself.

When we recycle materials, we are taking a leaf from nature's book and reusing materials for new purposes. When searching for new suppliers, see if you can find materials with some percentage of recycled content. Many different materials that are totally or partially sourced from recycled materials can be purchased; paper, metal, plastic, and fabric such as polyester are just a few examples.

Remember, recycling can be complicated, and you may hear that the recycling process is energy-intensive or requires a significant amount of cleaning and processing. For some materials, this is true. Depending on the amount of processing required and the value of the material, some materials can't be recycled economically. It is also true that recycling often means "downcycling" because when some materials are recycled, they degrade in quality until eventually they can no longer be recycled. This is true for materials like paper and plastic, but not true for materials like metal. Most metals can be recycled indefinitely without a loss of quality.

It is also worth noting here that when possible, reuse is better than recycling. If a product can be directly reused rather than recycled, you can rescue material from the landfill without a loss of quality or the expense and energy use of recycling. Glass, for example, is very easy to reuse—a glass jar or bottle can be washed and reused very easily—but it is more complicated to recycle. Glass is heavy, breaks easily, and can lose quality when colors are mixed. Many municipal recycling programs have stopped accepting it.

Ultimately, even with acknowledgement of the facts above and the understanding that recycling is no silver bullet, as a general rule, diverting waste from the landfill by sourcing recycled materials is still better than using virgin materials.

Source Locally—Know Your Suppliers

If you have the opportunity to source materials locally, sourcing from businesses located in close proximity to your business is a bit of a shortcut on ethical sourcing. Because of the proximity, you have the automatic guarantee that at least the environmental impact of transporting materials will be lower. Even if you are not able to source locally, the best way to know that you are sourcing materials responsibly is to actually know and trust your suppliers. Visit their facilities and see how they treat their workers, and check where they source *their* materials from and how they process their waste. Get to know the management—know their principles and values, where they draw lines, and where they cut corners.

Generally, sourcing materials from another country results in significantly higher carbon dioxide emissions from transportation than from a business within your state or region. The proximity of a local supplier also ensures that it is easier to have a personal relationship with your suppliers and have the chance to observe their business practices firsthand. You also have the added benefit of contributing to your local economy. Finally, sourcing locally requires no outside body to certify that the business is local to you—all you have to do is look at a map.

Even if you can't source locally, taking the time to know where your materials come from does more than ensure that your materials are being sourced responsibly (although it does that too!). Visiting your suppliers helps to ensure the quality of your products and protects your company from the bad media coverage and reputation hit that can happen if it turns out your suppliers are damaging the environment or treating their workers poorly (remember the Nike boycotts in the 1990s?). Finally, building a good relationship with the companies you depend on means that you are more likely to get a heads-up about shortages and price hikes that could be on the horizon.

Keep in mind that depending on what you are sourcing and where you live, it is not always possible to source locally. If you live in Kentucky and are trying to source bananas, you are out of luck. Even if sourcing locally is an option, it can often end up being more expensive than transporting the materials you need. Although this doesn't make logical sense (shouldn't it be cheaper if you don't have to ship a material around the world?), the difference in pricing often comes from lower wages paid in other countries, currency differences, and the ability for large factories to mass-produce a product. If you are not able to source locally, depending on how complicated your supply chain is, it can take a lot of time (and travel) to visit and get to know all of your suppliers.

Ultimately, if your goal is to source ethically, nothing can beat taking the time to know where your materials come from. Be sure to involve multiple people from the team so that the supplier relationships are not lost with staff changes. Set goals around ethical and environmental sourcing standards for your company. Remember, you don't have to meet these goals all at once. You can work up to them, and you should be honest with employees and customers about your progress (Patagonia does a particularly good job with this—see the Patagonia company profile on page 190 for more details). Another thing to remember is that you don't have to figure this all out by yourself. There are supply chain and manufacturing experts that can help. FORGE, for example, is a nonprofit organization that helps startups figure out their onshore supply chain and manufacturing.[4]

Source Creatively

One of the things I love about entrepreneurship is the idea that, if you look hard enough at any problem, you can find an opportunity inside it. There is no denying the fact that our society has a waste problem, but there is value to be found in this waste, and there is profit to be made for the innovative companies that can find a way to source part or all of their materials from a waste stream (see the Circular Economy Industry section on page 307).

There are three undeniable benefits to sourcing materials from a waste stream:

1. <u>Cost</u>: The first is the cost of new materials. If you can rescue materials from the trash rather than purchasing materials from suppliers, your bottom line is going to notice the difference in material expenses. If you can save another company money by taking a portion of their waste stream that they would otherwise have to pay a fee to dispose of, they may even pay you to take the materials.

2. <u>Your story</u>: The second benefit is to your company's story. If you are positioning yourself as a sustainable company, incorporating a waste stream into your product shows that you mean what you say. You can get excellent, straightforward metrics for your company's sustainability story by directly diverting waste from the landfill. Incorporating materials that were landfill-bound into your supply chain is a powerful addition to your story and brand identity (check out the company profiles of Patagonia and Interface for some examples).

3. <u>Your mission</u>: I'll say it again: our society has a major waste problem. We are generating millions of tons of waste per year, which is causing damage to bodies of water, wildlife habitats, sanitation, and human health. We are also running low on

precious natural resources such as fresh water, clean air, trees, metals, petroleum, topsoil, phosphorus, and much, much more. If you can use someone else's waste as a product input, you are both preventing new natural resources from being used and diverting waste from the landfill. In other words, you are helping to take our society a step in the right direction, toward a circular economy, where materials are reused and upcycled, rather than a linear economy, where natural resources are taken from the earth and then trashed.

The things that may trip you up when exploring the process of sourcing from waste streams are the logistics and processing involved. If you find a waste stream that you could use as a source of materials, collecting, transporting, and processing it can be a complicated equation to consider. The ideal situation would be to find another company or industry (preferably close to your manufacturing facility) that produces a consistent and reliable source of waste from a small number of locations. If post-consumer waste is what you're after, your best bet may be to partner with a municipal waste hauler or recycling company and pay them to collect and bale the material for you. Processing waste can also be tricky and potentially expensive because waste may need to go through additional processing and cleaning. Ideally, these costs will be offset by the amount saved from not purchasing new materials. However, if you are going to explore sourcing from waste, make sure you have someone skilled in supply chain logistics as part of your team or advisors.

Below are three recommendations to use as starting points for thinking through how to divert waste from the landfill and turn it into profit. Make sure to look at the company examples throughout the book for inspiration.

1. Take a close look at your bill of materials. Are there any inputs that, with some processing, could come from another company or industry's waste stream? Think carefully about what other companies may be generating as a regular waste stream: wood chips? Cloth scraps? Plastic packaging? Scrap metal?

2. If you can't imagine pulling any of your current materials from a waste stream, consider whether there are any materials that you could replace with something similar that did come from waste.

3. If you're having trouble finding other industries that produce the materials you need, remember that you know at least one company that uses these materials—yours! Consider methods to recapture and reuse the materials that go into your own products from your manufacturing process or after your customers are finished with them.

Company Profile: thredUP

Where the company integrates impact

- Products and services
- Material sourcing
- Packaging and shipping

Founder: James Reinhart

James Reinhart was a born entrepreneur. When he was ten years old, he started a lawn mowing company in his neighborhood. He charged fifteen dollars per lawn and then hired other kids to help him mow at ten dollars per lawn.[5] Like many social impact companies, thredUP was not initially founded with a social mission—that came later. thredUP was founded because James saw a need in his own life and thought it might translate to a larger market opportunity. In 2009, when James was in business school, he took a look in his closet and didn't see anything he wanted to wear. However, he was on a student budget and didn't want to spend money to get any new clothes. (I can relate to this feeling.) He guessed that other people might have the same issue, so he teamed up with some friends to create an online clothing swap for men and women's clothes. The platform did okay, but it wasn't taking off like they had hoped. They expanded to kids' clothing and saw increased interest and attracted some venture capital funding. The real growth came when they shifted the business model from a swap model, started selling used clothing, and introduced the Clean Out Kit that allows people to easily donate their old clothes.[6]

What they do

thredUP is an online secondhand clothing store. Secondhand clothing stores have been around for decades, but they are usually in brick-and-mortar locations, and patrons' options are limited to the clothes that other people in their community have donated. thredUP has taken the traditional consignment store model virtual. This means that customers anywhere can donate their clothes to thredUP, and customers have thousands of options to choose from, donated from people all around the country. As online shopping skyrockets in popularity, the thredUP model allows shoppers to purchase secondhand from their living rooms with added benefits usually not available to thrift shoppers, such as the luxury of searching for secondhand options by size, color, or brand.

thredUP has developed proprietary technology that allows the company to accept, process, and recirculate clothing at a remarkable speed. They have the capacity to process 100,000 unique items a day, list 2.4 million items online at a time, and house 5.5 million items in their distribution centers. In 2021, the company was seeing annual revenue of around $44 million.[7]

Business model

thredUP's core business model is what I would refer to as "Circular B2C," meaning that the company is selling directly to consumers and is also sourcing directly from the same consumers. What is magic about this model is that thredUP is offering a service on both sides of the business model. On the customer side, they are offering consumers fresh clothing options at a lower price with a lower environmental footprint (as compared to new clothing). On the supplier side, they are offering people a place to send the clothing that no longer fits or that they no longer wear. thredUP processes and catalogs the items, making them available to purchase online. When the items sell, the supplier gets a portion of the profits (offered on a sliding scale based on how much the item sells for) and can either choose to cash out or get store credit for thredUP. This means that thredUP basically has no supply costs aside from shipping, and that it encourages their suppliers to also become customers.

In addition to their core Circular B2C business model, thredUP is also exploring what they call a Retail as a Service model (or RAAS). Large clothing brands know that secondhand clothing purchases are on the rise and may ultimately threaten their business. Rather than treating these stores as competitors, thredUP has developed a model to partner with these stores in a way that benefits both businesses.

thredUP's RAAS option allows brands to integrate an online shop on their website where consumers can shop for secondhand options of that particular brand. thredUP handles all the logistics of accepting and selling the used clothing utilizing the same methods they already have in place. Consumers who purchase the secondhand clothing through the retailer's site get a credit to purchase more clothing from that particular brand. This model means that any brand could have their own resale store, similar to Patagonia's Worn Wear program (see company profile on page 190) and benefit from the success their products achieve in the secondhand economy while also adding to their sustainability story. The difference is that thredUP handles the logistics, meaning that this option is available to brands with very little risk or difficulty. thredUP benefits by gaining the eyes of these large clothing brand's customers. Some of thredUP's RAAS partners include Adidas, Gap, Vera Bradley, and Banana Republic.[8]

Because the core function of thredUP (enabling the purchase of secondhand clothes) has a huge benefit to the environment (as opposed to the purchase of new clothes), thredUP can engage in consumer education about the environmental impact of the fashion industry, which ultimately benefits the environment and also doubles as a means of advertising for thredUP. thredUP offers reports and education about the environmental impact of the fashion industry as well as a Fashion Footprint Calculator to help customers understand the impact of buying a new garment as opposed to a secondhand piece of clothing.

thredUP also embarks on initiatives and partnerships to generate enthusiasm about reuse and to overcome consumer skepticism and stigma around secondhand clothes. One popular initiative was the "Shop Their Closets" campaign that allowed customers to buy secondhand clothes from celebrities with the proceeds going to charity.[9]

Impact

PRODUCTS AND SERVICES

thredUP helps facilitate the circular economy for the fashion industry. It takes an average of seventy-seven gallons of water and creates seventeen pounds of carbon dioxide to create one item of clothing. That's a lot when you consider that approximately 100 billion new garments are produced every year. If, instead of buying a new item of clothing, someone fulfills the desire to spice up their wardrobe by purchasing a secondhand item instead, the carbon, waste, and water footprint of that piece of clothing is decreased by 82 percent.[10] The core function of thredUP is to facilitate the secondhand economy, allowing it to be a profitable business while also having a significant environmental and social impact. As the thredUP business continues to grow, the positive impact will continue to grow as well.

MATERIAL SOURCING

A 2022 Bloomberg report stated that people throw out their clothing after wearing it an average of seven to ten times![11] Unless that clothing was very poor quality, it should still have some good life in it after seven to ten wears, not to mention that that number was *an average*, meaning that many pieces of clothing are thrown away much earlier. However, one person's trash is another person's treasure, as they say. thredUP sources its merchandise from this unwanted clothing, effectively diverting clothing from the landfill and giving it a new life in someone else's closet.

PACKAGING AND SHIPPING

When you place an order from thredUP, your secondhand piece of clothing will arrive in a polka-dot poly mailer, an envelope made out of a thin plastic film. In this case, the film is made from recycled plastic. thredUP claims that its packaging is not only made of recycled material, but also 100 percent reusable and recyclable. I'd say this is a partial truth. And as discussed in the Packaging and Shipping chapter on page 139, plastic film is *technically* recyclable but is generally not collected with curbside municipal recycling and must be dropped off at a plastic film collection center (like at a grocery store), where it then *may* get recycled depending on what the plastics market is doing at the moment. All that said, packaging is a challenge, and I do commend thredUP for using mailers made of recycled plastic.

One of my favorite things about thredUP is their "Bundled" shipping option. It is a clever way to reduce the environmental impact of shipping and the costs of shipping for both the company and consumer. When you make a purchase from thredUP, you have the option to either have the item shipped to you right away, or, if you think you may purchase multiple things in the coming week, you can select the "Bundled" shipping option. This means that they will hold your purchase for seven days (unless you cancel it sooner), and anything else that you buy will be bundled and shipped with your original purchase, decreasing the amount of packaging needed as well as delivery miles and resulting carbon dioxide emissions.[12]

What I like about it

thredUP is such a clean example of using business for good. There's no sourcing of virgin materials, no manufacturing emissions to worry about—just the need to process and move resources around in an efficient way and take something that is no longer valuable to one person and sell it to someone else who does see value in it. According to my point of view as someone who both likes clothes and is very conscious of the environmental impact of producing unnecessary consumer goods, thredUP helps to fulfill a distinct need.

It should be noted that thredUP is not the first or only business to address this problem. Brick-and-mortar thrift stores around the world offer a similar service and are often run in conjunction with other mission-driven initiatives, such as Goodwill's job training program or Karm Stores' rescue and restoration programs. These brick-and-mortar options also provide an added "treasure hunting" experience that, like many things, is hard to recreate virtually. What thredUP has managed to do is add scale, connectivity, and infrastructure to help strengthen the foundations of the secondhand economy.

thredUP

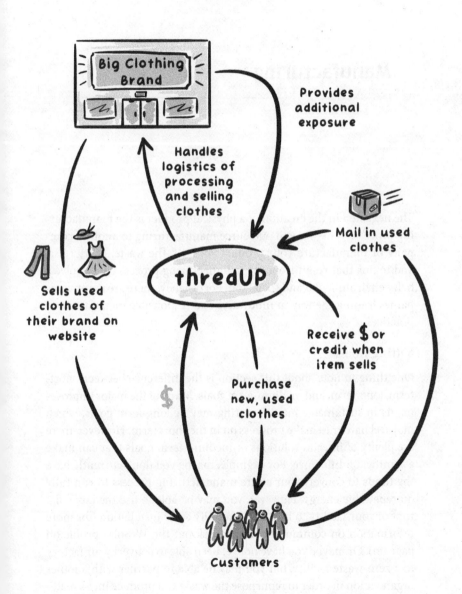

9

Manufacturing

The next step in the creation of a physical product is the manufacturing process. Whether you outsource manufacturing to another company or manufacture your product yourself, the waste, energy use, and toxins that result from the manufacturing process can involve a hefty environmental and social toll. Fortunately, there are many companies leading the way in innovative and responsible manufacturing practices.

Setting Goals

One thing to note about this section is the difference between short-term, long-term, and medium-term goals. Many of the major improvements in sustainable manufacturing may be long-term goals, which may feel harder to make progress on in the short term. However, there are plenty of interim solutions or medium-term goals that can make a significant difference. For example, maybe you don't currently have the funds to convert your entire manufacturing process to run fully on renewable energy. However, you may be able to use the large, flat roof of your facility to host a community solar installation (for more information on community solar, check out the WeSolar profile on page 181). Or maybe you have not yet been able to convert your factory to a zero-waste facility, but you may be able to partner with another organization in order to repurpose the waste you produce into a material that can be used by another industry.

Before You Begin

Some of the most important decisions around the social and environmental impact of your manufacturing process are made before you actually begin to manufacture anything. Product design and the materials you use will make a huge difference in the impact of your manufacturing process. Read more about material sourcing in chapter 8 and product design in chapter 7.

Stages of Manufacturing

If you are starting a new company and creating a physical product, manufacturing usually happens in three stages as you scale. Depending on the unique nature of your business and how large you plan to grow your business, you may stop at any one of these stages, or you may go through them in a different order. For example, if you offer a high-end, handcrafted product, you may never advance past stage 1, and that is perfectly okay. If you offer a product where the technology is particularly novel or trade secrets are essential, you may skip straight from stage 1 to stage 3—it all depends on what makes the most sense for your business. However, companies that create a physical product and plan to scale usually advance through manufacturing stages in this order:

1. Manufacturing by hand: At this stage, you or someone else on your team creates every product you offer by hand. This method is ideal for perfecting the design of your product, and it can also have benefits if being "handcrafted" increases the value of your product (this can be particularly true for artisans or food products). You are also able to keep a much closer eye on the environmental impact of your business because you are closely involved in the entire process. However, if you plan to scale your business, eventually you will likely need to move beyond this stage. Manufacturing by hand is generally slower, less precise, and more expensive per-unit than stages two and three.

2. Contract manufacturing: Contract manufacturing means that you work with another company that specializes in a particular kind of manufacturing to create your product. There are many

advantages to this method, namely that even as a small company you can benefit from the expertise, equipment, and established processes of a contract manufacturer. This is a less capital-intensive way to manufacture your product, although the per-unit cost of production would likely be higher than establishing your own manufacturing plant.

If you are working with a contract manufacturer, you may not be making many of the decisions about manufacturing processes, treatment of employees, or environmental impact. If you are a large business, you may have the ability to influence your contract manufacturers (see Patagonia company profile on 190), but if you are a small company, it may be harder to suggest changes. Because of this, it is important to select contract manufacturers that align with your values. Even if you are not making the decisions yourself, it is important to read this chapter fully so that you understand the questions to ask, the areas to evaluate a manufacturer in, and have the ability to select a contract manufacturer that fits your business.

3. Running your own manufacturing facility: When your company reaches a certain size, it may make sense to bring your manufacturing in-house and develop your own manufacturing facilities. Not only do you no longer have to pay the contract manufacturer's fee, but you can also benefit from economies of scale and have a higher level of control over product quality and the social and environmental impact of your manufacturing process. If you are running your own manufacturing facility, your company has direct control to make decisions about the manufacturing process to improve the environmental and social impact of your product.

Six Areas to Watch: Key Areas of Impact in Manufacturing

Below are the key areas of impact for manufacturing with tips to minimize negative impact and best practices from business leaders in sustainable manufacturing. Like most parts of this book, this section will contain disappointingly few silver bullets. About 1 percent of progress in sustainable manufacturing comes from exciting new innovation; the other 99 percent comes from practicing tried-and-true methods, setting goals, measuring progress, and making improvement a priority. Below are the key areas of impact within the manufacturing process and best practices for improving them.

1. Waste

How much waste is generated to create the things we buy every day? The unfortunate answer is *a lot*. A general rule is that for every one can of garbage put on the curb by a household, approximately seventy times that amount was generated in the process of manufacturing everything that went into that garbage can.[1] Remember, nature is able to create without generating any waste, so it must be possible to create new materials more efficiently. However, nature has had thousands of years to refine its processes and we humans are still learning the ropes. Luckily, there are several tools, systems, and pioneering entrepreneurs leading the way. Here are a few actions you can take:

MINIMIZING WASTE

The first step is to decrease the waste generated during manufacturing. The best way to do that is by increasing efficiency throughout the manufacturing process. Producing a new product without waste is difficult, but in a world where one-third of our planet's natural resources have already been consumed, it's worth the work.

REPURPOSING AND RECYCLING WASTE

When waste is produced through manufacturing, look for destinations other than the landfill. The path to the landfill is straight and ends at a dead end. We live in a circular planet, and the planet's resources should follow a circular path, too. The ideal circular paths to explore for waste are listed below. Eventually, these materials may not seem like waste at all, but just another resource.

- Reuse: The ideal path for waste is to be reused for another product or purpose. Compared to recycling, reuse often requires less processing and can save a company money by minimizing the amount of new or virgin materials that must be purchased. If you can sell the excess materials to another company, even better.

- Recycle: Recycling your waste products means breaking the waste down to the base materials (such as plastic resin or aluminum) and then using the material for another purpose. Some companies, like Eastman, have taken this a step further and are exploring recycling materials at the molecular level.[2] You could recycle in-house and reuse the materials yourself, recycle through municipal recycling in the city you are located in, or sell your product to another company either directly or through an intermediary like TerraCycle. Depending on the value of the waste stream and the complexity of recycling it, this could either make or cost you money.

- Compost: If you have natural waste streams such as food waste, untreated wood chips or cotton, or other biological materials, you can compost this material either onsite or through an industrial compost facility and give your waste new life as fertilizer for crops and gardens. Many breweries compost their own spent brewery grains onsite or partner with local farmers to use the spent grain as a supplement for animal feed.[3] (See the New Belgium Brewing profile on page 130).

2. Water

Water usage and contamination is another common area of social and environmental damage in manufacturing. Large amounts of water are used in the manufacturing process, even for products you may not think of as being particularly water-intensive. For example, approximately 180 liters of water is used in the manufacturing process to manufacture one pair of jeans (not counting the water it takes to grow the cotton).[4] High water usage is wasteful and expensive, particularly in areas where water is scarce. Water contamination that results from manufacturing can be detrimental to the local community and ecosystem if not properly cleaned and treated. Water usage in manufacturing can be improved in the following ways:

REDUCE AND REUSE

The first step is to reduce the amount of water used in the manufacturing process. This can be done through planning, water-efficient equipment, innovation, and reuse. By capturing and reusing water onsite, manufacturing facilities can decrease water use and save money on water bills and wastewater discharge fees.

PROCESSING AND CLEANING

For the wastewater that is produced by the manufacturing process, it is important to clean and treat the water before releasing it back into nature. The Environmental Protection Agency (EPA) regulates industrial water discharge with specific standards for different industries.[5] Some companies have gone above and beyond and found ways to benefit from cleaning their wastewater. In 2002, New Belgium Brewing (company profile on page 130) built an anaerobic digester to treat the wastewater they generate from their brewing process and capture the resulting biogas to use as a renewable energy source.[6] Which brings us to our next category . . .

3. Energy

Because of the equipment and processing required, manufacturing can be extremely energy-intensive. The manufacturing industry is responsible for approximately 23 percent of US greenhouse gas emissions; for context, commercial and residential energy use is responsible for only 13 percent.[7] There are four steps to making the manufacturing process more energy-efficient:

ENERGY REDUCTION

A significant amount of energy can be saved in the manufacturing process through simple efficiency modifications such as building weatherization and switching to LED lighting. These steps are the "low-hanging fruit" that will generally save a facility money over time in addition to reducing energy emissions. Switching to more energy-efficient equipment and machinery can also decrease energy emissions and improve bottom line over time. Educating employees about energy use and incorporating energy efficient practices, such as turning off equipment when not in use, can also result in significant energy savings. See the section on Lean Manufacturing on page 126 for processes and practices that improve resource efficiency in manufacturing.

USING RENEWABLE ENERGY SOURCES

For the energy use that cannot be reduced, try to source energy from renewable sources. Some manufacturing facilities generate their own electricity onsite. For example, the Method Soap factory in Chicago boasts a 230-foot onsite wind turbine that generates 600 kilowatts of energy, about 30 percent of the factory's energy use. It also has three solar trees which together can supply about 150 kilowatts of energy. These impressive facilities have an added benefit of being a marketing tool for the company, which offers grand tours of their factory.[8] If you don't have the capital to invest in the up-front costs of onsite renewable energy generation, there are other options. Community solar and wind initiatives allow you to subscribe to renewable energy installations generated elsewhere in your community.[9] Renewable energy options may even be offered by your local utility.

VERTICAL INTEGRATION

By doing more steps of the manufacturing process in one place, a manufacturer can cut down on transportation and shipping emissions of transporting product from facility to facility. To use Method Soap as an example again, the factory houses manufacturing, bottling, and distribution under one roof.[10]

CARBON OFFSETS

Finally, for the energy use that cannot be reduced or produced through renewable sources, "carbon offsets" or "carbon credits" are a tool utilized by many companies. Carbon offsets are a method companies use to "offset" their carbon emissions through paying for another organization to remove an equal or greater amount of carbon from the atmosphere. For example, a company may calculate their carbon footprint and find that through their manufacturing, shipping, and other business practices, they produce X tons of carbon dioxide per year. To "offset" this CO_2 production, the company would purchase carbon credits through a carbon marketplace that would then facilitate payment to another organization that has agreed to plant enough trees to absorb X tons of CO_2.

Carbon credits cover more than just planting trees—carbon credits can finance the construction of renewable energy infrastructure, the rehabilitation of natural spaces, and even farmers' adoption of sustainable agricultural practices.[11] While some argue that carbon offsets are problematic because they give companies a "pass" to continue environmentally harmful practices, others argue that carbon offsets are a necessary bridge in the transition to a cleaner economy.

There are a few important things to know about carbon offsets. The first is the principle of "additionality." This means that carbon offsets cannot be purchased by contributing to an initiative that was already happening without that funding. For example, if a company was planning to build a solar power plant anyway, contributing money to that initiative will not count as a carbon offset. Or if a farmer is already utilizing regenerative agricultural practices, paying them for it does not count as a carbon offset. This may seem unfair, because it does not reward people who are already doing good work; however, for carbon offsets to really work, they must be actively removing carbon from the atmosphere that would not otherwise be removed.

The second thing to know about the carbon market is that, as of now, it is unregulated in many countries, including the United States. This means that some carbon credits end up being of higher quality than others. So how can you tell if you're buying a good carbon credit? First of all, you can usually tell by the price. If it seems too good to be true, it probably is. The more effective and legitimate kinds of carbon credits are generally more expensive. For example, there are actually machines that pull carbon dioxide from the atmosphere and turn it into a solid, which is then buried in the ground or used for other purposes. No surprise, this is pretty expensive.[12] If you are considering purchasing carbon credits, you can assess the validity of the credit at the online Carbon Credit Quality Initiative, founded as a collaboration between the Environmental Defense Fund, the World Wildlife Fund, and Oeko-Institut.[13]

4. Toxins

This is a big one. The US manufacturing industry emits approximately three billion pounds of toxic chemicals a year.[14] *Yikes.* This number is particularly concerning because (1) these are just the chemical emissions that are reported, so it seems logical that there is an even larger number that goes unreported; (2) much of the manufacturing process for goods we consume in the United States occurs abroad, so the full chemical footprint is substantially larger; and (3) these chemicals that are released into our air, soil, and water are linked to health problems such as cancer and neurological, developmental, and respiratory illnesses and disorders.[15] No entrepreneur wants to be part of that. Identifying and removing toxic chemicals in your products or manufacturing process is not only important for the legacy and identity of your company; it also protects your company from expensive liability and a ruined reputation. So, put in the work to make sure that the production of your product is not releasing something into that atmosphere that looks like Hexxus from *FernGully*.[16]

ASSESS YOUR CHEMICAL FOOTPRINT

Getting an honest look at the chemical content of your product includes two steps that are simple in concept but complicated in practice:

1. Understanding your supply chain: Often, companies don't even know what chemicals may be lurking in their products or packaging or how different chemicals in their product may react with each other. Understanding the chemical footprint of your product involves increased supply chain transparency and a knowledge of exactly what goes into your product at different stages. Supply chain transparency is important for many reasons, not just tracking toxins. Accurate supply chain mapping allows companies to increase efficiency, flexibility, and responsiveness in the face of supply chain challenges.

2. Testing: Testing your products and packaging for dangerous chemicals and contaminants is next. Hire consultants or specialists to help you understand what to test for. The Environmental Defense Fund Supply Chain Solutions Center also offers guides and resources for assessing your chemical footprint and testing for common heavy metals and contaminants.[17]

USE FEWER CHEMICALS

Decreasing the number of synthetic chemicals used in your product can improve the environmental footprint of your company as well as the health of your customers, employees, and the community where your product is manufactured. Because of increased consumer awareness of the environmental and health impacts of synthetic chemicals, reducing chemical usage may also mean that consumers will be willing to pay a higher price for your product.

Reducing chemicals requires a combination of returning to old practices and ingredients (such as naturally derived dyes, scents, and additives) and embracing new innovation to increase the effectiveness, efficiency, and scalability of these practices. Innovative startups are also capitalizing on this trend as a business opportunity. For example, Stony Creek Colors, an agricultural startup out of Springfield, Tennessee, has developed a proprietary plant variety, as well as an innovative extraction and processing method to enable food and textile manufacturers to replace synthetic blue dye with a high-purity, natural blue dye made from indigo.[18] Stony Creek Colors allows denim manufacturers to replace synthetic blue dye, made with chemicals such as cyanide, formaldehyde, and benzene, with a 100 percent plant-based dye. In 2021, Stony Creek Colors successfully raised $9 million from investors to scale their business.[19] The startup sells dyes to companies such as Patagonia, Lucky, and Wrangler.[20]

USE SAFER INGREDIENTS

Once you have mapped the chemicals and ingredients used in your product and packaging, take time to understand why each chemical is used. Is it for color? Flavor? Scent? Preservation? See if you can get the same result through natural ingredients, safer chemicals, or better design. The Organization for Economic Co-operation and Development (OECD) offers a Substitution and Alternatives Assessment Toolbox to assess chemical hazards and find alternatives.[21]

CLEAN UP YOUR MESS

If your manufacturing process produces toxic emissions, spend the money to clean it up properly. Innovative startups are improving this process too. Startup companies such as Amplytica out of Canada use a process called bioremediation to use living organisms such as microbes and bacteria to assess damage to land and water and remove contaminants.[22]

5. Labor

I won't go into labor in depth in this chapter because it gets a full chapter starting on page 156; however, it's impossible to discuss the environmental and social impacts of manufacturing without mentioning labor. The manufacturing process is a huge opportunity for a business leader to create positive impact in the community and the world because a manufacturing facility is a job creator. What *kind* of job creator you are is up to you. If you approach this element of your business with intention and accountability, you can provide well-paid, much needed employment in the community where your facilities are located. Without proper attention paid to this part of your business, you may find your company's name included in horror stories in the news about inhumane treatment of factory workers. If you outsource manufacturing to a factory in another country, make your choice carefully and examine the working conditions in the factory you select. Manufacturing locally, in the country where you live, makes the process of monitoring your labor standards much easier. Local manufacturing also has the added benefit of protecting your supply chain from some of the vulnerabilities and long lag times that can occur with overseas manufacturing, while also decreasing the carbon emissions caused by shipping and transportation.

6. Location and land use

This one might slip by unnoticed if you don't plan for it, but selecting the physical location for your manufacturing facility and management of the building and land where it's located are also opportunities for integrating positive impact into your business.

SITE SELECTION

Taking over management of land is an opportunity to leave the land better than you found it. This can mean being willing to take on a location that is less than pristine. When New Belgium Brewing (company profile on page 130), well-known for beers such as Fat Tire Ale, opened their second brewery in 2012, they selected a property in Asheville, North Carolina, that was designated as a brownfield. A brownfield is a property that has previously been used for industrial purposes and contains potentially hazardous waste or pollution. Rather than being deterred by this designation, New Belgium used their production facility as an opportunity to rehabilitate and revitalize the land, leaving it better than they found it.[23]

LOCATION

Selecting the location of your facility can be a powerful opportunity for impact. Is it close enough to the locations where you ship product to minimize cost and emissions from shipping? Can you locate in an area where another facility recently closed and able workers have been left without jobs? Finally, is it possible to locate close to public transportation options or bikeable routes so that your facility is accessible to workers by means other than a car? How will the addition of a manufacturing facility affect the fabric and flow of the community in the area? Does the local community welcome or oppose the idea? How can you get community input before moving forward with your plans?

BUILDING AND FACILITIES

Building utilization is a good opportunity to consider how you can move beyond minimizing your own negative impact, and to consider innovative ways to use your building and facilities to create a net positive impact on the land and community. For example, Method Soap partners with Gotham Greens to utilize 75,000 square feet of their factory roof as a commercial greenhouse, growing 500 tons of fresh, pesticide-free produce to be sold to the local community and restaurants. Additionally, they use 1,520 feet of the roof as a green roof (growing plants directly on the roof rather than in the greenhouse), which decreases cooling costs inside the factory, improves air quality, and helps treat stormwater runoff.[24]

Some facilities, such as the Method Soap factory and New Belgium Brewing, have become Leadership in Energy and Environmental Design (LEED) certified. This green building certification, developed by the Green Building Council, holds the company accountable to a framework of green building standards and signals to the world that the company takes sustainability seriously.[25] If you want to take green buildings a step further, explore the Living Building Challenge. The Living Building Challenge is considered to be the most rigorous standard for green design. The idea of the Living Building framework is to create buildings that give more than they take, are self-sufficient, create a positive impact on the natural and human spaces that they interact with, and connect occupants to the community and to nature.[26]

4 Tips for Success: Recommendations & Tools

1. Adopt an environmental management system

An Environmental Management System (or EMS) is a process for an organization to assess, plan, and improve their social and environmental impact (check out measurement frameworks on page 245). Environmental Management Systems differ slightly in methodology, but the basic framework is something along these lines:

- Benchmark: Collect data and best practices from across the industry

- Assess: Do a thorough assessment of your current social and environmental impact. You can use the categories listed above for guidance.

- Set goals: Make short-, medium-, and long-term goals for improvement. Make sure your team is engaged in setting these goals and committed to seeing them through.

- Make a plan: Make a game plan for how you will reach your goals and set a timeline for implementing them. Once again, this should be a process you do in collaboration with your team.

- Create policy and programs: Develop policies to enforce your plan.

- Implement: Carry out your plan.

- Evaluate: Schedule assessments at regular intervals to see how the process is going. What is working? What isn't?

- Iterate: Adjust and improve your plan and goals as necessary.[27]

2. Lean manufacturing

Lean manufacturing is a production process that aims to eliminate waste in all forms: waste of materials, waste of energy, waste of time, waste of space, waste of flawed or damaged products, and so on. What I like about lean manufacturing is that it is an area where environmental and financial benefits naturally align. It also incorporates other positive workplace principles such as cleanliness and safety, employee involvement in decision-making, and continuous improvement. Lean manufacturing is a series of practices and methodologies that people spend years learning and implementing, so while I won't go in depth on all elements, the core methods are listed below:

- **Kaizen:** "Kaizen" is a word that encompasses a simple, yet highly powerful idea: "continuous improvement." Rather than accepting products and processes as they are, the Kaizen methodology encourages workers from all ranks and roles to continually seek methods of improvement, embracing the idea that small improvements add up to large improvements over time. In a Kaizen production system, workers must be encouraged and empowered to make suggestions, find solutions, and take ownership of the quality of their work.[28]

- **5S:** The 5S methodology encourages a clean and orderly workplace as a means of eliminating waste and increasing productivity. The five Ss of the 5S system stand for: "Sort, Set in order, Shine, Standardize, and Sustain." The idea of 5S is that in a clean and orderly workplace, everyone knows where all materials are, workers use and order the amount of material that they need, product flaws are lower, and work can happen more quickly and efficiently.[29]

- **Cellular manufacturing:** Cellular manufacturing is an alternate design and methodology for manufacturing production facilities. Unlike batch production or large-lot production, cellular manufacturing moves a product through production one piece at a time and arranges the manufacturing floor so that the "flow" is smooth and so that the concurrent steps of the manufacturing process are located close together in "cells." This aims to eliminate wasted time and materials that can occur when different steps of the process are separated from each other.[30]

- **JIT/Kanban:** "Just-in-Time" manufacturing or "Kanban" encourages production to happen at the pull of customer demands so that inventory is not wasted, and so that the production process can be flexible as needs and demands change. Most manufacturing happens with a "push" methodology, which involves trying to predict customer demands, creating the products and then pushing them on customers through aggressive advertising and marketing campaigns. Rather than creating excess inventory in advance, the Just-in-Time manufacturing process creates new products as they are demanded. This process results in less waste of products, time, money, and materials, but requires an agile, flexible, and efficient manufacturing process that relies heavily on the other lean manufacturing techniques. "Kanban" refers to a card or order that communicates exact production numbers and specifications for the next step in the production process.[31]

- **TPM:** "Total Productive Maintenance" (TPM) is a methodology for keeping all equipment and machinery in top working order and eliminating breakdowns, safety hazards, and production stoppages. The TPM methodology involves all workers in this process, effectively crowdsourcing maintenance of machinery, based on the belief that the workers on the ground who regularly interact with the machines will be the first ones to know of potential problems and stop them before they occur. TPM also includes eliminating breakdowns through constantly improving equipment, investing in automation, and "mistake-proofing" equipment so that all processes are as simple and straightforward as possible.[32]

- **Six Sigma:** Six Sigma is an analytical process and set of statistical tools to identify waste and weaknesses within processes and to predict and eliminate defects before they happen. The sequence of steps associated with the Six Sigma process are: "Define, Measure, Analyze, Improve, and Control."[33]

- **3P:** Unlike the other methods of lean manufacturing that focus on the production process, 3P focuses on designing products for the production process. The 3Ps stand for

"Production, Preparation, Process." The 3P process involves a multidisciplinary team that understands the manufacturing process, listens to customer desires and feedback, and designs a product that can be used and manufactured in the simplest way, designed to have few flaws in quality or functionality. 3P results in a product that is easy to manufacture, generates low waste, and meets customer needs. The typical steps in a 3P process include: "Define Product or Process Design Objectives/Needs, Diagramming, Find and Analyze Examples in Nature, Sketch and Evaluate the Process, Build, Present, and Select Process Prototypes, Hold Design Review, Develop Project Implementation plan."[34]

3. Consider working with a consultant

Manufacturing can be complex, and understanding the intricacies and implications of toxins, waste, and energy use is equally so. However, there are people who make understanding the complexities of social and environmental impact their business, and you may want to consider bringing a consultant onto your team to help assess and make a plan to improve the impact of your manufacturing process. However, as the decision maker in your organization, it is still important for you to have at least a high-level understanding of the factors at play in the manufacturing process and how manufacturing can be a deciding factor in whether your business is creating a net positive or negative impact on the world.

4. Look for grants and other funding assistance to get you started

Many sustainability investments, such as building retrofits, energy-efficient equipment, and wastewater treatment systems, cost a lot of money up front but can save money in the long run. If you have the capital to invest in these changes, it can be a sound business move for your company, because of both the future savings and the contribution to your company's story and brand. However, if you don't have this up-front capital, there are other ways to get creative about funding sustainability initiatives. New Belgium Brewing has partnered with the city of Asheville for some of their initiatives, such as restoring the brownfield where they built their second brewery and building a bus station near the facility. Employees often want to feel good about the impact of their employer as well; New Belgium also funds some of their renewable energy initiatives through an internal, voluntary energy tax of their employees.[35]

Company Profile: New Belgium Brewing

Where the company integrates impact

- Manufacturing
- Hiring and labor
- Operations and governance
- Profit
- Voice

Founders: Kim Jordan and Jeff Lebesch

In 1988, New Belgium Brewing co-founder Jeff Lebesch took a bike trip through Europe and was inspired by the rich culture of Belgian brewing. In 1991, he began brewing Belgian-style beer in the basement of the home he shared with his then wife, co-founder Kim Jordan, in Fort Collins, Colorado. The couple took out a second mortgage on their house to purchase the initial brewing equipment. Jeff quit his engineering job to focus on brewing the beer and Kim, who worked as a social worker during the day, bottled and delivered beer in the evening. Now, the company has grown to employ approximately seven hundred people in two primary locations, Fort Collins and Asheville, with an estimated revenue of $250 million.[36]

What they do

As you may have guessed, New Belgium Brewing brews beer! The certified B Corp is known for their Belgian-influenced beers such as Fat Tire and their IPA brand family, Voodoo Ranger, as well as their commitment to serving people, the planet, and the communities in which they live and work.

Business model

New Belgium follows the B2B and B2C models. New Belgium sells beer via a three-tiered system: first to distributors and wholesalers, who then sell to retailers, who then sell to consumers. The company also sells a smaller number of products directly to consumers (in states where this is legal). They are successful because their beer is delicious, but also because they have cultivated a strong brand based on their commitment to their mission and, as a result, a loyal customer following.

New Belgium has made investments in environmental sustainability through waste reduction and energy efficiency, which have lowered their operating expenses in the long term. They finance their social and environmental initiatives in creative ways, partnering with the cities in which their facilities are located to take on initiatives that benefit the local land and community. They also fund some of their environmental initiatives via an internal, voluntary energy tax from their coworkers. To maintain the freedom to experiment with running their business in the way they felt was right, the New Belgium founders did not take on any outside financing other than bank loans as they grew the company into the successful operation it is today. New Belgium is known for practicing a unique, open-book management style, communicating openly about finances and internal processes with employees and operating as an employee-owned business for many years until they sold to Lion Little World Beverages in 2020.

Impact

MANUFACTURING

Inspiring social and environmental change is one of New Belgium's core values, and they honor that commitment through their production process:

- Waste: New Belgium Brewing is a certified zero-waste brewery. In 2018, they were able to divert 99.8 percent of their waste from the landfill. Of the waste they produce, 97.9 percent is spent grain, which they sell to a farmer to feed cattle. This transaction means the farmer doesn't need to use virgin grain, which results in less water used for growing crops and less emissions from farm equipment, not to mention less waste sent to the landfill. Other than grain, New Belgium's waste is disposed of in the following ways: 81.9 percent is recycled, 7.4 percent is composted, 2.8 percent is reused, and 8 percent goes to landfill.[37]

- <u>Water</u>: In the New Belgium bottling plant, the bottles are rinsed before they are filled, and the rinse water is captured and reused for the external rinse after the beer is bottled and capped. This water recycling process saves millions of gallons of water per year. The brewery also treats their own wastewater onsite. The water they use to clean kettles and tanks is taken to their onsite anaerobic digester that uses microbes to eat the contaminants, producing methane. The methane is sent to a cogenerator, where it is used for fuel, providing 15 percent of the electricity needed at the company's Colorado facility.

  At their Asheville location, New Belgium harvests rainwater for irrigation and cooling tower makeup. The brewery has also invested in an onsite solar hot water heater in their brewing facility, as well as solar panels.[38]

- <u>Energy</u>: In 2010, New Belgium installed solar panels with a 200-kilowatt capacity at their flagship brewery in Fort Collins—at the time, the largest installation in Colorado. In addition to the fuel generated from their onsite wastewater treatment plant, the brewery helped fund their city utility's investment in wind power in Colorado in 1999.[39]

  The brewing process can be very energy-intensive, so New Belgium has invested in energy-efficient equipment and processes to help cut down on the energy toll. During the brewing process, the beer must be boiled. Boiling liquid at that scale requires a large amount of energy, but New Belgium uses a cone-shaped boiler kettle that uses about 65 percent less energy than a traditional unit, along with a heat exchanger to capture the steam from their kettle. The waste heat is then used to preheat the incoming water, reducing the energy needed to produce the next batch of beer.

  The Fort Collins brewery also boasts a window-covered wall three stories tall that lets in large amounts of natural light.

This design helps the brewery save money on electricity bills and provides a better working environment for employees.

- Pollution & Emissions: New Belgium tracks and publicly reports their Scope 1, Scope 2, and Scope 3 greenhouse gas emissions. Scope 1 emissions come from sources directly owned and controlled by the business. Scope 2 emissions are indirect emissions generated by the company's activities, such as the emissions generated during the production of the energy it uses. Scope 3 emissions are those emissions generated indirectly by the activities of the company; for example, emissions generated by the company's suppliers or by the company's customers when they use the product.[40] Scope 3 emissions are more difficult to track and understand; however, it is important for a company to do so because most of the emissions generated by the existence of a company are part of Scope 3. For example, 85.6 percent of New Belgium's emissions fall into the category of Scope 3, made up of emissions from the production of glass, growth and harvesting of barley, and malt, as well as the distribution and retail of the beer. New Belgium went above and beyond the industry norm by tracking Scope 3 emissions, setting reduction goals, and reporting them publicly, long before other businesses were doing so.[41] The entire company aims to be carbon-neutral and running on 100 percent renewable electricity by 2030.

- Location & Land Use: New Belgium's second brewery in Asheville, North Carolina, was built on land that had been designated as a brownfield, which is a property that has previously been used for industrial purposes and contains potentially hazardous waste or pollution. New Belgium actually chose the property in part *because* it was a brownfield and used it as an opportunity to leave the land they worked on better than they found it.

  The brewery partnered with the city of Asheville and local nonprofits to clean the land and the stream on the property, managing to salvage or recycle 97 percent of the waste they collected. They planted native plants along the stream, specifically chosen for their ability to help prevent erosion and manage pests naturally. The tables and chairs in the tasting room were crafted by local artisans from wood and metal salvaged from the property. New Belgium also partnered with the city to create a bus stop near to the facility along with a greenway so that employees and customers could access the brewery via bike or public transportation. The tasting room in Ashville is now certified LEED Platinum, and their brewery is certified LEED Gold.[42]

HIRING AND LABOR

Kim Jordan's background as a social worker defined New Belgium's founding philosophy to brew beer for *all*. As an extension of this philosophy, New Belgium strives to be a workplace where all feel welcome. The company has institutionalized inclusivity into their culture through programs and policies such as a Coworker Wellbeing & Culture Task Force and a DEI Coworker council, fueled by the fact that they are a female-founded business in a male-dominated industry. The brewery employs a director of Diversity, Equity, and Inclusion, and was the first to employ a DEI specialist in the craft beer industry. New Belgium holds mandatory Diversity, Equity, and Inclusion trainings for their staff as well as internal audits of their own hiring, coworker, and customer experience through the lens of equity and equality. They were ahead of the curve by offering spousal benefits to same-sex partners starting in the 1990s, before same-sex marriage was legal, and in 2021, they were recognized one of the best places to work for LGBTQ+ equality by the Human Rights Campaign.

The brewery extends this philosophy to pay equity through a narrowed gap between the top and the bottom company salaries. In the US the average CEO makes 356 times more than the average worker's salary. New Belgium's CEO, however, makes less than ten times the average coworker's salary.[43]

New Belgium prides itself on operating as a "human-powered" business. They make a point to take care of their employees (whom they refer to as coworkers), knowing that in the long run, this pays off for business through decreased turnover and increased employee satisfaction. As a brewery with a focus on wellness, fun, and the environment, New Belgium integrates these principles into their company culture. They provide a minimum wage of $18.50, paid caregiver leave, and have a wellness clinic onsite at their Colorado location. They offer wellness programs such as yoga and substance abuse counseling. Longevity at the company is rewarded through a New Belgium-branded bicycle on a coworker's one year anniversary, an all-expenses paid trip to Belgium at five years of employment, and at ten years, a paid sabbatical. The company also offers a Coworker Assistance Fund, a pooled fund to provide financial support to employees who need assistance due to a personal hardship or disaster.[44]

OPERATIONS

New Belgium has traditionally operated with an "open-book management" philosophy, teaching employees to understand financial statements and practicing transparency about the financial state of the business. Teaching employees to understand how the business works not only benefits employees in the long run, but it is also an important move for a company that asked their employees to act like owners of the business (because they were!).[45] Financial literacy across the organization helps New Belgium stay profitable and earn profit sharing, which can equal up to 10 percent of annual pay for every coworker.

In 2012, New Belgium CEO Kim Jordan announced to her 457 coworkers that the company was being sold. They were each handed an envelope and told to open it to learn who the new owners would be. Inside each envelope was a small mirror, demonstrating that she had sold the company to them.[46] In this regard, as well as many others, New Belgium was a leader in the industry, becoming the first 100 percent employee-owned craft brewery, to be followed in subsequent years by many other prominent breweries.

Many fans of the brewery were shocked in 2020 when the company was sold again to Lion Little World Beverages. While this meant that the company was no longer employee-owned, the important thing to know is that it was the employee-owners themselves who voted to move forward with the sale to Lion Co. Many coworkers benefited handsomely from this sale, with more than three hundred employees receiving over $100,000 in retirement funds and some receiving much more. In total, present and former coworkers of the company received nearly $190 million from the sale.

Did the sale to Lion Co. betray the ethos of the company? It depends on whom you ask. Owners of a company often make the decision to sell the company in order to gain the benefits of many years of hard work. Should this be any different if the owners are the employees? In my opinion, the decision to sell a company is the right of the owner, and if the people who will benefit the most from the sale (the owners) are also the same people who will be affected the most by the sale (the employees)—even better.[47]

GIVING BACK

Since the early 1990s, New Belgium has donated one dollar of every barrel of beer sold to organizations working to solve the world's most pressing issues. This approach ensures that when they do well as a business, their philanthropy efforts grow as well. The brewery provides contributions and grants to causes that are central to their core values and the personality of their business, including environmental education, sustainable agriculture, and bicycle activism. As of 2022, they have donated over $30 million.[48]

VOICE

New Belgium is a member of the Business for Innovative Climate Energy Policy (BICEP), a coalition of businesses coordinated by the environmental nonprofit organization Ceres, that aim to influence state and federal policy around climate change.[49]

In 2017, when President Trump pulled the United States out of the Paris Climate Agreement, an international treaty on climate change, a coalition of mayors, governors, tribes, businesses, and universities joined together to form a coalition called "We are Still In," to communicate to the world that many Americans were still committed to holding up the goals of the agreement. New Belgium Brewing was on the leadership committee for this coalition.[50]

In 2020, New Belgium Brewing's flagship beer Fat Tire became the first carbon-neutral-certified beer in America. Fat Tire also published a Carbon Neutral Toolkit for craft brewers to help other breweries follow suit. Using this platform, Fat Tire also tracks which Fortune 500 companies have a 2030 Climate Plan and gives consumers a platform to call out other companies (via Twitter) for not having a plan or to congratulate them for having one in place.

Finally, in 2021, Fat Tire released "Torched Earth Ale," a beer brewed to raise awareness of climate change and the major effects on agriculture and the availability of natural resources, including the ingredients used to brew beer! Torched Earth Ale was brewed using only ingredients that would be available on an earth severely damaged by increased temperatures caused by climate change, such as smoke-tainted water, drought-resistant grains, shelf-stable extracts, and dandelion weeds.[51]

What I like about it

New Belgium knows who they are, what they care about, and what they do well, and they stick to it. New Belgium brews beer and they sell it, and within this scope of work they have done just about everything in their power to honor their stated core values: "make world-class beer for everyone, do right by people, inspire social and environmental change, and have a hell of a lot of fun." With their new Torched Earth Ale, they even use beer as a way to raise awareness of climate change.

Someone once told me that "if you do everything you can to make change within your sphere of influence, your sphere of influence tends to grow." From their manufacturing to the treatment of their employees, to their impact in the community, New Belgium has worked to do as much as they can to create change within their sphere of influence, and their sphere of influence has indeed grown. They are considered a leader not only in the craft brewing industry, but also to mission-based businesses in other industries.

In 2016, Forbes named New Belgium as a "Small Giant," described as a company that, instead of attempting to grow as large and as quickly as it can, has instead chosen to be a standout in its industry. As a result of this strategic choice, small giants have consistently strong balance sheets, are considered appealing places to work, have strong customer service, and are often an asset to their community. To me, this definition describes New Belgium to a T. Whether or not this small, big-hearted giant will maintain their unique methodologies, innovative spirit, and commitment to mission as they transition to new ownership is yet to be seen.[52]

New Belgium

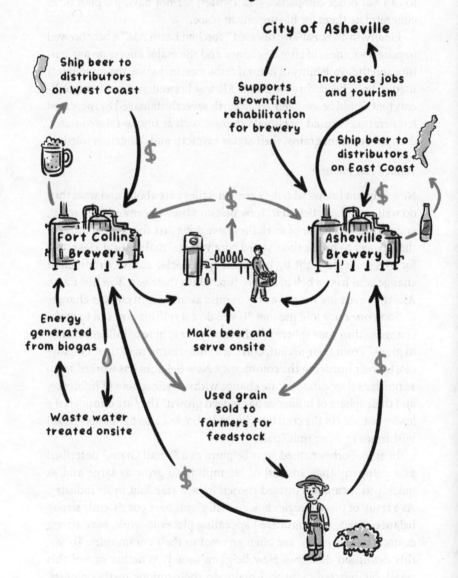

City of Asheville

Ship beer to distributors on West Coast

Supports Brownfield rehabilitation for brewery

Increases jobs and tourism

Ship beer to distributors on East Coast

Fort Collins Brewery

Asheville Brewery

$

$

$

$

$

Energy generated from biogas

Make beer and serve onsite

Waste water treated onsite

Used grain sold to farmers for feedstock

10

Packaging and Shipping

Once you've created your product, the next step is to actually get it to your customer. A large chunk of a product's carbon footprint can occur in this stage as a result of the choices made around shipping and packaging. Requirements for packaging and transportation will vary widely from product to product, but there are a few rules to keep in mind that will help you make more sustainable choices as you ship your product to your customer. There is also a lot of room for innovation in this area of the business. Some companies like thredUP (company profile on page 108) are making tweaks to traditional shipping and packaging processes to make them more sustainable, but there is still a long way to go and a lot of room for leadership in sustainability—maybe your company will be the one to lead the way.

Packaging

Packaging may seem like a very small part of the total product, but collectively, it can have a huge impact. The global plastic problem has escalated to become a real crisis, and packaging is a huge contributor. Approximately eight million tons of plastic waste escapes annually into the ocean; that is enough plastic to set five trash bags full of plastic on every foot of coastline in the world. *Yikes!* This plastic pollution kills millions of animals per year.[1] And let's not forget that humans eat aquatic animals, which means that these plastics wind up inside our bodies. Microplastics have been found inside human stomachs, lungs, and even our blood.[2] I could go on . . . but the point to realize here is that the plastic crisis is serious and that as entrepreneurs and business leaders, we have a responsibility to do our part to lessen this crisis.

Another point to keep in mind is that packaging is one of the most visible ways to communicate to your customer that you take the environmental impact of your product seriously. Your customer must directly interact with your chosen packaging, removing it from the product and disposing of it. How they feel about this process will have an impact on the associations they make with your company and brand. I've outlined some basic rules of sustainable packaging below:

1. <u>Less is more</u>: Have you ever opened a box and had to dig under what felt like a ton of Styrofoam packing peanuts to access that one, tiny thing you ordered? Don't be that company! Keeping packaging as minimal as possible is the first way to decrease its environmental impact. Where packaging is concerned, sleek and simple is good. Some companies over-package out of concern for the safety of the product or for brand promotion; but there are more sustainable ways to cushion and secure your product (see the section below) and to tote your brand without saddling your customer with additional trash. Less material also generally means less money spent on packaging.

2. <u>Keep the end in mind</u>: Use earth-friendly materials for packaging. Consider where the materials come from and where they will end up after they are used.

Where does the material come from?

This question is really an extension of thinking through material sourcing for your product (see the section on material sourcing on page 101). The primary factors to consider are:

- *Is the material recycled or reused?* Using packaging materials that have been used for something else and diverted from the landfill is always a win for sustainability. Look for products that have been made with post-consumer recycled content. Paper, plastic, and glass, among other materials, can be purchased with at least a percentage of recycled content.

- *Was the material sourced sustainably?* Look for key certifications relevant to your material. For example, if your packaging is paper, look for products with the Forest Stewardship Council certification (FSC).[3]

- *How much processing was involved?* Materials that have been highly processed generally take more energy and chemicals to get to their final state. Using raw and undyed materials is often a more sustainable choice.

Where will the materials end up after they are used?

When a customer removes the packaging from your product, what do they do with it? This part is trickier than it may sound. Many smart and well-meaning people have made mistakes here and ended up paying more for a material that is not actually more sustainable than the alternatives. Consider the following:

- *Can it be recycled?* It's not enough to use a material that could *technically* be recycled. It needs to be *commonly* recycled to increase the odds that your packaging actually gets turned into something else. Paper, metal, and plastic resins #1 & #2 are all things that are recyclable in most locations. Keeping materials pure and unmixed also helps recyclability. If your packaging is made of paper lined in aluminum, chances are that it cannot be recycled as paper or as aluminum.

- *Can it be reused?* More on this below, but some businesses have designed clever reusable or returnable options for their packaging.

- *Can it be composted?* This is one of the areas where choosing the sustainable option can get a little confusing. See page 89 of material sourcing to learn more about what materials can be composted.

Avoid common culprits

Here are a few common, wasteful packaging culprits to steer clear of:

- *Expanded Polystyrene or EPS (more commonly known as Styrofoam)*: this kind of plastic is very rarely recycled. It's too difficult to recycle and the end product has too low of a value for recycling it to make economic sense. EPS is also so light-weight that it often blows out of trash cans, trucks, and so on and ends up in waterways.

- *Plastic film:* Avoid plastic film when you can. Plastic film (think thin plastic bags and plastic wraps) is rarely recycled. It is not recyclable in municipal curbside recycling. If you bring plastic film to a plastic bag collection center, say at a grocery store, it *may* be recycled, but often it is not because it is a low-value product and plastic is fairly cheap.

- *Bioplastics:* I wish I could tell you this was a magic bullet, and that we could keep the convenience of plastic while also being sustainable, but usually when we're told we can have our cake and eat it too, there's a catch somewhere, and unfortunately bioplastics are no exception.

  There are so many organizations working on developing new types of bioplastics that I won't say it is impossible for someone to figure out a good solution. However, there are several issues with commonly used bioplastic options. First of all, bioplastics often break into tiny pieces rather than actually biodegrading, and microplastics are no good because they get into our food and our bodies. As I mentioned in the Material Sourcing chapter, *compostable* plastics can actually compost, which means that they can decompose into organic material and nutrients. However, most compostable plastics can only compost in an industrial composting facility where the process and temperature is highly regulated. This means that unless your customers live in a city with curbside compost pickup (like Seattle or San Francisco), then compostable plastic has no clear way to get to an industrial composting facility and will likely land in the garbage or muck up the recycling stream. Finally, even if there is a path to an industrial composting facility, not all facilities will accept compostable plastics.[4]

- *Coated paper:* Plastic- or wax-coated paper is often used to contain grease, protect from liquids, or give packaging an extra shine. Unfortunately, this kind of paper is another material that can't go to the recycling bin. You often see wax- or plastic-coated paper used as paper plates, coffee cups, take-out containers, and so on, but unfortunately, the fact that the wax or plastic cannot be easily removed from the paper makes it very difficult to recycle, and these products generally wind up in the garbage.

Get creative

Don't let the previous section get you down! There are plenty of good packaging options out there, and creative entrepreneurs are coming up with new options all the time. A few of my favorite innovative packaging solutions include:

- **Bamboo:** If you've ever been unfortunate enough to have bamboo growing near your home, you know that bamboo grows fast without chemicals, is highly resilient, and keeps coming back without being replanted. While this might not be a fun plant to have in your yard, these factors make it a good choice as a sustainable fiber. Bamboo reaches maturity in one to five years, much faster than trees, without the need for chemical fertilizers or pesticides. Unlike trees, harvesting does not kill bamboo, and it will continue to grow back and produce more fiber. Its complex root structure helps prevent flooding and erosion, and it also absorbs high amounts of carbon dioxide while releasing more oxygen than most trees. The problem with bamboo is that it is invasive in the United States and isn't grown on a large scale, which means you have to balance the benefits with the likelihood that it's probably being shipped from China, which of course includes some significant environmental impact.[5] PSA: despite bamboo's promising qualities, I wouldn't recommend planting it in your yard!

- **Seaweed:** The forests that exist under the sea play an equally important role in stopping climate change as the forests on land. In fact, seaweed is actually better at absorbing carbon dioxide than trees are, plus it can pull excess nutrients, such as nitrogen, from the ocean.[6] In addition to having health benefits for humans and animals, seaweed can be used for numerous other applications, including packaging. Several startups have developed packaging materials that look and function like plastic but are fully compostable in a backyard composting bin. Searo, a company founded by a UK-based husband-and-wife team, uses seaweed to produce clear polymer sheeting that can be heat-sealed, made into bags, and used for rigid packaging such as containers and lids.[7] Notpla (short for "Not Plastic"), another UK-based startup, uses seaweed to make single-use sauce packets and to coat cardboard for grease and liquid-proofing, creating fully compostable take-out containers.[8]

- **Mushrooms:** Ecovative is one of my favorite innovators in the packaging space. This New York-based company grows a Styrofoam replacement from mycelium (mushrooms!) and hemp hurd (a by-product of the hemp fiber industry). This foam-like packing material can stay shelf-stable almost indefinitely in dry, indoor conditions, but can compost within forty-five days when it is broken up and sprinkled into a backyard composting bin.[9]

- **Edible packaging:** One dream that innovators have been chasing for a while is edible packaging. The ultimate example of edible packaging is the ice cream cone. You can buy your ice cream from the shop, eat the ice cream, polish off the cone, and voilà! No waste! Other innovators have been working to replicate this success for other products. Notpla, mentioned above, offers edible seaweed pockets called Ooho! to replace plastic bottles for water or other beverages. In 2015, KFC piloted an edible coffee cup in the UK called the Scoff-ee Cup, made from a cookie lined in sugar paper and heat-resistant chocolate,[10] and in 2017, piloted edible rice bowls made from a hard tortilla shell in India.[11] Several other startups have generated considerable buzz around edible cups and cutlery, but have struggled to bring them to market.

Plan for reuse

In a society where we have become so accustomed to single-use packaging, it can be hard to imagine that reusable packaging would ever work at scale. However, it's important to remember that not only can it work, it *has* worked! Very recently, in fact. In the 1950s and 1960s, the milkman was a well-known character in the community who went door to door delivering milk in glass bottles and collecting the empty bottles so they could be cleaned and refilled. One-way bottles and cans (meaning that customers throw them away rather than send them back to the manufacturer) only became common in the 1960s. In fact, as they began to rise in popularity (with the trash levels rising right along with them), there were attempts at federal legislation that would have banned one-way bottles—hard to imagine that that's even a possibility, isn't it?[12]

We can still reuse packaging—it just involves a little more planning. There are a few different ways that reusable packaging can be managed. Reuse generally happens through one of the following methods:

- **The company that produced the product reuses the packaging:** The company that produces and ships the product can take back their own packaging in order to reuse it again. Beer companies used to sell their beer bottles with a bottle deposit. When you brought the bottles back to the store, you received the deposit back. This worked out reasonably well logistically, because when the new beer shipment arrived and was unloaded in the liquor store, the empty bottles could be loaded back into the truck and returned to the brewery. A modern-day example of this method would be the Soda-Stream refillable CO_2 canisters, mentioned previously. The customer can bring back their empty CO_2 canister and receive a discount on their next full canister.[13]

  Reuse by the company that created the product can happen "point-to-point" (as in, the customer brings or mails the packaging back to the company, or the company collects the packaging directly) or through a "hub-and-spoke" method, where the packaging is dropped off and/or refilled at a central location, such as a retailer.

- **The customer reuses the packaging:** In this scenario, the customer reuses the packaging for something else. An example of this would be jam sold in glass jars designed to be used as water glasses or storage containers afterwards. Another creative approach is the H&M paper bag designed to be deconstructed and refolded into a clothes hanger.[14]

  The issue with this method, of course, is that the company is basically providing the customer with an unsolicited item that they may or may not want or use. If extra resources go into making this packaging reusable, or if the product is something that the consumer would buy again and again, this packaging methodology could be problematic.

- **A third party facilitates the reuse:** In this arrangement, a third party facilitates the packaging reuse. A traditional example of this method would be the milkman who went door to door distributing and collecting milk bottles. A more modern example would be Loop, an initiative of TerraCycle that partners with major manufacturers and retailers to sell products such as Häagen-Dazs ice cream or Herbal Essences shampoo in durable, reusable packaging, and then facilitates the collection, cleaning, and transport of the packaging back to the manufacturers.[15]

- **BYO packaging:** BYO (bring your own) packaging means that the product is held at a central location and the customer brings their own packaging to collect it (such as glass jars, cloth bags, etc.) You'll see this at some eco-conscious stores where customers can fill their own containers from bulk bins of coffee beans, granola, nuts, etc. Some stores, like KnoxFill (company profile on page 152), have taken this method a step further and offer everything from shampoo to dish soap in bulk. Customers can come to the store with their preferred containers and fill them up with the products they want.

Educate your customer

This may be the most important section in this chapter. No matter how clever your packaging is, it most likely won't work if you don't explain the plan to your customer and let them know their role in the process. I cringe every time I see a bioplastic cup in the trash or the recycling, but this isn't the customer's fault—it's the company's fault for not clearly describing what the customer is supposed to do with it.

The thing about waste management is that it's complicated. If it wasn't, someone surely would have figured out a better recycling system than the number system. (By the way, if you ever wondered what the numbers are in the middle of the recycling triangles, these are the numbers of the plastic resin used. Theoretically, the consumer can check whether their local municipal recycling system recycles that resin number or not.) Leave a note on your packaging telling your customer what you want them to do with it. If it's complicated, you may have to use a headline like "How to Dispose of this Bottle" with a QR code that will bring them to a webpage explaining the disposal process for different locations. Some customers won't bother with complicated instructions, but many will. So, whether you want customers to recycle your packaging, eat it, or reuse it as a picnic basket, just make sure to let them know!

Transport

The impact of transporting products across the country or across the ocean often gets forgotten because we don't see it, but transportation is actually the leading cause of greenhouse gas emissions in the United States.[16] Transportation also results in air pollution that has a negative impact on human health.[17] There are four primary areas to consider when planning out the transportation of your product.

1. Location selection

The production of goods has become increasingly global. In fact, an estimated 90 percent of the world's goods are transported overseas.[18] That seems a little excessive, doesn't it? And of course, the Covid-19 pandemic showed us that the cost of a global supply chain goes beyond the environmental and health impacts. Our dependence on an intricate global supply chain makes us vulnerable. The success of an intercontinental supply chain depends on a lot of unpredictable things going right, and as we now know, that doesn't always happen.

One of the best things you can do to minimize the environmental impact *and* vulnerability of your supply chain is to be strategic about the location of your facility. If you can, try to locate close to the locations where you sell the most product. New Belgium Brewing (company profile on page 130) was originally based in Fort Collins, Colorado. When they opened up their second brewery, they chose Asheville, North Carolina as the location, in part so that they could better serve beer to the whole United States with less transport cost and emissions.

2. Route efficiency

Major savings in money and emissions can be achieved simply through more efficient shipping routes. This sounds like it would be simpler than it is. Just use Google Maps, right? But when you have multiple trucks with multiple pickup and drop-off points, it gets more complicated. There are many private companies that can help you optimize shipping routes. The EPA also offers a free tool for optimizing shipping routes, getting industry benchmark data around shipping emissions, and increasing fuel efficiency.[19]

3. Bundling

Bundling is a shipping method that allows customers that place multiple orders to have their full order shipped together rather than having each individual item shipped separately. Offering the customer the option to "bundle" their order means saving on packaging, shipping emissions, and shipping costs. For an example of a company that uses the bundling shipping technique, check out the thredUP company profile on page 108.

4. Trains, planes, and automobiles

The bad news is that the global impact of the shipping industry is a big deal. The good news is that there are a lot of smart people working on redesigning everything from truck engines to fuel sources to make shipping more sustainable. While the best way to decrease the impact of shipping is simply to decrease the miles that your product must be shipped, there are also a number of exciting technologies on the horizon to help make transportation less of a burden on our planet. A few of these include:

- *Electric vehicles:* Most large delivery services (such as FedEx, UPS, DHL, the US Postal Service, and Amazon) have made significant investments in electric vehicles. FedEx has committed to going 100 percent electric by 2040.[20] Switching to electric vehicles for the transportation of your products can feel intimidating, but also has a long-term payoff in financial savings and environmental impact. Luckily, there are plenty of tools and examples to help companies along the way. The Environmental Defense Fund, for example, offers a tool and roadmap called the Fleet Electrification Solution Center to help companies transition to an electric vehicle fleet.[21]

- *Biofuels:* Some companies are switching to renewable fuel options such as biofuel for both trucks and ships. Biofuels can be a bit controversial, because they are often associated with using crops for fuel instead of food. However, "biofuel" is a blanket term that encompasses many different kinds of fuel options, some that are much better for the environment and for people than others. There are three general categories of biofuel:

  - *First-generation:* First-generation biofuel is made from crops like corn, sugar, and wheat, and makes up the majority of biofuel used today. The problem with first-generation biofuel is that it uses land, crops, and resources that could otherwise be used for food. This theoretically increases the price of food, ultimately causing hardship for the poorest people. If we just produce more crops, this would likely involve clearing more forest land—also not good.

  - *Second-generation:* Second-generation biofuels are made from agricultural waste products and non-food products such as wood chips, grasses, corn stover (the leaves and stalks of the plant), and so on. Some breweries like Sierra Nevada have started converting their brewing waste into biofuels to fuel their trucks.[22] Second-generation fuels are generally considered a better option because they do not compete with food, but they also are not as well understood, and cannot (as of now) be produced at as large of a scale.

- ○ *Third-generation:* Third-generation biofuel is one of the most exciting alternatives to fossil fuel, in my opinion. Third-generation fuel is made from algae. Certain types of algae can be turned into a high-efficiency biofuel. An added benefit of algae is that it performs photosynthesis and effectively sequesters carbon dioxide from the atmosphere. Algae can consume up to 1.8 kilograms of carbon dioxide per kilogram of biomass. The byproduct from algal biofuel production can be used to make many other products such as fertilizers and cleaners.[23] Although algae biofuel seems as if it could be a silver bullet for both climate change and fuel shortages, there's a reason you aren't yet filling your car with algae fuel at the local gas station. Although algae's potential as a biofuel source has been studied since the 1950s, there is not yet an understanding of how to grow and produce algae at scale.[24]

- • *Hydrogen:* For a long time, hydrogen-powered vehicles sounded like a futuristic dream: a thing of science fiction, right up there next to flying cars. But today, hydrogen-powered vehicles are a reality and are increasingly available from vehicle manufacturers across the United States.

  Vehicles powered by hydrogen fuel cells use an electric motor much like electric vehicles do, rather than an internal combustion engine, but, unlike electric vehicles, they do not require a battery. In a hydrogen fuel cell vehicle (FCV), hydrogen from the fuel tank combines with oxygen in the air and produces electricity to power the car, with byproducts of only water and heat.[25] Hydrogen is an abundant element but it takes energy to isolate it from other elements, which can be produced from solar energy, wind energy, natural gas, nuclear energy, biomass, or even algae.[26]

So, has everything been figured out now? Can hydrogen fix the problem of massive amounts of emissions produced by transportation? Unfortunately, it is (of course) a little more complicated than that. As with electric vehicles, the success of hydrogen fuel cell vehicles depends in large part on the availability of nationwide infrastructure. However, the good news is that FCV infrastructure is becoming more available, especially in places like California, Hawaii, and the Northeast. In fact, if you've taken a public bus in Boston, Massachusetts or Flint, Michigan, there is a good chance that you have ridden in a hydrogen-powered vehicle.

- *Wind-powered ships*: Remember how I mentioned that over 90 percent of the world's goods are transported overseas? This means that millions of tons of carbon dioxide are produced from cargo ships. Luckily, wind-powered ships might help fix this. And I'm not just talking about tiny sailboats, I'm talking about huge sailing vessels that can transport over 1,000 metric tons of cargo across the ocean. This solution may seem a bit obvious. We've all seen depictions of pirates and fifteenth-century explorers cruising around the globe in giant wind-powered ships. But in order to meet expectations of speed, efficiency, safety, and reliability that our global economy has come to depend on, we must borrow ingenuity from both the past and the future. Wind-powered cargo ships are being developed by companies across the world and expected to be making sea voyages soon. Although completely wind-powered ships are possible, it may be that traditional cargo ships end up adopting wind propulsion technologies so that they are partially powered by wind, which would still take a significant chunk out of the carbon emissions of sea transport.

- *Carbon offsets*: And for those emissions that you're not able to erase through strategy, design, and technology, there is always the opportunity to offset your carbon footprint. See page 120 for the pros and cons and the wide variety of options around carbon offsets.

Company Profile: KnoxFill

Founder interview on page 266.

Where the company integrates impact

- Products and services
- Material sourcing
- Packaging and shipping

Founder: Michaela Barnett

Michaela became interested in waste at an early age. When she was growing up, her mother used to pull their van over to the side of the road a few times a week to look through the things that other people had put out in the trash. This fascination followed her through high school, where she started a recycling program at her school, to college, where she started a composting program in her cafeteria, and finally to adulthood, when she founded KnoxFill as an outgrowth of her PhD work focused on waste systems.[27] "I kept thinking, 'when is someone going to start a zero-waste store in Knoxville?'" Michaela said, describing her initial inspiration to start KnoxFill, "and I finally realized, that person was going to be me." Michaela started KnoxFill because she wanted it to exist, and because she believes that individual action that grows into collective action can be incredibly powerful. "If 20 percent of Knoxvillians reduced their waste by 20 percent we could keep almost 14 million pounds of waste out of the landfill each year."[28]

What they do

KnoxFill operates like a modern-day milkman, but instead of milk, they refill your shampoo bottles, your hand soap, your household cleaners, and more. They also sell other household essentials in no-waste or low-waste packaging, such as a solid bar of stain stick or tablets of toothpaste. KnoxFill opened in 2021, and within the first five months of operation, they had already served over 500 households.

Business model

KnoxFill operates primarily as a B2C business. The store, which currently operates out of the utility room of Michaela's house and at pickup spots across Knoxville through partnerships with local businesses, provides refillable containers of household products such as shampoo, laundry detergent, and cleaner. The customer uses the products, and then returns the containers to KnoxFill so that they can clean, sanitize, and refill them. Customers can select the products they would like to purchase online for pickup or home delivery. KnoxFill also offers pop-up opportunities at local stores where customers can bring their own containers and have them refilled on the spot. They charge by weight after subtracting the weight of the container. They will be launching a mobile refillery as well as a brick-and-mortar location in the near future.[29]

KnoxFill has also begun to sell products in bulk to eco-minded businesses such as coffee shops, bed-and-breakfasts, and yoga studios. Finally, the enterprising small business is also exploring collaborating with a refillery in a neighboring city to engage a cosmetics manufacturer to develop their own signature scents and products.

Impact

PRODUCTS AND SERVICES

KnoxFill allows residents of Knoxville and the surrounding region to purchase essential household and personal care products without the plastic waste that traditionally comes with purchasing these products. Plastic pollution is considered to be one of the biggest environmental threats to life on earth, and by 2050 it is predicted that there will be more plastic in the ocean than fish![30] Developing ongoing, accessible systems, such as refilleries, that allow people to avoid plastic in their daily lives is an essential part of the solution to avoid this future.

MATERIAL SOURCING

Knoxfill purchases from local and/or sustainable suppliers. They carefully vet all of their suppliers so that they can get as close to a zero-waste supply chain as possible. They also make a point to purchase from woman- and family-owned businesses when they can.

PACKAGING AND SHIPPING

The positive impact in this category is pretty straightforward. KnoxFill essentially eliminates packaging for their customers. There is, of course, an environmental impact from transporting the products and dropping off deliveries door to door. KnoxFill acknowledges this impact and mitigates it by purchasing carbon offsets through the Tennessee Nature Conservancy.[31]

What I like about it

There are a lot of things to love about this business. It is fulfilling a true customer need for household and personal care items without the waste usually associated with these products. It serves as a reminder that we don't *have* to create the amount of waste currently generated from day-to-day activities. Decreasing this waste just requires some planning and innovation. The fact that this company is a for-profit business that also provides sales channels to local makers and artisans is even better. However, what I like most about this business is that it is replicable. KnoxFill is not the first zero-waste store, and it won't be the last. While this business model is common enough to be tried and true, there are still many cities around the world that do not have the option of purchasing from a zero-waste store; this means opportunities for new sustainably minded entrepreneurs.

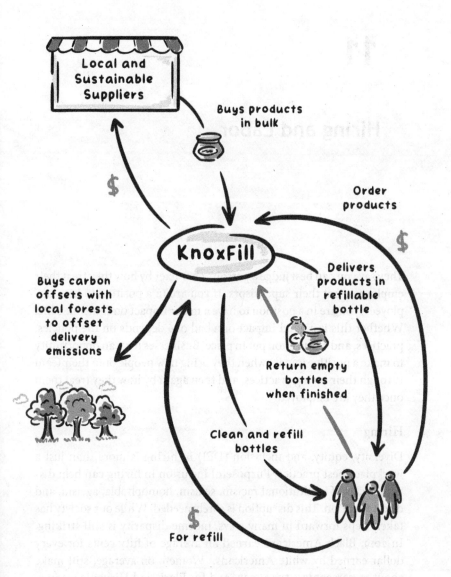

Local and
Sustainable
Suppliers

Buys products
in bulk

Order
products

KnoxFill

Buys carbon
offsets with
local forests
to offset
delivery
emissions

Delivers
products in
refillable
bottle

Return empty
bottles
when finished

Clean and refill
bottles

For refill

11

Hiring and Labor

They say you can best judge a person's character by how they treat their employees, not their supervisors. If you are in a position to hire employees, you are in a position to have a major impact on someone's life. Whether this is a good impact or a bad one depends on the policies, practices, and culture you put in place. Businesses have an opportunity to make a positive impact when they bring new people onto their team through their hiring practices, and then again by how they treat them once they are employed.

Hiring

Diversity, equity, and inclusion (DEI) in hiring is more than just a workplace best practice. Purposeful inclusion in hiring can help disrupt cycles of institutional racism, sexism, homophobia, ageism, and discrimination. This disruption is sorely needed. While our society has taken steps forward in many ways, income disparity is still striking. In 2019, Black Americans earned an average of fifty cents for every dollar earned by white Americans.[1] Women, on average, still make about 17 percent less than men, and for Black and Hispanic women, this number is even lower.[2]

Higher wages mean the ability to have a safety net, pay for better schooling for your children, buy property, pass on wealth, and other important factors that keep inequalities firmly in place from generation to generation. As an employer, you're in a position to help change this. However, the perpetuation of inequalities is embedded in our systems, and even with the best intentions it can be hard to avoid without putting purposeful systems in place. A few things to note as you begin to build out a hiring process:

We may not want to discriminate, but we do

The first thing to acknowledge when putting together a DEI plan is that even though most of us don't want to discriminate, we still do it in subtle and unconscious ways that we likely don't even notice, regardless of our race, gender, or background. It's possible to both really want diversity in the workplace and yet still actively discriminate without realizing it. That's why it's important to have policies and procedures in place to fight hiring discrimination, because good intentions are unfortunately not enough.

Embracing diversity goes beyond gender or skin color

Going back to those good intentions, many employers want a more diverse workplace, and even set goals around diversity, but find it challenging to meet those diversity goals. Why? Because they are looking for a specific type of person (most likely like themselves) with specific life experience, connections, and education, but hoping that person will come in a different color or gender. While not an impossible goal, there are many systemic issues at play that make this less likely. Systemic racism means that fewer people of color have advanced degrees.[3] Women may have résumé gaps because they have taken time off to raise children. BIPOC (Black, Indigenous, People of Color) candidates may not have advanced as quickly in their careers due to past discrimination and lack of a safety net. To truly embrace diversity in the workplace, businesses must be able to focus on skills and aptitude rather than credentials and embrace the benefits that come from having a team with true diversity of perspectives and life experiences (that may be different from yours!).

Tips for setting up a fair hiring process

1. *Use a formal process:* It's no secret that the best way to get a job is to "know someone." We prefer to hire someone who is

recommended by someone we know. This is a reasonable inclination; it's helpful to have someone we trust vouch for a future employee. Unfortunately, this process makes it more likely that the demographic of people currently in positions of power stay in positions of power. Our social circles often include people who look like us and who have had similar life experiences. As a result, when a person in power hires from within their own personal network, this means that there is less likely to be diversity in the workplace, and the barriers of systemic inequality continue to be barriers. So, even if it's tempting to give preference to your friend's neighbor, you're more likely to have an inclusive hiring process and a diverse workplace if you use a formal process for seeking job candidates and if you consider applicants you have no connection to. The good news is that it will ultimately benefit the business if people are chosen for their skills and abilities rather than who they know.

2. *Practice the "Blind CV":* Remember how I mentioned that people may have biases that they aren't even aware of? This can happen before even meeting an applicant. A reviewer may unconsciously be more biased against a woman's résumé for a position that involves hard math or science or may be less likely to call back someone with a name that sounds foreign. The National Bureau of Economic Research conducted an experiment where they sent out 80,000 fake resumes for entry-level positions at Fortune 500 companies. Applicants with distinctively Black names were 10 percent less likely to receive a call back than applicants with a comparable amount of experience with distinctively white names.[4]

One way to combat this bias is to hide the names of applicants when an application is being reviewed. This way the reviewer will be less likely to know the applicant's race or gender and will be more likely to review an applicant based on qualifications and experience, uninfluenced by the reviewer's internal bias.

3. *Use a diverse interview panel:* Using an interview panel made up of a diverse group of people of different races, genders, and

backgrounds can help an organization overcome bias and recognize potential in candidates.

4. *Set goals, strategize, measure, iterate:* As I mentioned in the
   introduction of this book, you can tell what a business prioritizes by what it measures. For a business to truly excel in DEI it
   must set goals, implement strategy to meet these goals, measure
   progress, then iterate on techniques. The tips above are some of
   many examples of strategies that may or may not work for your
   business—but you won't know unless you measure and track
   the results. No matter what strategies you use, it's important
   to educate and engage your employees as part of the process.
   Finally, remember that you don't have to do this alone. There
   are agencies and consultants that can help with this process.

Hiring as a Tool for Social Impact

Some organizations take inclusive hiring a step further and use their
hiring policies as a tool for making a positive social impact. Greyston
Bakery (profile on page 168) practices "open hiring," meaning that they
do not conduct interviews or background checks and do not require
résumés. Jobs are offered on a first-come, first-served basis. While
this wouldn't work for every company, there are many companies that
it can and does work for. This model is an effective way to empower
people who need a first or second chance and may not be able to get
one elsewhere.

Many social enterprises and nonprofit organizations use intentional hiring as a means of job training. Rewearable, a clothes recycling company on Long Island, New York, intentionally hires people
with learning and developmental disabilities to offer employment and
job training to individuals who otherwise may have difficulty finding employment and supporting themselves. Sama, the first Artificial
Intelligence company to receive a B Corp certification, trains young
people in digital skills. A recent study by researchers at MIT evaluating the Sama job training and placement programs in Nairobi, Kenya
found that participants experienced almost 40 percent higher earnings
and 10 percentage points lower unemployment than they those not in
the programs.[5]

Labor

"It's just a job" has never been true. The average person will spend 90,000 hours at work, or about one-third of their lives![6] How you treat your employees will have a massive direct impact on their lives and on the lives of their families. Keeping your employees happy makes financial sense as well. Think of the institutional knowledge that is lost each time an employee quits, or the number of productive hours that are lost training a new employee. It benefits the business to build employee loyalty.

When a business is just starting out, it's easy to treat employees well (assuming you have the funds to do so!). It's not hard to remember that your employees are human beings, not numbers, when there are only three of you and you're squeezed into a tiny office together. But what about when you grow and you don't see all of your employees every day or know them personally? Putting policies in place to ensure that the people who keep your business running are treated as your most valuable asset can help to ensure that those assets don't leave to work for your competitor. Here are some key factors to consider when designing your policies:

Pay

No surprise here—pay is important! It is incredibly challenging for people to thrive and be their best selves if they are not able to live comfortably, support their families, and save for emergencies and goals. Part of your legacy as an employer can be enabling people to be their best selves in the world and in your business.

DIRECT EMPLOYEES

You determine the wage of your direct employees, whether they are your executive team, administrators, or workers manufacturing your product. This means that you have a lot of power to improve the quality of life of those who make your business possible. However, pay is more nuanced and more complicated than just "paying people as well as you can." First of all, depending on where your workers are located, a "good wage" can mean very different things. If you have factories located overseas, the Global Living Wage Coalition can be a good source to look up living wage rates around the world. A living wage is defined as "remuneration received for a standard workweek by a worker in a particular [time and] place sufficient to afford a decent standard of living including food, water, housing, education, healthcare, transport, clothing and other essential needs including provision for unexpected events."[7]

Secondly, many founders would like to pay their employees top wages, but they are not yet at the point with their business that they are able to do so. Growing slowly and organically can help with this problem. By growing and bringing on new employees only when you know you are able to support them, you can avoid some of the massive layoff horror stories that make news headlines when startups grow too fast.

For early-stage companies that are not yet able to pay their team top wages, there are some other options. Many early startup founders pay their first employees partially through equity, or an ownership stake in the company. This means that if a company eventually exits (goes public or is acquired by another company), the early team members will get a percentage of this profit. To ensure that you don't give a portion of your company to an employee that only ends up staying six months, many founders use a vesting equity strategy, meaning that an employee gains equity in stages when they've worked a certain number of years with the company or they meet certain milestones.

SUPPLY CHAIN

Then, there's your supply chain to think about. Sometimes the people who are heavily involved in making your product, and maybe even manufacture your products or materials for your products, are not directly in your employment, and thus their wages and working conditions are not directly in your control. However, what you can control is who you decide to purchase from (see the material sourcing section on page 101). If you are a small company, set your own standards for who you purchase from and take the time to know your suppliers and ensure that their practices align with your values. If you're a larger company, and a large customer for your supplier, you may be able to influence suppliers and set standards for working conditions and wages.

WAGE GAP

The next difficult payment question for mission-driven employers is how to determine levels of payment: that is, how to differentiate between the pay of employees in positions that require a high level of skill and training and those in positions that do not. This pay gap is something that many employers have struggled with, and, in my opinion, have often landed on a result that hurts and divides our world a lot more than it helps. In 2018, new regulations in the US required that publicly traded companies disclose the wage that their CEO is making compared to their median worker. The information that was disclosed was pretty staggering. The largest CEO-to-worker pay gap was at an auto parts manufacturing company called Aptiv, where the pay ratio was 2,526 to 1.[8] *Yikes.* While it's reasonable for employees with more qualifications and more responsibility to make more money than those with less, a ratio of above 1,000 is pretty extreme, and it contributes to the rising wealth gap in our society (remember the 99 percent protests?). In the United States in 2019, the top 10 percent of families owned 76 percent of the wealth, while the bottom 50 percent of families collectively owned only 1 percent.[9]

An internal pay equity policy can limit the wage gap between the highest and lowest paid employees in your company, meaning that the highest paid employee can't make more than X times than the average worker. The value of "X" would be determined by what makes sense for your company. Some firms naturally have a higher ratio than others due to the nature of work done at their company. The US average ratio is around 300 to 1. New Belgium has a ratio of under 10 to 1 (see company profile on page 130). Equal Exchange, a for-profit worker cooperative that sells Fair Trade products, operates with a 5 to 1 top-to-bottom pay ratio.[10]

Setting a policy around your wage gap ratio ensures that business success will be shared by everyone who had a hand in it. When wages are locked together in a ratio like this, then if the business is doing well, the wages of the top-paid employees can still increase, but the wages of the lowest-paid employees will have to increase as well. In other words, business success can be the rising tide that lifts all boats, not just those few shiny boats in the C-suite.

Motivation

After reading the section above, a natural question may be, *but how will I attract and retain top talent if my employee salaries are limited by a wage gap ratio?* This is a reasonable question, and it may in fact be more complicated to attract and retain qualified employees if you don't offer them a higher salary than your competitors. But notice that I said "more complicated" not "impossible."

The truth is that humans are complex creatures. While money is certainly a motivator, it's not the only motivator. A 1940s experiment by psychologist Karl Dunker (recreated on a small scale by the BBC in 2018) set out to test whether people performed better when financial incentives were involved. The experiment divided participants into two groups and gave them tasks to complete that required ingenuity and creativity. One group was told that there was a financial incentive for completing the task, while money was not mentioned to the other group. The two groups performed similarly—in fact, in Karl Dunker's original experiment, the group without financial incentive actually performed better.[11]

Humans are motivated by all sorts of factors: prestige, social connection, a desire to have a positive impact, a desire to leave a legacy, a desire to create and discover, a desire to be challenged, a desire for fun, a desire to be loved and respected. Money is only one motivator, and not necessarily the strongest one. Motivating your employees through money alone means you may not be getting the most out of your employees, and you may still lose them to your competitors. The challenge for an employer that aims to motivate by means other than money is that they must be more creative and more attentive to their employees' needs and drivers. The positive side is that they will likely get a higher quality of work and more employee loyalty.

An employer that seeks to motivate their employees by more than a large check will ensure that their employees feel both challenged and valued and that they have an opportunity to learn and grow. The employees will feel like they have a voice and are listened to, as well as a certain amount of autonomy in their jobs. This employer will also make an effort to form social connections between employees and will make a point to regularly connect employees back to the mission of the company. Let's dig in on a few elements of motivation beyond money:

APPRECIATION AND ACKNOWLEDGMENT

Have you ever spent days working on a presentation that was never used and maybe not even looked at? I know I have! It's a terrible feeling. Acknowledgment and appreciation are especially important in a world where more and more people are working remotely. Make sure that your employees feel seen. Check in with them regularly, comment on their work, show them that you notice it and are grateful for it. Tell them what they've done particularly well and offer advice for improvement or change.

Behavioral economist Dan Ariely once conducted an experiment in which he asked participants to find words in a sheet of random letters. In the first round of the experiment, the participant wrote their name on the paper; the administrator took the paper, looked at it, scanned his eyes up and down the paper, nodded, and said, "Uh-huh!" Then he put it on the stack on his desk.

In the second round of the experiment, the participants were not asked to write their names; the administrator took the paper, didn't look at it, and put it on the stack of papers. In the third round of the experiment, the participants didn't write their name on the paper; the administrator didn't look at it, immediately putting the completed paper in the shredder.

In each round of the experiment, the participants were offered decreasing amounts of money for completing the papers. In the first round where the participants were merely acknowledged, they were willing to continue completing the exercise for fifteen cents. In the second round, where they were ignored, they were willing to work for twenty-eight cents. In the third round, where their work was shredded, they were willing to work for thirty cents. It is important to note not only that simple acknowledgment of their work inspired participants to work for half as little money, but also that being ignored was nearly as demotivating to participants as having their work immediately shredded.

CHALLENGE

It may feel like we as humans ultimately seek ease and relaxation, but our behavior says otherwise. I often feel like all I want is more time to relax, read books, and nap, and yet, here I am, writing this book. Why? Because humans actually crave a bit of challenge. This doesn't mean you should set employees up to fail or should assign employees tasks you don't believe they will be able to do—quite the opposite. However, a little bit of challenge and creative problem-solving can go a long way in helping people to feel engaged in an activity and more committed to seeing the project through to a positive outcome.

Ariely describes another interesting example of this principle in practice: cake mixes. Assuming that people craved the easiest solution, companies that first introduced boxed cake mixes made them as simple as possible. All you had to do was add water, dump the mix in a pan, stick it in the oven, and presto! A cake! Anyone could do it, and the taste and quality of the cake received positive reviews from consumers. One small problem: no one bought them. It turns out that they were *too* easy. No one felt proud of a cake that required zero effort to make, and they felt no ownership over the final product.

In order to address this problem, the manufacturers of cake mixes actually removed the eggs and oil from the mix so that the bakers had to add the eggs and oil themselves. The cake was still very easy to make and saved busy or inexperienced bakers a lot of time and effort; however, by adding a few extra steps, people felt like they had a bigger role in the process. As a result, bakers felt some pride and ownership over the resulting cake. By making the process slightly more difficult, companies made boxed cake mixes a big seller.[12]

FULFILLMENT AND MEANING

An increasing number of people are searching for a sense of fulfillment through their work. In fact, the Huffington Post reported that 94 percent of millennials are interested in using their skills to make a positive impact in the world.[13] If you run a company that has a social or environmental mission, it may seem like you've got this one down already. A social or environmental mission should be enough to keep employees intrinsically motivated, right? The truth is that if your job is looking at spreadsheets all day, it's easy to feel disconnected from that ultimate mission, no matter how grand it is. It's up to the employer to ensure that employees are regularly connected to the mission and the results of their work and reminded of the key part they play.

As we all know, there are an infinite number of moving parts and tasks that help a business to provide its services and to function as a whole. However, it is the employer's job not only to see this overall picture, but to help employees see the larger picture of the organization as well and to understand how they fit in. No one should become isolated within their particular role or project. It's also important to let employees know how their work is having an impact. Regularly share successes from the organization as a whole: how many people were served today? Can you share a personal story of how someone was helped? How many tons of carbon were sequestered this year? Better yet, can you show them the impacts of the company's work firsthand?

SOCIAL CONNECTION

Employees at mission-driven companies are often driven at least in part by socialization and the desire to be part of a community of like-minded people. Keep this in mind as you assign tasks, especially in the world of remote work. Assign teams and allow time for employees to naturally mingle and get to know each other. After a big event, you may want to schedule a regular expedition to a local bar or restaurant. Increasing socialization and building a community within your staff can help build motivation and accountability.

Increased community among employees has the added benefits of making work more fun, increasing the commitment and enthusiasm of workers and increasing accountability because people become accountable to each other as well as to you. Margaret Heffernan, entrepreneur and author, gives the example of a company that was able to increase profits by $15 million and increase employee satisfaction by 10 percent simply by synchronizing employee coffee breaks and allowing colleagues an opportunity to socialize and build trust and rapport with one another. In Sweden, they actually have a word for this: *fika*. Fika means "coffee break," but it has a deeper meaning as well. Fika cannot be taken alone at your desk. Fika means collective restoration; it means making time to take a break with your colleagues.[14]

Another key aspect of building community and team dynamics at work is to avoid creating a culture of competitiveness that pits workers against each other. This can be tricky, while also trying to acknowledge employee work and success, but setting teams up to succeed as a unit and acknowledging and celebrating their joint achievements can also accomplish this goal.

EMPOWERMENT

A study by *Harvard Business Review* on the best places to work and what makes company culture great identified that the best companies to work for treat their employees like owners. They give employees the opportunity to "rearrange, modify, and improve their assignments and feel possession over them." The analytics and software company SAS trains people to give presentations in a form similar to TED talks and gives them a platform to share their best ideas and encourage unconventional thinking. SAS employees are also given the freedom to pursue goals in the way that they see fit. On the SAS campus, even the landscapers are given their own acreage and the leeway to tend the section the way they see fit based on the terrain and architecture of the area.[15]

The other important thing to note here is that if employees are given the freedom to stretch, explore, and extend themselves, they must also be given the freedom to fail. A culture that accepts failure as an inevitable part of innovation is more likely to get outstanding results because employees are not afraid to fail. Companies that accept failure are also more likely to be alerted of mistakes early on and be given the ability to fix them promptly, because employees are not afraid that their job security depends on perfection.

Benefits

When we think of work benefits the things that usually come to mind are healthcare and 401(k) matching. While these are extremely important for employee well-being, companies are beginning to think beyond the standard benefits. What can they offer employees that will take them from being a good place to work to being an exceptional place to work? Flexibility, unlimited vacation days, remote or hybrid work options, and family leave are all becoming more common. The multinational nonprofit Save the Children recently started offering caregiver leave, which, among other things, can be used by working grandparents who need time off to help with a new grandchild. Some companies such as Patagonia (company profile on page 190) are beginning to offer daycare at their offices, a game changer for working parents. Other companies, such as New Belgium Brewing (company profile on page 130), are offering wellness and mental health programs or support to employees. The companies that will lead us into the future of work are showing through their benefits that they recognize that employees are not just workerbots or cogs in a machine. These companies recognize that their employees are full people with lives, pressures, and obligations outside of work.

Employee ownership

As I mentioned above, *Harvard Business Review* identified one of the key qualities of a great place to work is treating employees like owners. Employee ownership models take this a step further: in this model, employees actually *are* owners. Employee ownership can come in many different forms, such as worker-owned cooperatives, stock options, and equity compensation plans. The most common form is Employee Stock Ownership Plans (or ESOPs) in which employees own shares through a trust funded by the company. An ESOP is a type of retirement plan in which employees are granted stock in the company they work for. Employee ownership can range from 100 percent employee-owned to only a small percentage.[16]

Worker ownership comes with some pretty significant benefits to both workers and employers. For workers, belonging to an ESOP has resulted in 92 percent higher median household net wealth and 33 percent higher median income from wages. For employers, there are tax advantages, as well as a 53 percent longer median job tenure (meaning that employees stick around longer!) and an increased ability to preserve a company's legacy. Many founders choose a form of employee ownership because they want to ensure that after they leave the company, it will still be in the hands of the people who helped to build and shape it.[17]

Company Profile: Greyston Bakery
Where the company integrates impact
- Material sourcing
- Hiring and labor

- Community and mentorship
- Giving back

Founder: Bernie Glassman

Originally from Brooklyn, New York, Bernie Glassman took a circuitous route to founding a social enterprise bakery. He was living in California working to be an aeronautical engineer when he first discovered Zen Buddhism. Bernie found his place in the Zen community and ended up moving back to New York to live and work as a teacher in the Zen community of New York. Bernie's Zen name was Tetsugen, which translates to "penetrate the subtleties of life."[18]

Inspired by a Buddhist bakery he had seen in California, Bernie decided to open a bakery as a way to provide employment to his students at the Zen Center in New York in 1982. When the center relocated to Yonkers, Bernie and the bakery came with it, moving into an abandoned lasagna factory. Guided by his Buddhist beliefs, Bernie wanted to do more for the homeless and unemployed population of Yonkers and began hiring people from the community who lacked education, had formerly been in prison, or led unstable lives to work in the bakery. Ten years after opening Greyston Bakery, Bernie and his wife Sandra (also a Zen teacher) opened the Greyston Foundation, an associated nonprofit that provides additional services to address barriers to employment.[19] In the mid 1990s, Bernie left Greyston to pursue other endeavors, but the bakery, foundation, and legacy that he created continue on without him.

What they do

Greyston Bakery is a B Corp located in Yonkers, New York (the first B Corp in New York!) that makes and sells brownies. On the surface, that's pretty simple. However, behind the scenes, there is much more to this innovative, socially-minded company. In fact, the business is less about the brownies and more about the people. Their website proudly states this fact: "We don't hire people to bake brownies, we bake brownies to hire people." Although their brownies are delicious (I can vouch for them personally), their success—think millions of dollars in sales per year—is due as much to their social mission as to their baking prowess. Greyston integrates impact into several elements of their business, but they are most known for their Open Hiring model, described in more detail in the following Impact section.

Business model

For a company that is relatively straightforward in their offering (brownies!), their business model is quite complex. The elements to the Greyston business model are:

- B2C:
  - E-commerce: Anyone can purchase Greyston Bakery brownies or brownie gift packs directly on the company's website.
  - Retail: Greyston brownies are sold through various retail stores and distributors.
- B2B:
  - B2B (Brownie to Business): Greyston sells brownies directly to businesses for integration into their product line. If you've tried Ben & Jerry's Chocolate Fudge Brownie ice cream, you've tried a Greyston Bakery brownie. Greyston has also partnered with Whole Foods to co-create a single-serve Whole Planet brownie.
  - Inclusive Hiring Services: Greyston offers tools and training to support other companies interested in adopting their Open Hiring model. The company provides mentoring, an e-learning portal, data collection, and recruitment services for businesses interested in adopting inclusive hiring practices. They've worked with companies such as Rhino Foods, Bonduelle, and the Body Shop.[20]
- For-profit / Nonprofit hybrid:
  Finally, Greyston is a for-profit / nonprofit hybrid organization. Their for-profit, B Corp Bakery is owned by their nonprofit foundation, Greyston, which provides additional services and workforce development programs funded by the for-profit entity as well as by outside grants.

Impact

MATERIAL SOURCING

Greyston brownies are made with Fair Trade certified chocolate and sugar and kosher salt.[21]

HIRING AND LABOR

Greyston Bakery practices "Open Hiring," which means that they do not check references or look at résumés and you don't need a "connection" to get through the door. If you want to work, you are put on a waiting list and offered the next available job. Employees are given the chance to advance into other roles within Greyston or use the skills, coaching, and experience they've gained to find jobs elsewhere. This model is a daring way to run a business, and one that is starkly in contrast to standard hiring practices. But this model is a lifeline for many people looking for someone to give them a chance. Through this model, Greyston has given jobs to 1,350 people and trained 116 people through their workforce development program, as of 2022. Workers that have completed the Greyston training earn an average of 24 percent above minimum wage.[22]

The Greyston Open Hiring model serves the business as well as the workers. According to Greyston, in addition to making a positive impact in the community, inclusive hiring practices (such as Open Hiring) reduce hiring time by 80 percent, reduce hiring costs by 93 percent, and increase positive work culture and trust in the employer.[23]

COMMUNITY

Greyston serves their community in several ways. First of all, they provide brownies (essential!) as well as employment to a segment of the population that may not otherwise be able to find it. Although the "Open Hiring" term is trademarked, Greyston does not hold the model close to their chest. They actively work to help other for-profit companies follow in their footsteps and develop their own inclusive hiring models.

GIVING BACK

Greyston Bakery uses their profits to fund their foundation work, including workforce development programs outside of the bakery, such as Greyston Rangers, a re-entry program which employs formerly incarcerated individuals for community beautification projects and apprenticeships. In addition to employment, the programs offer social services, skill-building opportunities, and workforce training. These programs also benefit the community through cleaner streets and neighborhoods and less unemployment.[24]

What I like about it

One of my favorite things about Greyston Bakery is that their mission has been instrumental to their success. If they were not a mission-focused company—that is to say, if they were only a bakery that made brownies—they would probably not have reached the success they have achieved today. Their mission has been a key draw for crucial partners like Ben & Jerry's and Whole Foods. Their foundational mission of employment and workforce development also allows them to gain additional income through supporting other companies in developing inclusive hiring models and has allowed them to receive additional grant funding to support and expand their work. The company's mission has also allowed them to become a pillar in their community and a beacon for other social enterprises. In other words, if they had not been willing to take a risk on people, they would not be where they are today.

Greyston Bakery

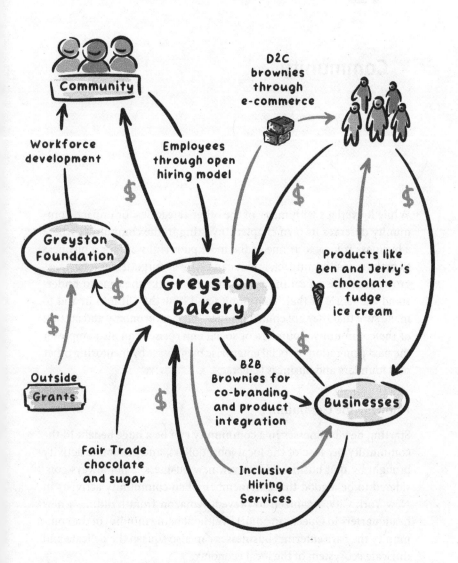

Community

D2C brownies through e-commerce

Workforce development

Employees through open hiring model

Greyston Foundation

$

$

Greyston Bakery

Outside Grants

$

Products like Ben and Jerry's chocolate fudge ice cream

$

B2B Brownies for co-branding and product integration

$

Businesses

Fair Trade chocolate and sugar

Inclusive Hiring Services

12

Community

While it overlaps with many of the other categories for impact, community deserves its own chapter. Investing in the community where a business is located is one of the most powerful ways for a business to make a positive impact, and it can easily be forgotten as a business grows and scales. Leading social enterprises take the time to understand the fabric of their community and how they fit into it, and to make sure that they are contributing to the local economy and culture of the community. Founders of social enterprises can also empower the next generation of social enterprise businesses by mentoring other new founders and business leaders.

Knowing the Community

Starting new businesses in a community can be a huge benefit to the community because of the local jobs, dollars, and economic activity brought by that business. However, new business is not always considered to be a good thing (remember when community activists in New York City organized to prevent Amazon from building a new headquarters in Queens in 2019?).[1] Without being mindful of the community they are entering, businesses can also squash the delicate and intricate ecosystem of the local economy.

A business that will benefit a community and a region will take the time to get to know the community before trying to integrate into it. A helpful tool for this process is to complete a SWOT analysis of the community (Strengths, Weaknesses, Opportunities, and Threats). Strengths and weaknesses are existing internal assets or struggles of a community, and opportunities and threats are external forces acting upon a community.

Strengths

Natural assets in a region or community such as rivers, mountains, and forests are a strength and could help draw customers or provide better quality of life to your workers to help attract and retain talent. Existing local industry and workforce could also be a strength. Locating your business in an area where there are other complementary businesses nearby could benefit your business and contribute to the local economy. For example, a company that conducts extensive research and development in material science may want to locate close to a university with a strong material science program, and may also look for a place with local manufacturing and prototyping facilities that they could contract with.

One tool to assess the strength of different industries within a region is a metric called the Location Quotient (LQ). The LQ measures an area's industrial specialization as compared to the rest of the nation. For example, an LQ of 1 in food manufacturing means that the region is on par with the rest of the nation in the food manufacturing industry. However, a LQ of greater than 1 for food manufacturing means that the area has a stronger than average food manufacturing industry, which could indicate an advantage to a new company in this industry in terms of suppliers, facilities, transportation hubs, and labor pools.[2] If your company is part of this industry, it means that there is a good chance your business would complement and contribute to the local economy of the region.

Opportunities

Thinking of a community in terms of opportunities means considering what outside forces are acting on a community that could result in a positive business opportunity. For example, have mountaintop removal sites left flat ground ideal for putting up wind turbines? Does a river running through town create an opportunity for watersport equipment rental? Or is there a gap or need in the community that is currently not

being met that you could fill? Michaela Barnett, the founder of Knox-
Fill (profile on page 152 and founder interview on page 266), had seen
zero-waste refillery stores in other cities, but not in the city where she
was living, and saw an opportunity to start a new business.

Weaknesses

What is a community struggling with? How could your business help?
Is there high unemployment? Could you explore an open hiring model
like Greyston Bakery (company profile on page 168)? Does the community have a large amount of pollution? Your business could sponsor
cleanups or, even better, find a way to turn the waste into profit like
Phinite is doing with the waste from livestock farms (profile on page
79). Or, you could work with the city to restore a polluted area into a
location for your company's facilities, like New Belgium Brewing did
when they worked with the city of Asheville to rehabilitate a brownfield and use it as a site for their next brewery (profile on page 130).

Threats

What outside forces threaten a community? Is a new mining site
threatening the drinking water of the area? Is opioid addiction increasing in the region? Are droughts hurting the local agriculture
industry? What can your business do to help alleviate these threats or
support solutions? Can your business use its voice as a local employer
to advocate for better policies? Or make financial contributions to local
solutions? (See more about using your business's profit and voice for
positive change on pages 199 and 210, respectively).

The Local Economy

An economy is like an ecosystem. It is made up of the businesses and
people in a given place and the ways they interact, and how they create
and exchange resources. A business should be part of the economic
ecosystem where they are located and try to contribute in a positive
way to the flows of money, resources, talent, and energy that makes an
economic ecosystem healthy; this means hiring local talent, purchasing from local suppliers whenever possible, and investing and engaging
in the local economy.

There's this magic thing that happens when money is spent within a local economy (all right, maybe not magic, just economics) called Local Multiplier 3, named by the New Economics Foundation, that describes the multiplying effect of money that is spent locally. When a dollar is earned within a local economy, spent within a local economy, and then re-spent within that same geographic area, the impact of that dollar has a multiplied impact on the local economy.[3] That means that having a business that interacts with the local economy through offering goods and services, employing local community members, and purchasing from other local businesses is a chance to get more bang for your buck in terms of positive economic impact.

A Connection to Place

Business is not inherently bad; in fact, it can be very good. Business is inherently about solving problems. The issue is when people leave their morals at home and think only with their brains at work, instead of with their brains and their hearts simultaneously. When you live in the community where you work, and you are around the people who are impacted by your business on a daily basis, it's a lot harder to leave your morals at the door.

Local ownership and decision-making power isn't just important because of the community and regional knowledge, although that's important too; local ownership means that the owner's family breathes the air and drinks the water that is impacted by the business. You'll run into your employees at the supermarket and your kids may be on the same softball team. The intimacy and accountability of living and working in the same community can be intimidating, but it can also be an antidote for the isolation and lack of connection that so many of us feel. When a business and the people who run it feel a sense of place and connection to the community, it can be as good for people in the business as it is for the community.

Community-Based Growth

Businesses are often told to "grow or die." As soon as a business reaches one horizon, it is pushed to start reaching towards the next. In fact, this is one downside of taking outside money from investors. Venture capitalists in particular are not looking to fund a healthy, self-sustaining business; they are looking to fund a blockbuster that will bring them tenfold returns on their investments. For this reason, they may push an entrepreneur to try to take their business large, even if the risk is higher, while the business could be quite successful and profitable with a smaller operation.

So, is it bad to grow? No, it's not. But for a social enterprise, growth must be planned mindfully so that the core of the mission is not lost in the growth. Community impact and relationships are particularly hard to maintain as a business scales. How can a founder intimately understand the economic ecosystem of more than one community? It's not impossible, but it's not easy. Here are a few tips for growing while preserving your mission and the ethos of your company.

Grow vertically, not horizontally

A common growth pattern for a business is to spread to new cities. As you can imagine, the community impact becomes difficult to manage, because the leaders and decision-makers of a business may not live in the community where the business operates. When Judy Wicks, founder of White Dog Cafe, was pushed to turn her successful restaurant into a chain, she decided to grow deeper instead of wider. "Nature doesn't grow like chains do. . . . Chains are like invasive species," said Wicks. "They go into other people's neighborhoods and smother out those local businesses. Nature grows in a place, in an ecosystem." So instead of expanding her business to other cities, she found new ways to expand within her own city, such as by opening a partner store called Black Cat that sold local and Fair Trade Products.[4]

This strategy can be used more directly within an existing business too. Many businesses decide to expand vertically rather than horizontally. So, rather than a coffee shop deciding to expand to more locations, they may decide to start roasting their own coffee and becoming their own supplier. By expanding vertically, rather than horizontally, a business can gain more control of its own supply chain and also increase its margins without losing track of its sense of place. The Method Soap factory, for example, operates their manufacturing, bottling, and distribution in one location, which cuts down on their carbon footprint, saves money on transport, and means that they don't have to share profit margins with contractors. They also started producing a large amount of the energy they use on site.[5] Vertical expansion can be particularly beneficial for companies with proprietary processes and trade secrets that they want to keep in house.

Give autonomy to different branches

If you are going to expand your business to different cities, consider allowing each branch to have the autonomy to integrate into their community in a positive way. Spend some time identifying the core elements of your business that must stay the same across all branches; outside of those core elements, give each branch the ability to make their own decisions and to find their unique strengths and identity within the community they are located in. One study from ESPC Business School in France found a positive correlation between the performance of franchises and the level of autonomy they are given.[6] This level of success is also dependent on choosing the correct person or team to lead your business in different locations. They must share and understand your vision and also have the level of competence necessary to carry out business functions with a high level of autonomy.

Goodwill Industries, for example, despite being a national organization with a well-known and recognizable brand, operates with a unique CEO and board of directors in each location. The branches operate under the same mission and goals, but function independently in order to better serve the needs of the unique communities in which they operate.[7]

License and social contract

If you plan to sell or license your business to others, consider including social and environmental commitments to the contract. When Judy Wicks decided to sell White Dog Cafe, she drew up a social contract with the new owner that laid out core elements of the business that must be maintained, such as local ownership and independence of each White Dog Cafe location and a maximum pay ratio between the highest paid and lowest paid employee.[8] When Ben & Jerry's was acquired by Unilever, the agreement included a provision that the social mission, brand integrity, and product quality would be preserved by the leadership of an independent board of directors, and that the company would spend at least $1.1 million each year on activism.

Mentorship

Mentoring other founders

Another powerful tool that entrepreneurs have at their disposal for positive impact is mentorship. When it comes to starting a new business, no one can advise you quite as well as someone that has done it before; that's why entrepreneurs make exceptionally good mentors to other entrepreneurs. A good mentor can help a startup avoid key pitfalls, give difficult feedback, and be a cheerleader, confidant, and sounding board for difficult decisions. Being an entrepreneur can be a lonely road, so having an experienced mentor that has gone down it before can be a game changer for a new startup.

Serving as a mentor can be a fun and empowering experience as well. Helping to build the next generation of social enterprises is a valuable service to the world, and even if the startup ends up failing (which, let's face it, is a common outcome), if you can help founders figure out the gaps in their business earlier, rather than later, you will have saved them money, energy, and possibly years of their lives.

If you're interested in serving as a mentor to other startups, you can check for programs at your local entrepreneur center to support entrepreneurs in your community (just enter the name of your city or state and "entrepreneur center" into a search engine and I'll bet something will come up). Or you can mentor other startups in your industry through organizations that are specific to that industry. For example, AgLaunch offers a mentor program specifically for startups in agricultural innovation,[9] and the Cleantech Open offers mentorship to cleantech startups through their annual accelerator program.[10] On the flip side, if you're a startup founder that could *use* a mentor, you can also apply to these programs as a mentee!

Mentoring other businesses

There's no way to sugarcoat it; starting a business is hard. Starting a social enterprise can be even more complicated (if it weren't, there would be no need for this book). However, the good news is that there is no shortage of problems to be solved, or of value to be added to the world, and we don't have to keep recreating the wheel on difficult questions like circular supply chains, inclusive hiring practices, and sustainable packaging. When one company figures out key elements, they can help other companies to do the same.

This approach may feel counterintuitive to capitalist strategy, but the good news is that business is actually not a zero-sum game. Many very successful businesses commit significant amounts of time to helping other businesses that are trying to improve their own impact in the world. Judy Wicks, the founder of White Dog Cafe in Philadelphia, was one of the founders of Common Future (formerly the Business Alliance for Local Living Economies, or BALLE), a network specifically designed for founders and leaders to lift up other founders and leaders.[11] Patagonia helped create the Regenerative Organic Alliance, a nonprofit organization committed to making regenerative farming practices more commonplace and making materials like regenerative, organic cotton more accessible.[12] New Belgium Brewing created a publicly accessible guide for other breweries to become carbon-neutral.[13] When you're facing a difficult business or mission-related problem, seek out other businesses who might have navigated the same issue. And don't forget to return the favor!

Company Profile: WeSolar

Founder interview on page 249.

Where the company integrates impact

- Products and services
- Community

Founder: Kristal Hansley

Originally from Brooklyn, New York, Kristal had always been passionate about serving her community and standing up for the rights of others, particularly low-income communities and people of color. Originally, Kristal pursued this personal mission through involvement in politics. Kristal studied political science and sociology in college and began a political career that led her to serve as a liaison to Senator

Harry Reid, to work as program manager for the Senate Democratic Diversity Initiative, and to oversee Community Affairs for Congresswoman Eleanor Holmes Norton.

When Maryland and other states began to make changes to legislation that incentivized the use of solar power and also helped deregulate the solar market, Kristal saw this moment as an opportunity and began working at a community solar firm. While she loved the model and the work, she noticed that the people working in the industry, the customers, and even the renewable energy organizations and nonprofits were primarily white. This meant that communities of color that would gain the most from the benefits of community solar were not included. Kristal founded WeSolar in 2020 with the goal of providing access to clean energy for under-resourced communities and closing the energy divide.

What they do

WeSolar is a community solar company located in Baltimore. Community solar enables "shared solar" or "virtual solar," which is the ability for an energy customer to purchase solar energy that is generated from a shared solar array. This means that consumers can have access to renewable power without having solar panels installed directly on their homes. This is a game changer for those who are interested in the benefits of renewable energy but are not able to afford the upfront costs of purchasing or installing solar equipment, do not own their homes, or do not live in an environment conducive to installing solar power (such as a shared apartment building or a heavily shaded area). WeSolar acts as a solar developer as well as a platform and intermediary to facilitate the community solar model, allowing multiple individual consumers to subscribe to renewable energy from a shared solar development.[14]

Business model

WeSolar has three tiers to their business model: 1) WeSolar is hired to facilitate new community solar installations; 2) They develop their own solar installations; and 3) They are paid by other solar developers to sign on new customers and to handle the billing and energy allocations to enable a community solar model. Customers who subscribe to community solar projects can typically save from 5 to 20 percent on their electric bills.[15] The energy captured by the solar installments is generally distributed through the existing utility provider, with WeSolar acting as an intermediary. The final player in this business model is the government. While the government is not a direct customer, government legislation and incentives make this business model possible.

Impact

PRODUCTS AND SERVICES

Switching to renewable energy sources is essential for avoiding the worst impacts of climate change and maintaining a planet that can sustain life as we know it for future generations. The average US household emits between 0.4 and 10.8 metric tons of carbon dioxide via energy use each year. Switching to renewable energy sources can drastically mitigate this.[16] However, large-scale clean energy adoption depends on new business models, like WeSolar, to make clean energy sources like solar available to the masses, rather than just to those who have the funds and roof access to install solar panels directly on their homes.

COMMUNITY

In addition to the lack of infrastructure and business models, another reason that low income and under-resourced communities do not have access to clean energy is due to a lack of communication, outreach, and trust. Often the people who own and work for clean energy companies do not come from the community and do not look like the people who live in the community. Kristal is helping to break this mold by being the first Black woman to launch a community solar company, in an industry whose senior executives are 80 percent white men.[17]

Because of deeply entrenched disparities and historical inequalities, members of low-income communities and communities of color are understandably skeptical when they receive an offer that seems "too good to be true," such as community solar's promise to save money on their energy bills and support clean energy with no catch. However, underserved communities are also missing out on new opportunities for energy savings and increased efficiencies. Kristal aims to forge this divide and build the necessary trust within under-resourced communities. To demonstrate the company's commitment to this mission,

WeSolar was launched on Juneteenth, the day that historically marks the end of slavery.

What I like about it

The businesses that will lead us into a more sustainable and equitable future will do so by focusing on both environmental and social justice, implementing the necessary structures and business models to advance the new technologies that our earth needs without leaving anyone behind. WeSolar is a perfect example of a company that has boldly taken on this integrated social and environmental mission that, while it may be more challenging at the onset, is the only true path forward.

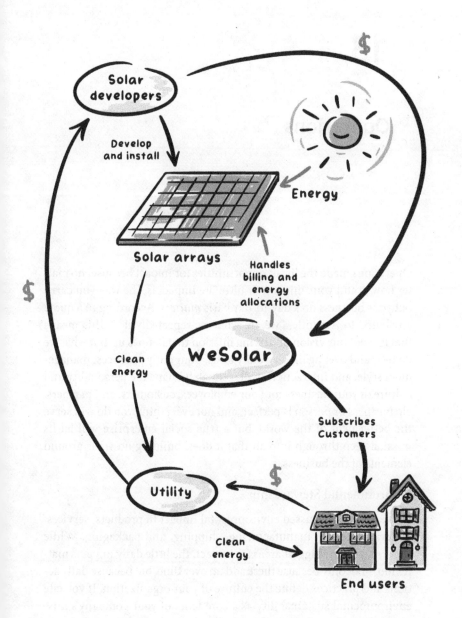

Solar developers

Develop and install

Energy

Solar arrays

Handles billing and energy allocations

Clean energy

WeSolar

$

$

Subscribes Customers

Utility

$

Clean energy

End users

13

Operations

Operations made the list of opportunities for impact because, no matter how grand your mission or ultimate impact is, the way you carry out your business on a day-to-day basis *matters*. According to a quote attributed to Aristotle, "we are what we repeatedly do." This means that it is not our vision or driving mission that defines us, but what we do over and over again on a daily basis. Your daily practices, management style, and interactions will ultimately shape the personality and culture of your business for your employees, customers, and partners. No business or person is perfect, and not everything you do will serve the betterment of the world, but a true social enterprise will let its mission seep through into all that it does, building no walls around elements of the business.

Environmental Stewardship

We've already discussed environmental impact in products, services, materials, design, manufacturing, shipping, and packaging. While these may be the biggest areas for impact, the little daily impacts matter too—not only because these add up over time, but because daily actions and practices define the culture of your organization. If you cite environmental sustainability as a core tenet of your company's mission, but use Styrofoam in the office kitchen, employees may be given the impression that the mission is surface-level only. This impression could corrode employees' trust and commitment to the organization, as well as the likelihood that they will continue to carry out the mission in the daily business decisions they make individually.

Kindness

Somewhere along the twists and turns of our history and cultural development, kindness became associated with weakness. There is probably nothing in our culture that harms us more than this misconception. Creating a culture of kindness at work boosts quality of life, increases productivity, and brings an improved perception of others as well as of one's own self-worth. *Harvard Business Review* credits kindness as improving the happiness of both those on the receiving end of kind gestures, such as voicing praise and gratitude, as well as those on the giving end of kindness. Being kind to others helps to create well-being and a sense of meaning.[1] In addition to the individual benefits of kindness, there are organizational benefits as well. One study of over 3,500 businesses and 50,000 individuals found that an organization that cultivates a culture of kindness through actions of courtesy, helping, and praise benefits through improved productivity, efficiency, and lower turnover rates.[2]

So how do you create a culture of kindness in a business? There are many theories and tactics for this, but the most powerful method is by example. When figures in authority positions make a point to practice kindness, others are more likely to follow suit. Because a leader can't be everywhere at once, there are also practices that can be built into work culture, such as setting aside time during a weekly meeting for co-workers to recognize each other for work well done.

Transparency

Transparency in business used to be a unique attribute, but now in the age of social media and online review boards, transparency is increasingly a must. At the end of the day, no person or business is perfect. The question is: are they brave enough to admit it? Transparency is no easy thing, but those business leaders who are willing to share information about their challenges, goals, and social and environmental impact often see advantages of increased trust and loyalty from employees, partners, and customers. The most important areas of business transparency include:

Internal transparency

Have you ever found out about huge organizational changes at your workplace through the rumor mill? Or learned that someone lower on the organizational chart earns a higher salary than you? Speaking from experience, I can say it's a terrible feeling! And every time something like that happens, trust and loyalty between employee and employer erodes. As an employer, you can get ahead of these scenarios by talking about the hard things with your employees before someone else does.

"Open Book Management" is a management strategy originally outlined by Jack Stack in the book *The Great Game of Business*, and famously adopted by companies such as New Belgium Brewing (company profile on page 130) that have been known for taking the practices to heart. Open Book Management is a step beyond just sharing financial information with employees; it also involves teaching employees to understand the financial information they're seeing and how to evaluate the impact of their work on the success of the business. In other words, the goal is to teach all employees to "think like owners," with the goal that employees are then empowered to make better decisions and feel a greater sense of loyalty to the business.[3]

Transparency is sometimes easier in a smaller team, where a founder will likely have a personal relationship with each employee, but as a business grows, transparency often has to be built into the structure of the organization through practices such as regular meetings, internal newsletters, or intentional communication channels such as passing information through managers.

External transparency

Trust is hard-earned these days. With social media, consumer blogs, and media exposés, not to mention an onslaught of "fake news," consumers have begun to approach brands with an increased level of skepticism. According to the 2019 Edelman Trust Barometer report, 67 percent of consumers agreed with the statement "a good reputation may get me to try a product, but unless I come to trust the company behind the product, I will soon stop buying it."[4] To win customer loyalty, businesses have to have more than a catchy advertising campaign.

The increased availability of information has led to a more informed customer who now cares about factors such as ingredients in a product, the way it was made, the social and environmental impact of the business, the way workers are treated, and price transparency—just to name a few! Couple that with a skepticism about whether or not the information they hear is true, and businesses are hard put to win over a customer's trust.

However, increased consumer skepticism is not without cause. Customers remember learning about child labor in sweatshops overseas and horror stories of worker treatment and facilities, like the fires that killed dozens of workers in locked-door factories in Bangladesh in 2012 and again in 2021.[5] Along with an increase in environmental awareness and concern has come an onslaught of "greenwashing" from businesses, to the point that almost every company claims environmentally responsible practices, and consumers are left scratching their heads about which claims are legitimate and which aren't.

To win consumer trust in today's muddled and skeptical world, companies have to take transparency to a whole new level. In addition to practices like public sustainability reports, diversity metrics, carbon accounting, and financial disclosures, some brands, such as clothing brand Patagonia (company profile on page 190), make a point to disclose the bad as well as the good. Patagonia does not shy away from the fact that, despite their environmental efforts, it's still better for customers to mend their old clothes than to purchase new clothes; in fact, Patagonia has run ad campaigns making this point. They also disclose extensive information about their sustainability and social impact on their website, citing their goals and progress across the areas of material sourcing, manufacturing, and worker payment and well-being. Patagonia is rewarded for their transparency through fierce customer loyalty and a high level of consumer and employee trust.

Another clothing company, Everlane, took a similar path in 2012 by sharing the "real cost" online of making a new T-shirt. Their first product sold out and the company was rewarded with 20,000 new followers.[6] In a confusing world, people are hungry for truth and transparency, and leading the charge in this effort pays off.

In addition to being an expectation of customers, transparency is increasingly demanded by regulatory bodies. Around the world, companies are increasingly required to disclose their finances, their ingredient lists, their carbon emissions . . . the list continues. Those companies that disclose this information voluntarily before they are required to do so can get ahead of their own stories and have time to shape their messaging, gaining consumer trust through early disclosure rather than waiting until disclosure is required.

Company Profile: Patagonia

Where the company integrates impact

- Material sourcing
- Operations
- Giving back
- Voice

Founder: Yvon Chouinard

Yvon Chouinard never planned to run a company. An avid rock climber, Yvon spent part of the 1960s living out of his car and eating damaged cans of cat food that he bought for five cents. He initially started his business in 1965 by selling handmade climbing equipment from the back of his car, mostly to fund his own climbing expeditions. Eventually, after successfully importing rugby shirts from England and selling them to American climbers, he began to focus on apparel more than gear, initiating the business that eventually grew into what is now Patagonia. For Yvon, concern about the environmental damage he was seeing in wild spaces was a natural extension of his love of the outdoors. He began to consider the idea that he could use his company as a platform to make a positive environmental impact in the world—an idea still relatively new for the business world. Under Yvon's leadership, Patagonia began contributing to environmental groups and speaking out against international free trade agreements such as NAFTA and GATT due to a distrust of the promises regarding environmental and social protections that were part of the agreements. This was the beginning of a company that now stands out as a leader to other mission-oriented companies: a company that somehow manages to straddle the line between being a profitable apparel company and discouraging consumerism with grace and integrity.[7]

What they do

Patagonia designs and sells outdoor gear and apparel. The company has built a strong and profitable business on the principle that people should consume less but consume better. Although consumers may pay more for Patagonia apparel than for competitors' products, Patagonia's clothes are made to last. Consumers are also paying for the Patagonia brand and mission, and they are willing to pay more because they believe in the company's commitment to social and environmental impact.

Patagonia is known for "practicing what they preach," especially when it comes to the environment. They have been rewarded for this commitment through the loyalty of both consumers and employees. In 2021, Patagonia employees rated the company with 4.3 stars out of 5 on Glassdoor (a site where employees anonymously provide feedback about employers), with 83 percent saying they would recommend the company to a friend. Patagonia's bottom line has also benefited from their positive reputation, with annual sales of over $1 billion each year between 2019 and 2021.[8]

In 2022, Yvon Chouinard surprised the world again when he transferred ownership of the company to charity. Until this time, Patagonia had been a privately owned, for-profit company. As Yvon aged, he wanted to make sure that the company remained true to its values after he and his family were no longer involved. Rather than selling the company or going public, Yvon, with support from his family and the company's chief executive Ryan Gellert, decided to donate the family's ownership of the company (approximately $3 billion) to a nonprofit and specially designed trust that will ensure that Patagonia's profits will go towards fighting climate change and protecting the environment.[9]

Business model

From a business model perspective, Patagonia is relatively straightforward. They sell outdoor clothing and gear to consumers, both directly and through distributors. What is unique about Patagonia is all the ways they integrate impact into their business model along the way. For large consumer goods companies, Patagonia leads the way in ethical sourcing. They also use their profits to support environmental causes and speak out about environmental issues.

Although they are an apparel company that depends on selling new goods to make a profit, Patagonia encourages customers to reuse and repair clothing, and even provides resources and services to help customers donate or repair their clothing. In a world where planned obsolescence (purposefully designing a product to break after a certain amount of time so that a customer must purchase it again) is a common business practice, Patagonia stands out for its commitment to its values and its authenticity.

Impact

MATERIAL SOURCING

Patagonia is a leader in their industry in sustainable and ethical sourcing of material. They use a combination of recycled materials and carefully chosen certifications to make their products as sustainable and ethical as possible. A few of their notable sourcing achievements include the following:

- **Cotton:** Cotton is used in many of Patagonia's products. However, depending on how it is grown, cotton production can use large amounts of water and can have a substantial carbon footprint, and is often grown using a large amount of pesticides. In the fall of 2021, 36 percent of the cotton fabric Patagonia used in their products was made from recycled cotton. This is possible through a partnership with their supply chain partners who collect pre-consumer fabric scraps from their factories, shred the scrap fabric, and re-spin it into yarn. Most of this cotton is blended with recycled polyester. For the other 64 percent of cotton in their products, Patagonia uses either organic cotton, "Cotton in Conversion" (cotton from farmers who are transitioning their cotton from traditional to organic), or Organic Regenerative Certified cotton from farms practicing "regenerative agriculture," a combination of farming practices that help to regenerate soil and sequester carbon from the atmosphere.[10]

- **Down:** Down is the fluffy insulative material used in jackets and comforters that is made of goose or duck feathers. Patagonia uses down in many of their coats and jackets. In the fall of 2021, forty-seven Patagonia styles (a number they aim to increase) were made using 100 percent recycled down, which is taken from old cushions, bedding, and other used items that were diverted from the landfill.[11] The remainder of the down they use is certified by the Global Traceable Down Standard, which ensures that the geese and ducks are treated humanely and are neither force-fed nor live-plucked.[12]

- **Nylon:** Nylon is a strong plastic used in many of Patagonia's lightweight fabrics. Producing nylon has a high energy cost and produces a large amount of greenhouse gases. Patagonia is working to use as much recycled nylon as they can in their products. Recycled nylon is made from nylon waste products such as weaving mill discards and used fishing nets. In the fall of 2021, Patagonia used at least some percentage of recycled nylon in 90 percent of their products that contain nylon.[13]

- **Fair Trade:** Patagonia clothing is manufactured in factories around the world that are not owned by Patagonia. In an effort to ensure that the laborers in these factories are treated humanely and paid a living wage, Patagonia partners with Fair Trade USA to offer Fair Trade Certified sewn products. Patagonia helps incentivize factories to get the Fair Trade certification by paying a premium for items that are Fair Trade Certified. They are currently offering more Fair Trade Certified sewn styles than any other apparel brand.[14]

OPERATIONS

Patagonia is also a leader in integrating positive impact into their business operations and the running of their facilities. The points below are not an exhaustive list of how they integrate impact into their operations, but they are some of the aspects that make the Patagonia operations stand out.

- **Operation of Patagonia-owned facilities:** Patagonia does not own their own manufacturing facilities; however, they do operate offices, distribution facilities, and stores around the world. At the facilities they fully own and operate, Patagonia has made a major effort to minimize their environmental footprint. In the United States, they operate with 100 percent renewable energy in their facilities through a combination of onsite and offsite solar panel installations. This means that they have some solar panels directly on their buildings and offset the rest of their electricity through renewable energy certificates created by installing solar panels on residential homes and on farmland.

  The company is conscious of minimizing the water usage at their facilities and have built a bioswale at their headquarters in Ventura, California that naturally filters rain and stormwater runoff before it drains back to the ocean. Patagonia also makes an effort to minimize waste by installing composting systems at all facilities, educating employees about waste and recycling, and phasing out single-use plastics. They have developed principles (listed on their website) about responsibly sourcing service providers, preferable purchasing, procurement, and recycling principles.[15]

  Patagonia also makes the health and well-being of their employees a priority. They provide company-paid health care and sick-leave time for all employees, as well as paid maternity and paternity leave, and offer onsite childcare at their headquarters in Ventura and their distribution center in Reno.[16] Treating their employees well and connecting them to their environmental mission by incorporating the Patagonia values into their day-to-day operations is key to their strategy for employee loyalty, satisfaction, and retention.

- **Resources and services for repairing and reusing clothing:** Even with all the responsible sourcing and in-house sustainability practices, there is no denying that Patagonia is an apparel company—ultimately, they are creating more consumer goods in a world that is already chock-full of consumer goods.

Do we need apparel? Yes. Do we need as much apparel as is currently created and sold? Definitely not. We could probably repair and reuse the apparel that is already in the world for several generations to come without making any more, and we would be just fine. What I appreciate about Patagonia is that they do not shy away from this fact. They recommend that consumers buy less. They go so far in this recommendation that, if I were an investor in the company, I might start to get nervous. Their famous "Don't Buy This Jacket" campaign of 2011 encouraged consumers to consider buying used Patagonia products instead of new and to be conscientious about their purchases (of course their sales actually increased as a result!).

However, their commitment to buying less and buying used is more than just a clever marketing campaign. On the homepage of the Patagonia website, there are videos and resources showing consumers how to patch the insulation on their jacket or to repair a broken zipper or missing button. They offer a mail-in repair service and run an entity called Worn Wear where they facilitate the buying and selling of used Patagonia clothing. Consumers can send in their used Patagonia apparel in exchange for store credit (to be used on new or used clothes) or buy used apparel from the Worn Wear website.[17] In this way they are able to facilitate the reuse of apparel (a win for the environment) and profit from apparel twice (a win for the business).

- **Transparency:** The transparency with which Patagonia operates speaks to their authenticity and commitment to their mission. On their public website, you can access information regarding their factories, suppliers, sustainability and social impact goals, and *where they are with these goals*. This last part is particularly impressive. Many of the stories and statistics they share around their social and environmental goals are exciting and inspiring—but not all of them. On the Social Responsibility section of their site they disclose that while they believe that earning a Living Wage is a basic human right, as of 2020, on average, only 39 percent of their apparel assembly factories were paying their workers a living wage (as estimated by the Anker Methodology).[18]

This statistic is shocking coming from a company that is generally known as being socially and environmentally conscious with their practices. However, these low numbers speak to the inherent problems in the apparel industry and to the global issues of poverty and inequality. Patagonia does not own their factories, which means they cannot mandate practices such as wage levels. Because these factories also make products for other brands, there is a negotiation process that goes along with any changes. Patagonia is a founding member of the Fair Labor Association and has developed an approach to work with their factories to improve these numbers. Although they have a long way to go, I applaud Patagonia for being honest about these numbers and working to improve.

PROFIT

Patagonia has a self-imposed "Earth Tax." Patagonia founder Yvon Chouinard started "1% for the Planet" along with fellow founder and environmentalist Craig Matthews. The organization advocates for businesses to give at least 1 percent of their revenues to an environmental cause. Over 5,000 businesses now participate, and $435 million has been donated through this program. Patagonia donates to environmental nonprofits working to defend air, land, and water around the globe.

In addition, Patagonia has established Tin Shed Ventures, a fund to help like-minded startup companies that have a mission to protect the environment. These contributions have the dual benefit of supporting environmental causes and increasing the loyalty of Patagonia customers and employees through the knowledge that their contributions are furthering important environmental work.

Finally, the newest addition to the Patagonia-driven impact organizations is the Holdfast Collective, the 501(c)4 that came out of the Patagonia ownership transfer in September 2022. Holdfast is different from 1% For the Planet in that it receives *all* excess profits after Patagonia takes care of other obligations, such as reinvesting in the business, donating to 1% For the Planet, etc., and disperses the money to groups working on finding nature-based solutions to the climate crisis.

VOICE

In addition to donating directly to environmental nonprofits, Patagonia runs a Global Sports Activism program that funds well-known outdoor sports activists such as surfers and climbers to speak out on environmental issues. Patagonia also makes films that are a mixture of advocacy for environmental issues and inspirational stories about athletes. Patagonia encourages customers to engage in activism by hosting petitions on their website. The company has also made a practice of participating directly in activism. In 2017, for example, Patagonia was part of a coalition of conservationists and indigenous people that sued the Trump Administration for proclamations to revoke the status of two national monuments.[19] Using their voice through films, athletes, and direct activism has the dual benefit of advocating for environmental issues and spreading awareness of the Patagonia brand.

What I like about it

Patagonia is a large, global, apparel company; they are not perfect. That said, their commitment to their mission is clear, and they are undeniably industry leaders in many areas such as sustainable sourcing and environmental activism. In an industry full of greenwashing, their transparency around their social and environmental practices, both the good and the bad, sets them apart.

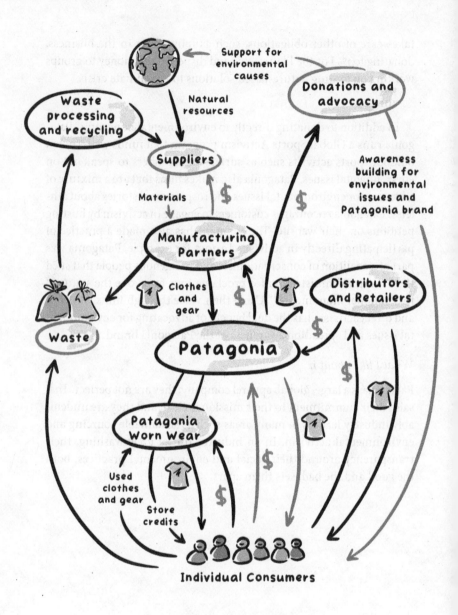

Support for
environmental
causes

Waste
processing
and recycling

Natural
resources

Donations and
advocacy

Suppliers

Awareness
building for
environmental
issues and
Patagonia brand

Materials

$

$

Manufacturing
Partners

Clothes
and
gear

$

Distributors
and Retailers

$

Waste

Patagonia

$

$

Patagonia
Worn Wear

$

Used
clothes
and gear

Store
credits

$

Individual Consumers

14

Giving Back

This is the category that comes to mind most often when people think about how businesses can make a difference— money! While this is an entirely viable and effective way to make a positive impact, I will give the disclaimer that this is the least interesting category to me. This strategy aligns with the ideology that businesses are money-making machines that will do whatever they can to make a profit, and can *then* think about making a positive impact, right at the very end, by throwing money at some cause. I believe that this is generally an uncreative strategy that lets businesses get away with not trying to do good through the services and products they provide and the impact of their operations. That aside, contributing profit towards a good cause can be very powerful, especially when coupled with the other strategies in this section. There are many companies who are contributing their profits in creative ways and utilizing unique strategies to make their donations more impactful.

What to Contribute

Let's start with *what* to contribute. A business has many valuable re-sources at its disposal that can be utilized to make a positive impact in the community and world. The most common resources to contribute are:

Money! (Your own)

You guessed it, money makes the top spot on the list of things busi-nesses can contribute to good causes. A business donating its own funds to a good cause is one of the most common and most effective ways to give back. You can find more information on different ways to structure this below.

Money! (Someone else's)

This one may sound a little surprising, but businesses actually do this all the time—in fact, you've probably participated in this strategy. Any time you're invited to "round up" at the checkout counter or asked if you'd like to kick in a dollar for a local charity, you've participated in a fundraising campaign facilitated by a business. Businesses will also engage in a version of this strategy with their own employees, presenting them with the option to donate a small percentage of their paycheck to a good cause. This strategy may seem like a cop-out, but it can be an effective way for a business to engage customers and employees in their mission, especially if the business agrees to match the funds raised.

Product or service

Another common mode of giving back is to donate a portion of your services or product for free to a good cause. This strategy can be effective because it allows a business to do what it does best (delivering its core service or product) to those who wouldn't ordinarily be able to pay for it, while also doubling as an advertising strategy. For example, the athletic brand Champion donates products and apparel to causes like the Special Olympics and youth summer camps.[1] For every product sold, Soapbox Soaps donates one bar of soap to someone in need through a network of nonprofit partners.[2] Another way to contribute is by allowing your employees to donate their time and expertise. Some law firms like Chapman in Chicago allow their lawyers to include a certain amount of pro bono services as billable hours.[3]

How to Contribute

Now that we've covered the options of what to contribute, the next question is how to go about it. There are many different strategies for making donations, some that tend to be more effective than others.

One-time donations and sponsorship

One-time donations may be the most common form of contributions from businesses to nonprofit organizations. These contributions could happen at the end of the fiscal year, around a specific marketing campaign, or as a sponsorship for a special event or initiative. Although few nonprofits are likely to ever turn down a one-time donation, I would venture to say that these are generally the least effective form of charitable contribution. Just like businesses, nonprofit organizations like to plan! Having a reasonable estimation of what their funds will be over time allows them to budget, schedule future initiatives, make hires, and so on. That's why an ongoing relationship between a nonprofit and a business can be a more effective way of giving.

Recurring donations through partnership

Recurring donations are generally a more strategic and effective method of donating to a good cause for both the business and the nonprofit. The business is able to incorporate this ongoing relationship into its brand identity. For example, Revivn (company profile on page 205) has an ongoing relationship with nonprofit partners such as First Tech Fund and the Boys and Girls Club; these relationships allow Revivn to distribute refurbished technology to kids who need it, making Revivn's sustainability and community impact goals a reality, but also functioning as a core part of Revivn's business and brand identity, attracting customers who are drawn by the mission of the company.

Likewise Coffee, a coffee shop in Knoxville, Tennessee, is wholly owned by the nonprofit Raising a Voice, which works to combat human trafficking, and serves as a method of bringing more a more sustainable source of funding to the nonprofit.[4] With an ongoing and predictable source of funding, nonprofits are better able to budget and plan for the future.

Funds and foundations

Some businesses set up a foundation or a fund as a means of facilitating mission-driven contributions. These are similar but distinct strategies:

- A foundation is generally a grant-making entity that sets aside a certain amount of money to be given away to good causes (each foundation has different guidelines about what exactly they contribute to, but often it's to nonprofit organizations). Organizations apply for grants, specifying why they need a particular amount of money and what impact they will have, and the organization selects a few proposals to fund, generally requiring a certain amount of reporting for the organization to describe what they did with the money and what the result was.

- A fund is more likely to contribute to for-profit initiatives and startup companies. Instead of donations, these contributions are usually either loans or investments. If the contribution is a loan, there will likely be an expectation of repayment, with a specified interest rate. If it is an investment, the fund will likely take a small percentage of equity in the company in exchange for a certain amount of money; then if or when the startup is eventually sold or goes public, the fund will receive a financial payout determined by the amount of shares they own in the company. Funds owned by companies often invest in startups with a purpose that aligns with the company's mission or with a function that could be useful to the company if the startup succeeds. For example, Bayer invests in biological and agricultural technologies, while Unilever invests in beauty, wellness, and commerce companies. Patagonia (company profile on page 190) actually operates both a foundation and a fund. Patagonia's foundation arm provides grants for communities and environmental organizations,[5] while its venture fund (called Tin Shed Ventures) invests in socially and environmentally responsible startup companies.[6]

Tying donation to business success

Some companies make donations in ways that are tied directly to the company's success, meaning that the better the company is doing, the more they will donate, and vice versa. The most common ways of doing this are:

- **Percentage of sales or profits**: Some companies commit to donating a set percentage of their sales or profits to a good cause. 1% for the Planet is a membership platform that asks companies to commit 1 percent of their annual sales to environmental causes and helps to facilitate the process. This effort has resulted in contributions of over $435 million. There are over 5,000 business members including companies such as Patagonia, New Belgium Brewing, and Honest Tea.[7] Members of 1% for the Planet are certainly not the only companies that donate a percentage of their profits to a good cause; many companies use this strategy as a means of weaving impact into their business model. Some companies will let customers or employees determine where these funds will be donated as a means of increasing engagement.

- **Set donation per item sold**: Finally, there's the method of donating a specific amount of money or product per item sold. This can be a monetary donation: for example, New Belgium Brewing has donated $1 per barrel of beer they sell to charity since the early 1990s, resulting in over $29 million given to charity. Other companies commit to donating products: TOMS Shoes is well known for pioneering the one-for-one model, donating one pair of shoes to someone in need for every pair purchased (it's worth noting that TOMS has since shifted away from this model and now gives one-third of total profits to charity; see more on this on page 16). Sometimes this strategy will be used for the company as a whole or for a particular product line or limited time only.

Who to Contribute to

Once a company has determined their donation structure, the final question is, *who* to donate to. There's no right or wrong answer, of course, but some companies have found strategies for making their donation more impactful for the recipient of the donation and for the business. These strategies fall into three primary categories:

- **Contributing to your own community**: When you give back in the community where you live and where your business is located, you get the extra benefit of living in the place that you are working to improve, meaning that you, your business, and your employees also benefit from community improvements. The other important element of giving back in your own community is that you are more likely to understand the intricacies and nuances of the challenges faced by the community and are more likely to be able to direct resources to positive solutions. Finally, local giving also increases the visibility of your company in the community, which is helpful for business development, community relationships, and employee recruitment. For more on this topic, see the Community chapter on page 174.

- **Contributing to causes connected to your mission and business model:** When your donations align with your core business model and mission of your business, the donations strengthen the ethos and brand of your company, showing employees, customers, and partners that your mission is more than an advertising campaign. Donations that are unrelated to the business model and mission of the company can also be impactful but run the risk of feeling "tacked on" rather than incorporating giving back as a core element of your company's brand and operations. Greyston Bakery, for example (company profile on page 168), uses their charitable giving to develop workforce development and re-entry programs. This makes sense for Greyston because workforce development is core to their mission and business model—workforce development is what they know and what they do; therefore, they are uniquely qualified and effective at developing additional re-entry programs with a portion of their profits.

- **Contributing to new innovators / changemakers connected to your business model:** As mentioned above in the Funds and Foundations section, some businesses give back by contributing to innovators and changemakers that are making a difference in their industry or within the focus of their mission. This can look many different ways—fellowships for individuals, grants to organizations, or investments in startups—but the goal is similar: support new work and innovation that would be beneficial for your business and for the world that you want to help build. For example, Patagonia's investment fund, Tin Shed Ventures, has invested in multiple sustainable textile companies because they intimately understand the challenges in sustainable textile manufacturing, and also because Patagonia would likely like to use the new technologies once they are viable. For example, Bureo, one of the companies Tin Shed Ventures invests in, converts discarded fishnets into the first 100 percent post-industrial nylon: a technology that Patagonia has now incorporated into some of their product lines.[8]

A Word of Caution—and Why Partnerships Are Essential in Charitable Giving

I couldn't end this chapter without also voicing a word of caution around charitable giving. Although charitable giving is almost always well-intentioned, when organizations or individuals contribute to causes, situations, and communities that they don't understand, the result can be ineffective or, at worst, harmful. Read the story of TOMS Shoes on page 16 to demonstrate this point. That doesn't mean that businesses shouldn't give. What it does mean is that it is important to either 1) give to causes you understand well (either in your own community or closely related to the work you do), or 2) give through an organization that is deeply immersed in the issue you are working on, doing the on-the-ground work, and understands the complications and nuances of the issues. If you are giving to an organization that does work in a developing country, make sure that there are people from that country on the leadership team of the organization.

It's okay to give to causes you are passionate about even if you don't have an intimate familiarity with the issues, but you should lean heavily on partnerships with organizations and people who are already working on this issue to make sure that the funds or resources you are giving are used in the most effective and beneficial way.

Company Profile: Revivn

Where the company integrates impact

- Material sourcing
- Community
- Giving back

Founders: John Fazzolari and Anthony Serina

John and Anthony met during their freshman year of college at Villanova University. After graduating, they became roommates in New York City and began to notice the large amount of old electronics and hardware that were piling up both in their apartment and at their offices. Old electronics would stack up when new models were introduced, charging cords changed, employees turned over, and so on. Everyone seemed to know that these electronics were not exactly trash, but they also didn't quite know what to do with them or have the time to figure it out. Inspired by this problem, John and Anthony initially started collecting and selling old iPhones and iPads out of their apartment and learned through their own research how to refurbish the electronics they received. Throughout the years they've taken what worked from this original model and pivoted on what did not to grow Revivn into the company it is today.

What they do

Revivn is a public-benefit corporation that recycles and repurposes technology and then distributes a portion of it to people in need through community partnerships. The Brooklyn-based company has offices across the country and provides used electronic collection services and software to businesses, schools, and residential buildings. They then wipe the data from the technology, refurbish it if possible, and distribute a portion of it to those who would not otherwise have access to a computer, helping to close the digital divide while also keeping used hardware out of the landfill.

Business model

Revin utilizes a B2B model. They charge companies for the service of repurposing and recycling their technology solutions. This is a valuable service, but it also depends on companies placing value on keeping technology waste out of the landfill and getting technology into the hands of those who need it. In addition to technology collection, Revivn also provides full data sanitation for security purposes, provides a software platform to manage donations, and offers a Certificate of Data Clearing & Ethical Recycling as well as a Revivn Transparency Report, which includes a count of technology recycled, the make, model and serial numbers of the items recycled, and the pounds of material recycled. Companies can include these metrics in their sustainability reporting.

Impact

MATERIAL SOURCING

In 2009, the EPA estimated that US households and businesses threw out 2.37 *million tons* of electronics waste (think TVs, computers, printers, phones, etc.).[9] For reference, a blue whale, the largest mammal on earth, weighs around 196 tons. It was estimated that about 25 percent of the tossed electronics were recycled, and the rest went to the landfill.

Every part of that picture is problematic. First off, that is *a lot* of electronics, meaning that we're buying a lot of new electronics and throwing away a lot of old electronics, when in reality old electronics can often be repaired and refurbished (if you don't believe me, take a look at the company iFixit).[10] Second, when electronics are "recycled" in the United States, that often means that they are shipped overseas to developing nations where they are picked apart for the valuable metals and materials inside. This is a problem because this "recycling" often takes place in very unsafe conditions, with processes such as open burning and acid baths being utilized to access the valuable materials. This exposes workers to high levels of toxins and carcinogens and allows toxic chemicals to leach into the environment. Finally, that's still about 1.8 million tons going to the landfill. This is a massive amount of trash, and a lot of valuable metals that are not being reclaimed, which means we will have to keep mining more virgin metals to make all of the new electronics we're buying.

The beauty of the Revivn model is that it addresses every aspect of this problem. 1) By collecting used electronics, the company effectively diverts electronics from the landfill. 2) By refurbishing electronics, they decrease the number of electronics that end up going overseas to dangerous recycling operations. 3) By providing a supply of refurbished electronics to schools and nonprofits they are helping to decrease the number of electronics that will be purchased new.

COMMUNITY

Revivn's partnerships with local nonprofits within the communities they work in (more in the Giving Back section below) help to ensure that donations are being used effectively and appropriately. These partnerships create direct lines for Revivn to get computers into the hands of people who need them, people that the company may not otherwise have had access to or even been aware of.

GIVING BACK

Revivn could sell all the electronics they salvage and they would still have a business that offers a positive environmental impact. But they don't. Instead, they donate a portion of the refurbished electronics in an effort to help bridge the digital divide that occurs between those that have access to technology and those that do not. Those that do not have access to technology are not given the same opportunities for learning, connection, and developing job skills. By donating refurbished electronics through community organizations and nonprofits like the First Tech Fund, Emergent Works, and Digital Girl, Revivn helps to narrow the digital divide.

What I like about it

I love a business model that serves as a missing link between someone that doesn't want something and someone that does. There are a lot of businesses out there like this (for example, see the thredUP company profile on page 108 and Phinite on page 79), but usually the money is paid by the receiving party. One of the things that's unique about this model is that the party disposing of the product is the one that pays for the service and funds the transaction, making it an ideal model for a social enterprise. Our society currently sends a lot of materials to the landfill. We know that this is not because there is no value in these items; it's because a convenient infrastructure to collect, process, and deliver these materials to a party that values them has not been developed. That means there are a lot of business opportunities out there for creative entrepreneurs, and the Revivn model can be used as a roadmap for others to learn from.

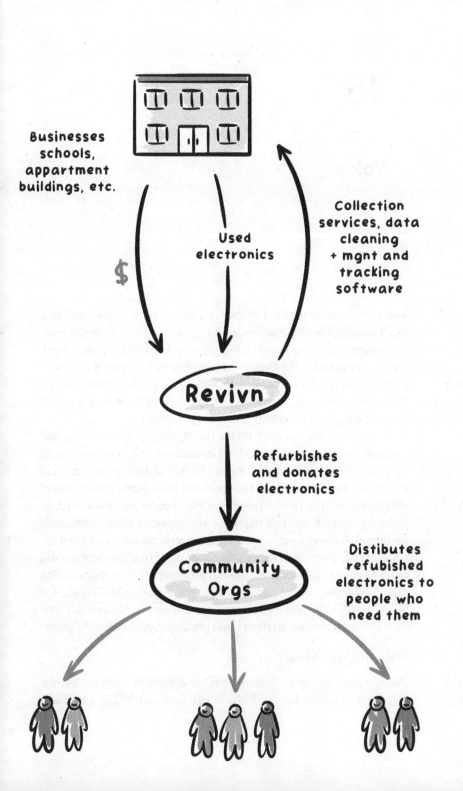

Businesses
schools,
appartment
buildings, etc.

$

Used
electronics

Collection
services, data
cleaning
+ mgnt and
tracking
software

Revivn

Refurbishes
and donates
electronics

Community
Orgs

Distibutes
refubished
electronics to
people who
need them

15

Voice

And now, we enter the final chapter in this section, where we will talk about one of the least frequently used, but perhaps most powerful tools a company can use for social change: their voice. We don't often think about companies having a voice; voices are for individuals. It has traditionally been considered taboo for businesses to speak out about issues. Businesses used to be discouraged from putting their nose where it doesn't belong and potentially alienating customers.

However, in recent years, with the rise of a millennial workforce and customer base, business activism has become more and more common, to the point where you might say it is almost expected. Eighty-one percent of millennials expect their favorite companies to make public declarations of their corporate citizenship.[1] This means that if companies want to retain top talent and customer loyalty, they need to speak up. What's more, with the invention of social media and the mainstream nature of social and environmental justice conversations, for a company to remain silent can still be seen as making a statement. This has left many companies scrambling to craft public responses to topics such as climate change, Me Too, and the Black Lives Matter movement. Businesses that are already in touch with their own activist voice, strategies, and principles are ahead of the game.

What to Speak About

The first question for a company that has decided to embrace its own voice as a changemaker is *what* to speak up about. While a business can of course speak up about any issue it feels called to, there are so many social issues out there that it can be overwhelming to choose where to begin. There are, however, certain issues where a company is likely to be more informed, more persuasive, and more effective. These issues include:

- Issues in your community: A business can be a powerful force for good when they speak up about issues that affect the community, state, or region where they operate. It's important that businesses remain on top of local issues because these decisions may not only affect how the company can operate, but also affect a company's employees and potentially its customers. For example, in 2022, over sixty businesses added their signature to an open letter condemning local anti-transgender laws proposed in Texas.[2] In 2018, over 200 local businesses signed on to support New York City's ban of Styrofoam food containers.[3] Businesses can be a powerful voice for change in their own communities because they play a part in the area's economic health.

- Issues related to your work: Another natural and impactful space for communities to exercise their voice is in issues related to their work. For example, SK-II is a cosmetics brand based in Japan whose primary customer base and audience is women. The company engages their customer base by releasing films that explore issues and societal pressures placed on women, such as the pressure to marry.[4] In 2017, Interface, a company that makes carpet and flooring and an industry leader in sustainability (company profile on page 93), lobbied for a recycling bill mandating that carpet manufacturers in California implement a system that sets a goal of recycling 24 percent of carpet by 2020.

- Issues that impact us all: Finally, businesses speak up about issues that are too big to ignore and that affect the business because they affect the world. We saw this on a large scale in 2017 when President Trump backed out of the Paris Climate Agreement. Businesses across the country joined local governments, universities, and faith groups to form a coalition called "We are Still In" to demonstrate to the world that many Americans remained committed to the climate goals outlined by the Paris Agreement. Together this coalition represented $9.46 trillion in GDP.[5]

In 2020, companies spoke out on an unprecedented level in support of the Black Lives Matter movement, posting black squares on their social media and making public statements about racial justice. It is important to note here that public statements were accepted with varying levels of public scrutiny, based on whether or not the company's actions aligned with their words (see the "When to use your voice" section below).

How to Use your Voice

So, how can companies use their voice? What does being an activist business look like? There are five primary ways that businesses can utilize their voice.

1. Advocate for (or against) governmental policy: A good example of this was the 2016 uproar around the House Bill 2 in North Carolina, also referred to as "The Bathroom Bill." The proposed bill would have prevented cities and states from putting ordinances in place to protect the LGBTQ+ community. Along with celebrities, sports teams, and the general public, businesses also stepped up to protest this bill. Companies such as Adidas, PayPal, and Deutsche Bank announced that they would halt plans for expansion in North Carolina in response to the bill. All in all, the economic loss to North Carolina of passing the bill was estimated to be $3.6 billion and nearly 3,000 jobs.[6]

2. Advocate for industry change: Businesses can also be change agents within their respective industries through leadership, collaboration, education, and lobbying for regulation. As mentioned in their company profiles, New Belgium Brewing (company profile on page 130) has produced guidelines and toolkits

to help other breweries to lower their environmental impact, and Patagonia (company profile on page 190) was a founding member of the Fair Labor Association, helping to hold apparel companies accountable for the treatment of their workers. As mentioned above, Interface lobbied for more stringent environmental regulations on carpet producers.

3. Educating and engaging your audience: Businesses can offer a platform for social justice and environmental education, which also serves as a means of building connection and engaging your audience. Ben & Jerry's has been mixing activism with its products since 1988 when they joined the movement that criticized the Reagan administration for devoting so much of the federal budget to developing nuclear weapons rather than to fighting poverty. They released the "Peace Pop," a chocolate-covered ice cream bar with a wrapper describing the "1% for Peace" campaign that advocated for the government to spend at least 1 percent of the money it spent on weaponry to build international bonds of understanding.[7] Ben & Jerry's continues to advocate for social and environmental change through its products today, recently with the Justice ReMix'd flavor, which advocates for criminal justice reform, and Home Sweet Honeycomb, which states support for legislation that would resettle refugees across the United Kingdom.[8]

4. Educating and engaging your employees: A company arguably has no audience as readily available as their own employees. As discussed on page 165, engaging employees in your mission is also a great way to increase employee loyalty and retention. Patagonia goes above and beyond with this by offering an "Employee Internship" program where they allow employees to take two months off from their regular jobs to volunteer with and learn from an environmental group (while continuing to earn their Patagonia paycheck and benefits).[9] Ben & Jerry's directly engages their employees in their activism campaigns, allowing them to support the campaigns of the advocacy groups they partner with, such as Close the Workhouse in St. Louis

(see more about this in the Ben & Jerry's Company Profile on page 218).

5. <u>General public</u>: This is the one that people think of most frequently when they think of businesses using their voice. Businesses supporting social or environmental causes on their social media accounts or by funding Public Service Announcements (PSAs) are probably the practices that come to mind when you think about business activism. While this kind of advocacy can be very impactful, it is also probably the method that gets the most public scrutiny, especially if companies are not taking the actions inside their own business to back up the public statements they are making. Greenwashing has been prevalent in this kind of advocacy as well as a trend of big corporations pointing the finger at individual littering or water waste as the major environmental culprits to detract attention from the environmental impact of industry (if you've never heard it, the full story behind the Make America Beautiful Campaign referred to as the "Crying Indian" is fascinating).[10]

That said, a lot of good can actually come from businesses adding their voices to social and environmental campaigns. Businesses' voices can be loud (thanks to marketing budgets), and when businesses begin to speak out about a movement, they can play a significant role in normalizing social and environmental issues and bringing them to the forefront of conversation.

Speaking out about issues can be good for business too. If a business crafts their message well, a good advocacy campaign can result in people sharing a business's message on social media, talking about it with their friends, and building a sense of connection and loyalty with the brand itself. For example, in 2018, Nike ran an ad campaign with Colin Kaepernick, the football player who became a controversial figure because of his choice to kneel during the national anthem to protest the criminal justice system in the United States and the treatment of Black Americans. It was a controversial move that was met with outrage and even shoe-burning from some—however, in the week the ad was posted, it was viewed over 14 million times and Nike's online sales increased 27 percent.[11] The company later won an Emmy for the campaign.

When to Use Your Voice: "Winning-Driven" vs. "Value-Driven" Activism

The story about Nike's controversial campaign with Colin Kaepernick is a great lead-in to this final and important section: *when* to use your voice. Businesses are often shy about speaking out about controversial issues because of a fear of alienating their customers, just as individuals are often hesitant to speak about social or environmental issues around friends and family out of fear of making people angry or uncomfortable. As a result of this feeling, individuals often speak about social issues around people they already know agree with them, and businesses often speak out about issues that have already entered the mainstream. For example, these days it's fairly commonplace for businesses to post statements about what they are doing to prevent climate change; likewise, it's not unexpected to see corporate floats in a local Pride parade. Gay rights and climate change are issues that, while certainly not agreed upon by everyone, are fairly mainstream in the United States. Depending on the business's customer base, they can feel relatively certain that these statements will resonate with more people than they will upset. However, a company speaking up about gay rights in a country like Egypt, where same-sex marriage is still banned as of 2022, would be a different matter. A company risks more backlash for a more controversial statement, but also has the opportunity to do more good.

Entrepreneur and activist Gijs Corstens refers to this phenomenon as "victory-driven" versus "value-driven" activism. "Victory-driven" activism refers to a company publicly supporting a cause once it has already passed the tipping point of public support and is relatively established within mainstream society, allowing the company to be fairly certain that they are joining the "winning side of history." Victory-driven activism is not bad. The companies that speak out with this strategy still probably believe in the cause they are supporting, but they have also run the numbers on whether it will help or hurt their sales revenue. Victory-driven activism is still helpful for pushing issues further and making them more firmly cemented in mainstream society.[12]

However, in order for a cause to reach the point where it is considered to be on the "winning side of history," a lot of hard work is required of the activists, organizations, businesses, and politicians that *are* willing to take risks. When a business speaks out about an issue before it is popular, simply because they believe it is the right thing to do, they play a more significant role in pushing an issue closer to the tipping point of mainstream acceptance. From a business perspective, just like any early mover, they have the opportunity to be seen as a leader on a particular issue rather than one voice of many. They also have the opportunity to attract more attention per dollar spent and generate more word of mouth and viral sharing of their content. They will likely face more backlash but also gain more loyalty.

Ben & Jerry's, for example, a company that practices value-driven activism, has been known for speaking out about social and environmental issues *before* they have crossed the tipping point, when they are not yet widely accepted by society. In 2018, after a rainbow installation in Zbawiciela Square in Warsaw, Poland (a place where gay marriage is not legally recognized) was vandalized, Ben & Jerry's installed a light and water hologram rainbow in its place in celebration of Pride month. As a result of the company's history with value-driven activism, social justice is baked into Ben & Jerry's brand, and they have been seen as a genuine leader on many social and environmental causes.

The previously mentioned Nike campaign is an example of a brand campaign right on the line between victory-driven and value-driven activism. The company knew they would face backlash, and they did; however, you can feel pretty sure they had run the numbers before taking a calculated risk, meaning the accompanying boost in sales was also not a surprise. The decision of where on the activism spectrum to speak up is a choice that each company must make for themselves, but as with many aspects of business, it often pays to be bold.

Tips for Success

Push your Advantage: As a business owner, you are in a strong position to speak out about the economic impact of policy decisions. As a job creator and part of the economic fabric of the community, the country, and even the world, you have a powerful voice to utilize. As discussed earlier in this chapter, businesses have been some of the strongest voices speaking against discriminatory politics. In New

York City, during the debate around plastic bag and Styrofoam bans, businesses were some of the loudest voices on both sides of the discussion. Everyone wants to know how policies will affect the economy and how they will affect jobs. So speak up! Tell your story and why you support or don't support an issue. Supporting small businesses is one of the few things that just about everyone agrees on. Use this to your advantage when it comes time to utilize your voice to speak out about something that matters to you, your business, and your mission.

Go to the boring-sounding meetings

I'm sure you've heard people complain that it's impossible to influence politics or reach decision-makers. My generation (millennials) is famous for being very outspoken about politics on social media . . . and stopping there. There's even a word for it: "clicktivism." The interesting thing about how passionate people are about political issues and the dissatisfaction of not being able to reach decision-makers is that when you actually check out a meeting called something like "Public sub-committee hearing on local law S648," the room will probably be occupied by the local elected officials who have to be there along with about three concerned citizens. However boring and opaque these meetings may sound, they are actually the official time set aside to talk about specific community issues, let opinions be heard, and make decisions. By actually attending these meetings and speaking up, your likelihood of having your voice heard and listened to increases by about 1,000 percent.

Stay informed

If you plan to get involved in activism, make sure you follow the issues closely and talk to people directly affected by the policies (ideally people with opposing views!) before deciding what points you want to make. Find local newsletters to subscribe to in order to stay on top of issues. It's important to stay informed if you are going to speak up. However, at the same time, don't let the fear of not knowing *everything* there is to know about an issue paralyze you or keep you silent.

Company Profile: Ben & Jerry's

Where the company integrates impact

- Material sourcing
- Packaging
- Labor
- Operations
- Giving back
- Voice

Founders: Ben Cohen and Jerry Greenfield

Ben and Jerry have been friends since they met in gym class in seventh grade. In 1978, they decided to take their life savings of $8,000 (plus $4,000 more that they borrowed) to start an ice cream company in a former gas station in Burlington, Vermont. As with several other major for-profit companies with a social and/or environmental mission, such as Interface, activism did not become a significant part of Ben & Jerry's business model until many years later. In the case of Ben & Jerry's, they started to integrate activism into their work after ten years, in 1988, when the founders began to feel that they were not doing enough to support their values and considered giving the ice cream company up. Instead, they decided to see if they could use the resources and structure of their business to further the causes they believed in.

What they do

Ben & Jerry's makes and sells ice cream. They are particularly well known for integrating bold public stances on social and environmental justice into their products with playful names such as Justice ReMix'd (a flavor that was paired with a campaign for criminal justice reform) and Change is Brewing (a flavor launched in support of the People's Response Act, calling for investment in mental health, violence interruption, and youth programs for Black communities). Rather than the vague references to social and environmental justice used by so many companies, Ben & Jerry's stands out with their specific campaigns and demands, inviting customers to sign petitions for legislative change directly on the Ben & Jerry's website. They are also known for aligning their spending with their words, investing millions of dollars in support of social and environmental causes.

In 2000, the company was acquired by Unilever, against the stated desires of the founders, an occurrence that brought light to the fact that companies are legally bound to make the decision that maximizes profit for their shareholders even if it goes against other company priorities and founder wishes. This acquisition was used by many as an example case for the launch of the Benefit Corporation, a legal entity that is permitted to consider social impact alongside shareholder interests. In 2012, Ben & Jerry's joined the movement they helped inspire, becoming the first subsidiary of a publicly traded company to become a Benefit Corporation.[13]

Despite the rocky start, the acquisition agreement serves as an example for other companies that aim to be acquired but maintain their mission. The acquisition contract included an agreement that an independent board of directors would be responsible for providing leadership focused on preserving and expanding Ben & Jerry's social mission, brand integrity, and product quality.[14] The contract also stated that Ben & Jerry's would continue to spend at least $1.1 million on social and environmental causes, a goal that they often surpass despite the new ownership.[15]

Business model

Ben & Jerry's is a B Corp wholly owned by Unilever that operates through a B2C franchise model. Their ice cream is sold in brick-and-mortar stores and on the shelves of supermarkets in thirty-three countries around the world. As the company has grown, they have decided to focus on their core offering (ice cream) and expand globally through franchise partners rather than expanding into other product markets. Ben & Jerry's operates with a linked prosperity model, meaning that as Ben & Jerry's prospers, they aim to ensure that their suppliers and stakeholders prosper as well.

Impact

MATERIAL SOURCING

As of 2015, Ben & Jerry's sources all of its bananas, cocoa, vanilla, sugar, and coffee from Fair Trade certified sources. They were the first ice cream company to use Fair Trade ingredients (in 2005) making them a leader in the impact space. In addition to purchasing Fair Trade ingredients, they also pay a "Fair Trade Social Premium," which means they pay a higher price to the farmer to allow them to invest back in their own community.

As you might guess, a major ingredient on the Ben & Jerry's supply chain is milk. Ben & Jerry's runs a "Caring Dairy" program, where they partner with the dairy farmers making their milk to implement a series of practices around animal health, participation in the Milk with Dignity program (described in more detail below in the Labor section), and regenerative agricultural practices, which mean that the farmers participate in sustainable practices that help to regenerate the soil, such as cover crops, crop rotation, and animal foraging.[16]

Ben & Jerry's partners with an organization called Certified Humane to ensure that the eggs used in Ben & Jerry's in the United States are from cage-free hens.[17] They also make an effort to support other like-minded social enterprises; for example, they purchase brownies from the B Corp Greyston Bakery (company profile on page 168).

PACKAGING

As a company whose primary business is selling "to-go" food, Ben & Jerry's struggles with significant amounts of waste created from their disposable packaging. There are currently large amounts of paper and plastic used in Ben & Jerry's ice cream tubs, to-go containers, wrappers, and more. However, Ben & Jerry's has set goals around reducing the amount of their packaging that lands in the landfill or in nature by aiming for their packaging to be 100 percent free of petroleum-based plastic (this means they are still open to considering bioplastics) and switching to packaging that is fully reusable, recyclable, or compostable by 2025.

For their paper packaging, they have partnered with the Canopy Pack4Good Initiative to ensure the pulp used in their packaging does not come from ancient or endangered forests. They also use Forest Stewardship Council certified paper in their pint containers.

The company is also working to transition away from petroleum-based plastic by no longer offering plastic straws or spoons in their scoop shops and by transitioning the petroleum-based plastic coating on their paper containers to a plant-based plastic (which will be recyclable in many parts of Europe, although not yet in the United States). The company is transitioning many of their wrappings on products such as the Peace Pop and Cookie Dough Chunk pouches from plastic to paper, and, in the European Union, they are transitioning their bulk ice cream tubs from virgin plastic to 100 percent post-consumer recycled plastic.[18]

LABOR

Ben & Jerry's works to ensure that fair labor practices are used across their supply chain. As mentioned above, they purchase Fair Trade products when they can, with an extra contribution given to their farmers to help them invest in their own communities.

They also participate in the Milk with Dignity program, coordinated by an organization called Migrant Justice (or Justicia Migrante), which requires participating farms to comply with the Milk with Dignity Code of Conduct, outlining standards and stipulations for worker treatment.[19]

The company's Vermont-based employees start at $18.13 an hour ($8.17 above the state's minimum wage), and workers are allowed to take home three pints of ice cream a day. In 2015, in an effort to make hiring more equitable, Ben & Jerry's removed the box that asked if an employer had ever been convicted of a crime from their initial employment application, in an attempt to prevent applicants with a criminal record from being filtered out of the application process before being given an opportunity to prove themselves.[20]

Ben & Jerry's is getting a lot of things right, but they've also got room for improvement. Although the company's Livable Wage policy applies to Vermont-based employees, the wages of the workers in their scoop shop franchises vary based on the decisions of individual owners and the laws of the state the business is located in, something Ben & Jerry's has received some criticism for. Furthermore, despite their public support of racial equity campaigns, the company itself remains primarily white. As of 2020, 93 percent of Ben & Jerry's US-based employees were white. The company has publicly recognized their own need to integrate diversity and equity within their own business operations and supply chain.[21]

OPERATIONS

Ben & Jerry's gets a shoutout in the Operations section because of their bold transparency. As mentioned above, despite the fact that racial justice is one of the company's core values, their operations remain 93 percent white in the United States. There's clearly some work to be done. But what should be noted here is that I did not locate that number in some online smear campaign or corporate exposé—I read it on Ben & Jerry's own website. In fact, these numbers are listed front and center at the top of their 2020 Social and Environmental Impact Report, along with an improvement plan, right below the letter from their current CEO Matthew McCarthy.[22]

No business can be expected to be perfect, but what can be expected is that a business is transparent about the areas where they are or are not meeting their goals, and that they have established a plan to improve the areas where their business operations are not aligned with their values. Within the 2020 Impact Report, Ben & Jerry's shares results from an internal assessment of the practices they have in place that have prevented their business from meeting diversity goals and outlined a plan for implementing changes to align their business metrics and incentives with their goals.

GIVING BACK

Ben & Jerry's runs their own foundation where they make grants for both national and Vermont-based organizations working in social and environmental justice. The foundation was given 50,000 shares of the company when it was first created and is supported by 7.5 percent of the company's pre-tax profits. To date, the foundation has contributed over $50 million in grant donations.

In addition to monetary donations, the company also partners directly with nonprofit organizations to use the skills of their employees and the reach of their brand to help support their partner's advocacy campaigns. For example, Ben & Jerry's has supported Close the Workhouse in St. Louis, a campaign to urge representatives to shut a St. Louis jail. A team of Ben & Jerry's employees has helped to support direct action campaigns from Close the Workhouse on social media, and co-founder & former CEO Ben Cohen traveled to St. Louis to support the campaign through a press conference.[23]

VOICE

While many businesses are likely to speak out about social and environmental causes these days, there are a much smaller number that are comfortable speaking frankly about political issues. Ben & Jerry's is one of these rare companies that does not bat an eye at taking their key issues from the abstract level to direct political and policy discussion.

Ben & Jerry's has swirled activism with ice cream since the launch of the Peace Pop in 1988. Even after the sale to Unilever, Ben & Jerry's activism is still going strong. In 2018, right before the midterm elections during Donald Trump's presidency, the statement printed on the label of the limited-edition flavor Pecan Resist read: "Welcome to the resistance. Together, Pecan Resist! We honor & stand with women, immigrants, people of color, & the millions of activists and allies who are courageously resisting the President's attack on our values, humanity & environment. We celebrate the diversity of our glorious nation & raise our spoons in solidarity for all Americans." As can be expected, this flavor met with onslaughts of both support and criticism, including a #boycottbenandjerrys campaign; however, it's worth noting that in the days after the release, the company's stock went up 4.74 percent.[24]

When the company was sold to Unilever in 2000, supporters worried that the new corporate ownership would dilute Ben & Jerry's activism. While the new ownership has not been without its bumps (Ben & Jerry's sued Unilever in 2022 for selling its product in Israeli-occupied West Bank, because it said this decision clashed with its values), Unilever has seemed to understand that activism is part of Ben & Jerry's brand and that to stifle it would mean hurting sales.[25]

What I like about it

Ben & Jerry's is one of best examples of a company that utilizes its voice for value-driven activism, and they do this while managing to operate in countries around the world and bringing in hundreds of millions of dollars in revenue ($681.5 million in 2019). To me, Ben & Jerry's proves three important things: 1) A company can speak out on controversial issues and still keep sales high. Although there is no precise way to test it, I would even guess that the integration of activism into the brand and identity of the company has actually made it more financially successful because of its strong brand identity, loyal following, and earned media. 2) Any company can use its business platform and products to speak up on issues that are important. Although I'm not knocking the importance of ice cream, the product does not naturally have a clear connection with the causes and campaigns Ben & Jerry's supports. However, the company has been able to seamlessly integrate activism into its products, utilizing the launch of new flavors to bring attention to important issues and offer opportunities for customers and employees to engage with their campaigns. The ability to do this and retain respect and loyalty from customers and activists is directly tied to the fact that the company makes a genuine effort to back up its values with its actions and business practices. 3) Finally, Ben & Jerry's manages to toe the line between speaking frankly about difficult issues while maintaining a brand that comes off as happy and playful, and yet does not trivialize the important causes it aims to address.

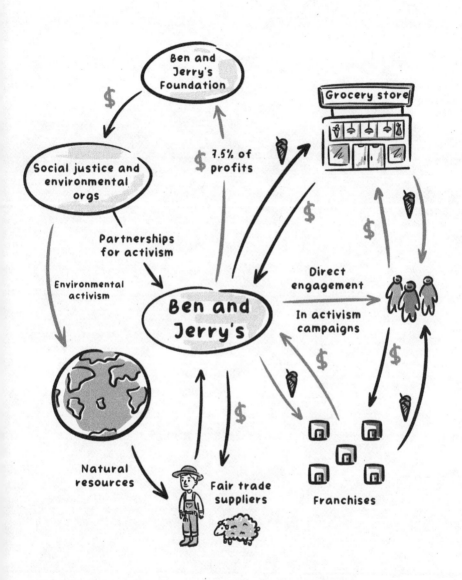

PART 3

Guidance to Help You on Your Path

. . . A lot of it you just have to do. I can give whatever advice that people could have given me, and did give to me, but you also have to honor that spark within you that's telling you to do this thing, and you're going to figure it out on the way.

—MICHAELA BARNETT, FOUNDER OF KNOXFILL

16

Balancing Mission and Money

Thus far, the topics covered in this book have focused primarily on strategies and business models designed to embrace both profitability and mission. But what happens when those two goals diverge? No matter how well-oiled a social enterprise is, there will be times when a founder will have to make a decision that prioritizes either the financial profitability or the social mission of their business.

Balancing mission and money is a difficult task, and it's easy to avoid thinking about it until a decision is thrust upon you. However, this is how you can find yourself in situations you don't want to be in, conflicting with either the profitability of your business or with your own morals and the legacy you want to leave in the world. It is important to determine where you stand and develop your own protocols ahead of time so that when the time comes, you have a process and guidelines to fall back on and help you with difficult decisions.

Exercise: Your Line in the Sand

For your business

Step 1: Determine your line in the sand for your business. Where would you stop considering your mission to protect the viability of your business? Make it clear, specific, and honest. For example: "When the cost of producing my product sustainably means I can no longer achieve a profit for selling my product."

Step 2: Determine your key indicators. What are the key indicators that would show you that you were close to crossing your line in the sand? For example, this could be when the cost to produce your product becomes higher than the price you can sell it for.

For your mission

Step 1: Determine your line in the sand for your mission. At what point would you consider shutting down your business or making a major pivot? This can be a difficult one to think about. Feel free to think in extreme terms. Sometimes using the "headline test" can help. Imagine a situation where you were compromising your mission, and imagine a story about it in the headlines of a newspaper. At what point is the headline so bad that you would not want to continue to operate? Some examples include: "When I can no longer pay my workers a living wage and stay profitable," or "When my product is detrimental to human health." These should be customized to your business risks and also to your own personal morals and the legacy you want to leave in the world.

Step 2: Determine your key indicators. When would you know you had crossed your mission line in the sand? An example could be "if a peer-reviewed scientific study shows that my product is causing major damage to the environment or human health." This is a good time to say again that this exercise is hard. If you feel uncomfortable thinking about this, you are not alone. But it is important because, as a business owner, you are responsible for impacting the world and people's lives, so you need to ask yourself the hard questions.

Determine your protocol for decision-making when these lines cross

Now that you know where you stand on your business and your mission, it is important to develop your own protocol of what to do when these two priorities conflict. Your protocol will be unique to you and your business, and it can be as detailed or short as you like, as long as it can guide you when you are faced with a tough decision. As I mentioned, your protocol will be unique to you, but here is a basic protocol that I recommend as a starting point:

1. *When your **mission** crosses your **business line**—choose your business.* Your mission is important, but if it causes you to no longer be able to operate as a business, you will no longer be able to make an impact of any kind.

2. *When your **business** crosses your **mission line**—choose your mission.* If making the best business decision means majorly compromising your own mission and morals, it is time to take a hit on the business side. Staying true to your own vision and mission will benefit you in the long run through maintaining the respect of your employees, your customers, and yourself.

3. *When your **business line** crosses your **mission line**—choose your mission.* This means that you are facing an extreme decision where you must cross either your business line or your mission line. If it comes down to it, and it is a choice between staying viable as a business and being the person you want to be, it is time for a change. Life is short. Consider making a major pivot or even ceasing to operate, but don't cross the ultimate line in the sand you drew for your mission.

4. *For everything in between . . .* this is where it gets tricky, because there is a lot of gray area. Sometimes making a choice that is better for the environment won't cause you to no longer be profitable, but it will hurt your bottom line a bit. How do you judge this? This a choice that only you can make, but drawing your ultimate lines in the sand for your business and your mission will give you parameters to work within, ground you in your decisions, and make sure that you don't compromise your business or your mission in a way you cannot come back from.

Other Tips for Balancing Mission and Money

Keeping mission top of mind

Of the two, I would say that it is easier to lose track of your mission than it is to lose track of your financial goals. Finances tend to have a way of making themselves front and center in your mind. Monthly bills, rent, payroll, lenders, and investors make your financial goals hard to forget. It is up to the leadership of a company to ensure that mission also remains top of mind for all employees. If the leadership of a company does not prioritize mission, it will be hard to make anyone else do so. This means that it falls upon the founder or CEO of a company to make sure that your mission is brought up to your team with as much regularity as your revenue numbers. The leaders of social enterprises can take a leaf out of the book of nonprofit organizations by remembering to share success stories and metrics, discuss strategies for maximizing impact, and regularly bring the team's attention back to why you do this work in the first place.

Measure

The next chapter will talk about measurement in more depth, but it's important to mention here as well because it is exceedingly difficult to prioritize something that you don't measure. Mission can be more nebulous and more difficult to measure than your bottom line, but once you determine your key indicators, it's important to measure them with the same amount of rigor and regularity as you do your finances if you want them to stand a chance of being equal in standing.

Report

To follow on the discussion of measurement above, it is equally important to ensure that the numbers that are being measured are being reported somewhere with regularity. You can instruct people to measure all sorts of things, but if no one ever looks at the results, it's easy for those measurements to slowly taper off and become out of date. Mission metrics should be reported at staff meetings alongside financials. Each mission metric should also be associated with target goals so that it's possible to assess progress. Employees who are able to share success stories serving your mission should feel as encouraged as those who are able to report high sales numbers. Many companies publish regular social or environmental reports that they share with their customers and stakeholders. This is a good way to stay connected to your audience and also hold your business accountable.

Let your heart and your mind share the wheel

The manager of a successful social enterprise manages with both their heart and their mind. You don't have to choose one or the other. Many social enterprises are successful not in spite of their mission, but because of their mission. I'll go out on a limb and say that TOMS Shoes, Greyston Bakery, and Method Soap would not be as successful as they are today if it weren't for their social mission. These companies were not successful because the world badly needed more shoes, brownies, and soap; I think we probably have plenty of each (okay, maybe not brownies); they were successful because the vision and mission that was an integral part of their business model resonated with customers. So don't be afraid to let your heart into your business philosophy and day-to-day operations. However, it's equally important not to *only* run your business with your heart—that's how well-meaning enterprises go out of business. A strong mission should be coupled with sound business strategy.

This is easier said than done. To start, it means *listening* to both your heart and your mind at the same time, which is intrinsically difficult to do, like rubbing your stomach and patting your head simultaneously. I recommend an exercise to practice:

Step 1: When you find yourself facing a difficult dilemma, find some quiet time to yourself and practice letting your head and your heart share the mic. Let them take turns.

Step 2: First, listen exclusively to what your head has to say. What does it want? What are its concerns? Desires? Fears? What does it suggest? Write it down.

Step 3: Now do the same for your heart. Let your mind quiet down now that it has said its piece. Let your heart speak. What does it want? What are its concerns? Desires? Fears? What does it suggest? Write it down. If you feel vulnerable and a little silly, then you know you're on the right track. No one did anything great by staying in their comfort zones.

Step 4: Take a deep breath. Try to find a comfortable resting place in between the two voices. Read back over what each has to say. Which concerns are valid? Which are based in fear? Is there middle ground to be found? Can you make a decision that honors both voices?

Watch the larger trends

A founder has the unique and difficult job of watching the details, like the day-to-day sales numbers, while also keeping their eye on the horizon and paying attention to the larger trends. The fact that more and more investors and customers are beginning to care about ESG (Environmental, Social, and Governance) goals or that climate change is affecting weather patterns and thus our global supply chains can matter just as much to the future of your business as your current manufacturing costs, team issues, or whatever other immediate need is demanding your attention. In spite of the hundreds of fires that need to be put out every day, the founder has the responsibility of watching the larger trends to guide the company's strategy and mission.

17

Pricing for Social Enterprise

While I was writing this book, I asked several entrepreneurs to look over the outline of the book and let me know if there was any topic missing. The answer that came up multiple times was "pricing." I've heard many social entrepreneurs say that they struggle with determining the appropriate price for their product. This is a hard thing to do for any entrepreneur, but it is especially difficult for social entrepreneurs because they also tend to be particularly concerned about making their product accessible—in other words, not only selling their product to rich people. And yet, they still need to be able to run a profitable business. This is a difficult problem, and the answer will be different for every entrepreneur, but here are a few strategies and ideas to help you find the right answer for your business.

Pricing Strategically

First, we'll look at traditional pricing strategies, because, at the end of the day, you must be able to have a profitable business if you hope to be able to continue offering your product or service. There are three primary factors to look at when determining the best strategic price for your product:

Your costs

How much does it cost you to deliver one product or service to one customer? Your costs will break down into two categories: Variable costs and fixed costs. Variable costs change as the quantity of goods or services increase. So, for example, if you work with a contract manufacturer and they charge you per product, that would be a variable cost. The higher the number of products you order, the higher your costs are. Fixed costs, on the other hand, refer to costs that you will pay regardless of how many products or services you sell. If you run your own manufacturing facility, the costs of the equipment you purchased, the rent for the building, and the salaries of your employees will all be the same no matter how many units of product you make.

Spend some time looking at your costs and determining what your cost structure looks like. Are most of your costs variable or fixed? The answer to this question can affect your pricing strategy and whether you should price low with the goal of selling as many products or services as possible, or price high with the goal of selling fewer products or services but for a higher rate. Keep in mind that cost is not the *only* thing to consider here. Your market and your customer demographic, preferences, and price sensitivity also make a big difference as well, which we will discuss below. Looking at cost alone, however, your ideal pricing strategy based on your cost structure will generally look like this:

- High variable costs and low fixed costs = high price, fewer customers
- Low variable costs and high fixed costs = low price, more customers

If your variable costs are high and your fixed costs are low, meaning that your costs increase significantly the more product you sell, it will generally work out that it makes sense for you to have a premium product and sell fewer units for a higher price. If you have low variable costs and high fixed costs, meaning that your costs will not increase drastically no matter how many units you sell, you will generally want to price lower with the goal of selling as many units as possible. However, keep in mind that this is a generalization. Do the math using your actual costs and projected profit at different price points and sales numbers and model it out.

Your customers

The next essential part of your pricing equation is to dig deeply into your customer's traits and buying preferences. Answer the five questions below about your customer. You can guess at first, but don't stop there. Go and speak to your customers and run small tests to help validate your answers.

1. *Who are your customers?* A business owner needs to be obsessed with their customers. It's important to understand who your customer is, what they care about, how much expendable income they have, what their habits are, who they are influenced by, and so on. And finally, how many of them are there?

2. *What can they pay? What are they willing to pay?* The answers to these two questions might be different. A business owner needs to understand both. What is your customer's budget? What do they spend on comparable products or services?

3. *How many do they want? How frequently?* Are you selling something that is a one-time purchase? Or something they may buy every month? Will they buy more if they have a larger family?

4. *How price-sensitive are they?* How much does your customer base notice price changes? If you increase or lower your price by a few dollars, will it change how many units they purchase or how frequently they purchase? (See more details on this under "pricing for an essential good or service" in the following section.)

5. *How do they want to pay?* Finally, consider *how* your customer wants to pay. There are many different pricing tactics such as:
   A. *Subscription pricing:* Charging a set amount for a recurring product or service over a set amount of time
   B. *Volume pricing:* Providing discounted pricing if your customer purchases in larger amounts
   C. *"Razor blade" pricing:* Selling one item (such as a razor) and continuing to sell add-ons to the product (such as razor blades) to the customer as needed

D. *Time / hourly billing:* Charging a set amount for each hour of service provided
E. *Freemium:* Providing certain elements of your product for free to introduce your customer to your good or service and providing additional services or features for an increased price
F. *Leasing:* Rather than selling a product outright, your customer pays you for the use of a product for a set amount of time.

To determine the pricing structure that is best for your business, consider both what makes sense for your company financially, and how your customer prefers to pay. Test different models with small groups and see what resonates.

Your market

Finally, when determining your price, it is helpful to know what your competitors are charging. You don't necessarily have to charge the same or less, because presumably your product offering is different (and hopefully better!), but you do want to make pricing decisions that are informed by a knowledge of your market and an understanding of what customers are currently paying.

Pricing Socially

Many social enterprises get stuck between the desire to price high to stay in business, and the desire to price low to make their product more accessible to more people. There are many different factors to consider here, including the topics in the previous section about determining the most strategic price for your business. However, since a social enterprise also cares about more than maximizing profit, there are additional factors to consider. Below are a few general guidelines to help you make this difficult decision:

Pricing for an essential good or service

Most goods and services have what is called an "elastic demand curve," meaning that the more an item costs, the fewer items customers can be expected to buy. The more elastic a demand curve is, the more price-sensitive the customer base is. When a demand curve is "inelastic," that means that customers will be willing to pay any price. The demand curve is often inelastic for essential goods like food, water, and medical care. This means that no matter what the price, people will likely find a way to pay it because they must. This means that when your business involves selling an essential good or service, you cannot morally depend on traditional pricing strategies to select your selling price. You must take the time to understand your customer and what they are able to pay, knowing that you may need to explore more complex business models such as the Subsidized B2C Model (page 15) and creative financing options (page 36).

Pricing differently for different groups

In an ideal world, you would be able to ask every customer what the maximum is that they are able and willing to pay, and then charge them that amount. For obvious reasons, this is trickier in reality! (Although do check out the "Pay What You Can" model discussed on page 15). If you read the previous section and determined that strategically, your product really needs to be a premium product with a higher price point, but you also would like to make product available to groups of people that cannot pay the high prices of a premium product, here are a few ideas:

- *Offer a premium and non-premium version:* You know how sometimes in the grocery store, you'll see two different products, such as two boxes of cereal, that look quite similar except for the fact that the price is lower on one product and the lower-priced product looks like someone's twelve-year-old child designed the packaging using PowerPoint, whereas the higher-priced product looks sleek and appealing? Often, if you examine the fine print of the label, you'll see that the two products were made by the same company. There may be little to no difference in the actual quality of the two products; however, they are designed to appeal to two different customer bases: those who are able and willing to pay more for a premium product, and those who are not. This is a strategic way for the company to reach a broader customer base with a similar product.

- *Distribute coupons or discounts through a community partner:* If you want to price high but also make your product available to those that cannot pay that high price, you may want to consider teaming up with an organization that works closely with the lower- income demographic you would like to make your product available to, and working through this partner to provide discount codes, coupons, or even discounted or donated product.

- *Explore alternative models:* Finally, look at chapter 1 for B2C and chapter 2 for B2B to learn more about alternative models, such as the pay-what-you-can, subsidized pricing, and one-for-one models.

18

Measuring Impact

In the introduction of this book, "impact measurement" is listed as one of the three key indicators that marks a business as a social enterprise. Mission cannot be a true priority for a business until it is measured with as much rigor and precision as profit. And yet, there can be a dark side to measurement. The "soul" of a mission can be hard to capture with data. There are so many potential elements of impact to measure that if you're not careful, impact measurement can be overwhelming and incredibly time-consuming. So how do you make sure you are collecting key data and holding your business accountable to your own standards without measuring the soul right out of your mission?

Measuring What Matters

There are so many metrics and frameworks for measuring the ESG (Environmental, Social, and Governance) impact of a business that selecting what to measure and how can feel very overwhelming. While all of the indicators and frameworks out there highlight important areas of impact for a business, the best place to start is internally. What matters most for *your* business? This means some personal reflection as well as some digging to make sure you understand the priorities of your key stakeholders. Start by using these steps:

1. <u>Identify your key stakeholders</u>: Whose opinion truly matters to your business? While the impact will be unique for each business, it will likely be some combination of the following:

company leadership (including you), customers, employees, and investors.

2. Figure out what matters to each group of stakeholders: Spend some time identifying which areas of mission matter to each of these stakeholders. Start by selecting three areas for each group. What does your business stand for? Why does it exist? What elements of impact are key to the mission? Remember, it's essential that you don't *guess* here. Spend time interviewing each of these stakeholders to make sure you truly understand their priorities and motivations. You can reference the chapters in this book to help you identify different areas of impact to consider.

3. What metrics impact your top and bottom lines? Some metrics will be more important to the financial health of your business than others. In an ideal world, all the metrics that contribute to your mission will also contribute to the health of your business. While this might not always be the case (see the chapter on balancing mission and money on page 229), it's a good goal to shoot for.

4. Determine your key areas of impact: Put your list together. What areas of impact rose to the top? Hopefully there will be some overlap on the priority areas of impact reported by each of your stakeholder groups (and if not, you may have some issues with stakeholder misalignment). Try to keep your final list to ten areas or fewer.

5. Identify metrics or key performance indicators: Determine the key performance indicators (KPIs) or metrics for each category on your list. What metrics will demonstrate whether you are successful in working toward your goal? It can be helpful to break these metrics down into four categories:
   a. Inputs: These are the resources your company is putting in, such as staff time, money, R&D, etc.
   b. Activities: These metrics describe what you are doing with the inputs, such as programs, projects, outreach, education, etc.
   c. Outputs: These are the direct results of your activities, such as number of people fed, amount of carbon emissions reduced, number of workers trained, and so on.

d. Outcomes: Whereas outputs describe the short-term impacts of your work, you can think of the "outcome" areas as the long-term impacts, such as improved quality of life, economic development, environmental preservation, and so on.[1]

Breaking your metrics into these four distinct categories can help you pinpoint why you are or are not getting the outcomes you desire. The frameworks described later in this chapter can help you with identifying key indicators.

6. Determine your data collection strategy: Now that you know what metrics you want to count, you must determine how you will collect the data behind these metrics. The more you can automate this process, the better. It can be tempting in this phase of your strategy to start mandating that your employees, partners, or customers fill out a new survey at every turn, but the best data collection strategy will focus on the data that is most important and minimize time spent collecting data.

7. Determine your data analysis strategy: Data alone doesn't get you very far. You must have a strategy for analyzing the data you have collected and pulling out key insights. Data will not be of any benefit to you if it is interpreted incorrectly. Do you have a data analyst on your team? If not, could you work with a consultant or invest in software? Depending on the type of data, and the amount that you are collecting, this could be a more or less complicated process.

8. Identify your reporting structure: And finally—what will you do with the information you have collected? What process will you have in place for sharing your impact with your key stakeholders? Will it be available to the public? Many companies include impact data on their website, in their annual reports, and even in marketing campaigns. Remember the importance of transparency here: although you may only want to include the metrics you are most proud of in your social media campaign, it's also important to be transparent about the areas you are still working on. Transparency helps to build trust with customers, employees, investors, and other stakeholders.

Tips for Success

- <u>Mix qualitative and quantitative</u>: Although the previous section focuses primarily on collecting and analyzing quantitative metrics, qualitative measurement can be just as important. In fact, the two types of measurement (qualitative and quantitative) are important to balance each other and tell the full story. Qualitative measurement helps to capture your story and the "soul" of your mission. Telling the story of a single person that has been helped through the mission of your business or of a forest that your organization has helped to restore can be much more powerful than any collection of numbers and metrics could ever be. However, the quantitative is an important balance to the qualitative to provide the full picture of impact, be fully transparent with your stakeholders, and offer important insights to determine whether your strategy is working and where you may need to pivot.

- <u>Start small and build</u>: When you begin to look at ESG frameworks (described in more detail below), you'll see that there are hundreds of areas that you could potentially be measuring. However, don't feel like you need to measure everything at once. Start small and measure what is most relevant and important to your business (complete the stakeholder exercise described previously and check out the following section on choosing a framework). As your business grows and you grow in capacity, you can expand on your impact measurement as well.

- <u>Rise to the challenge</u>: When selecting what areas you want to measure, it can be tempting to choose only those areas in which you already excel. If you know your company is strong in environmental impact, it may be tempting to focus solely on environmental impact metrics and ignore areas such as Diversity, Equity, and Inclusion (DEI) and worker well-being. Be honest with yourself about what areas are important to you and your business, where you are doing well, and where you need to improve. Metrics are not just a way to brag, get certifications, or tell your story; they are also a way to hold yourself accountable, identify areas for improvement, and measure progress.

- <u>People can help you!</u> Impact measurement can be a lot of work, especially if you're not familiar with the concepts and tools. Eventually, this may be something your company would like to hire a person or a team to help with. In the interim, there are consulting firms that specialize in this work that can help you set up your strategies and processes.

- <u>Don't forget about your product impact</u>: When you begin to dig through all the impact frameworks and metrics out there, remember not to lose sight of the core purpose of your business. If your business exists to provide fintech solutions to unbankable communities, don't get so caught up in measuring the rainwater recycling at your office that you don't measure how many individuals you're serving and what the impact is. This may seem like an obvious suggestion, but you'd be surprised how many impact reports dance around the core impact of the business.

Frameworks

There are many tools and frameworks for measuring social and environmental impact. Unfortunately, at this point there is not one set of globally recognized standards that everyone uses, which can make it hard for a business to choose what framework is best for them. Here are a few of the most well-known impact measurement frameworks:

B Corp

You've probably heard of this one. B Corp is one of the most well-known forms of impact measurement, and it may be the option that is best for a small company or startup. However, getting B Corp certification is still a very rigorous process.

First of all, there is some clarification necessary, because a B Corp is different than a Public Benefit Corporation, although it is possible for a business to be both. A Public Benefit Corporation is a legal structure (like an LLC or a C Corp), recognized by most states, that allows a company to prioritize mission alongside shareholder profits when making business decisions. While companies can generally make whatever business decisions they deem necessary, there are certain situations where a business is obligated to make a choice that maximizes wealth for their shareholders (the story of Ben & Jerry's selling to Unilever is a common example of this).

A B Corp, on the other hand, is a certification provided by the nonprofit organization B Lab. Being a B Corp is a way to signal to customers, partners, employees, and investors that your company is committed to social and environmental good as well as profit. To become a certified B Corp, companies must complete the online B Impact Assessment (this is a free, confidential tool that can be used by companies to assess your impact even if you don't plan to submit for B Corp certification). You then submit your assessment to B Lab for review. If you score above an 80, you can sign the B Corp Declaration of Interdependence, pay an annual fee, and disclose your score publicly. You then become a certified B Corp and are added to the B Corp Directory. Companies must recertify every three years.

The B Impact Assessment asks a series of questions about your business, focusing on five key categories: governance, workers, community, environment, and customers. The assessment is customized slightly depending on what industry the business is in. Companies that complete the assessment are then able to benchmark and track their own impact and also to compare their results to other companies that have completed the survey.[2]

Impact Reporting and Investment Standards (IRIS+)

IRIS+ is a free, publicly available software managed by GIIN (Global Impact Investing Network) with the goal of making a standardized system for investors and companies to measure, compare, and communicate impact data. IRIS+ is based on the United Nations Sustainable Development Goals, organized by impact categories such as Water, Climate, Energy, and Employment. IRIS+ also provides research and background information about impact areas and advice about how to determine metrics and collect data.[3]

Sustainability Accounting Standards Board (SASB)

SASB provides a set of standards that focus on environmental, social, and governance issues most likely to affect financial performance in different industries. SASB specializes in integrating financial accounting and impact accounting and also providing different sets of standards for different industries such as consumer goods, food and beverage, etc.[4] SASB is a tool that would most likely be more suited to large enterprises and investors than to startups.

ISO

ISO (International Organization for Standardization) creates standards and certifications for all sorts of things from quality management to information security. You've probably heard the term "ISO" followed by some number and then the word "certified." The ISO 14000 family deals with environmental management.[5] ISO 14000 claims to be applicable to organizations of any size in any industry. ISO 14001 is a popular framework used to measure and manage environmental impact, based on a Plan-Do-Check-Act methodology.[6]

GRI

GRI (Global Reporting Initiative) standards are created by an independent, international organization with input from a variety of stakeholders, from businesses to policy makers to investors, with the goal of making a common language and set of standards from which to measure and communicate impact and report on human rights and environmental practices. GRI offers "sector standards" to allow businesses to have access to the standards most relevant to them. These standards may be especially well-suited for companies working across multiple countries.[7]

Choosing a Framework

Keep in mind that the list above is not exhaustive, and you can utilize multiple impact frameworks. There are many sets of standards out there that may be most well-suited for different types of companies. As you can tell by reading the descriptions of the frameworks above, there is a need for a globally recognized set of standards from which to measure and benchmark impact. This is a goal many different organizations are working toward and the suggestion for the best option will likely change depending on who you talk to. Unfortunately, at this time, there is no one right answer to the question of which impact measurement framework is the best choice, and the decision can be rather overwhelming. Below are a few tips for selecting a framework that works best for you and your organization:

- What matters to your business? Refer to the exercise at the beginning of this chapter. What are the impact categories and the metrics that matter most to you, your company, and your stakeholders? Have these in hand when you start exploring framework options so that you can choose a tool that best fits your needs, rather than shaping your needs to best fit a tool.

- Don't make the choice in a vacuum: The last thing you want to do here is make this decision from your desk without talking to stakeholders and gathering information from other organizations. Find out what your partners are using, what similar organizations are using, and most of all, what your key stakeholders—like major customers or investors—are using and what they prefer. Impact measurement is a lot of work, and you certainly don't want to go through all the trouble only to find out that your key customer requires a different set of metrics guided by a framework that doesn't work well with the tool you selected. Do your homework and evaluate the methodologies your key stakeholders are using before jumping in.

- Think strategically: Spend time thinking about where your company is now, where you are going in the future, and what the goals of impact measurement are. Is it to keep your company accountable? Which framework could your employees be most engaged in? What standards would be most accessible to your customer base? Are there particular certifications relevant to your industry that would allow you to reach new customers? What kind of impact assessment do they require? Government regulations you need to comply with? What data do they ask for? Are you seeking investment from a particular impact investor? What impact assessment do they require? Are there particular requirements mandated in countries where you plan to do business? Take your time to think through these key considerations when selecting the impact measurement framework that is the best fit for your business.

19

Lessons Learned: Interviews with Social Entrepreneurs

In this section, I share interviews I conducted and recorded with four social entrepreneurs. While it's one thing to hear me talk about these businesses, it's a whole different experience to hear from these entrepreneurs in their own words. These interviews help to shed light on some of the incredibly difficult and incredibly rewarding parts of being an entrepreneur with a social and environmental mission. Reading these interviews may help you to understand why I have so much personal admiration for these people and am committed to supporting them and helping them to achieve their goals in whatever way I can—and one of these ways is by sharing their stories and lessons learned with others.

Interview #1 with Kristal Hansley

Founder of WeSolar, a community solar company located in Baltimore, MD.

Interview conducted on December 19, 2022.
The WeSolar company profile can be found on page 181.

ME: In a nutshell, can you tell me what your business does?

KRISTAL: WeSolar is a woman- and minority-owned renewable energy firm. We focus on increasing affordability and accessibility to solar energy. We do that in several ways, but primarily through community solar. Community solar is the latest vertical within the solar industry that allows up to 80 percent of American households to tap into existing solar farms, meaning systems built outside of their home that power the local grid. Now households can have access to those solar farms and receive a renewable energy credit directly on their utility bill, eliminating the issue of being able to afford and develop their own solar system on their roof. Without the option of community solar, many low-income families cannot access renewable energy because they cannot reach past the barriers of not owning their homes or having a good credit score. WeSolar is growing quickly and increasing awareness around community solar and renewable energy projects.

ME: Thank you. And will you tell me the story of how you started your business?

KRISTAL: Yes. I will go all the way back to childhood. I am like a third-generation community organizer. I was always passionate about community and politics and making sure that the resources in underrepresented communities were advocated for. My grandmother actually started the largest vegetable garden in Bushwick, in Brooklyn, New York on Linden Street. And that's where I really got my calling to serve and to be a public servant. We did a lot of mobilization and grassroots work, knocking on doors, going to a lot of community meetings. She was the president of the block association. So from the time I was about three years old to high school, I probably attended anywhere between three to five community meetings a week, my entire childhood. And I think that ingrained a seed of curiosity in me and made me want to get a professional lens in theory. So I went to DC and I majored in political science, and I worked on Capitol Hill for about eight to ten years. I did some lobbying work for nonprofits as a public servant lobbyist, and then I also worked in the United States Senate and House of Representatives.

During the time I was working on Capitol Hill, we had an administration change and Donald Trump was elected. After that point, there wasn't a lot of mobility around environmental justice, and there wasn't a lot of room for advancement, career-wise, for the progressive side of the political ideology spectrum. And that's also when I noticed that a lot of states were passing sweeping clean energy legislation across the board. And Maryland, our neighboring jurisdiction, had just passed their Community Solar Act of 2015. I thought it was a great opportunity to leverage my community and political background, so I joined a local community solar firm that was located in Silver Spring, really close to DC. And I just took to it. I enjoyed the work, and I enjoyed the mission of community solar. About three years into that gig, that's when the pandemic hit. But even before the pandemic, I had started to think that I should go out on my own because I had a different cultural lens than others in the industry, and I started to think that the only way for me to really expand and scale industry-wide may be to go on my own. I wanted to have agency over my ideas. My CEO actually agreed, and we determined that I would work as a 1099 and start WeSolar. So my previous employer was actually my first client, and that was really the foundation to WeSolar. You have to remember that during this time, everything was shut down. I launched on Juneteenth of 2020, when we were in the middle of racial riots and protests across the country, as well as the pandemic, and there were also a lot of calls for action for renewable energy and solar. And WeSolar just found itself right at the height of those intersections of energy, justice, environmental racism, and discrimination. And WeSolar was a shining star as it relates to making sure that underrepresented groups were a part of this transition to renewables. That's our calling, that's our purpose.

We're able to bring all these collaborators and institutions together and say we all have a common goal, no matter where you are politically. When you look at the policies around community solar, I think it's really unique in the sense that it brings together progressive activists and rural conservative farmers on the Eastern shore who are like, "I don't know about solar. However, this business model, and the opportunity to build a solar farm on my land, gives me more options. I don't want anyone telling me what to do with my land, and I like having this option that doesn't destroy the land." And especially now with inflation, it's really difficult for farmers, so to have this option is something they're really excited about. Community solar is very bipartisan. Having worked in politics, I always like to find common ground. Community solar is not polarizing: the overall mission helps so many people, from the landowners to the off-takers (aka the subscribers), and also our planet because we're decarbonizing our footprint and also keeping those resources in local communities, and supporting green jobs and Black-owned businesses.

ME: The full spectrum!

KRISTAL: Yes! (Laughs) I could go on. So many pros!

ME: Absolutely. That's awesome. So, my next question is, could you tell me more about the business model? Who is making money, and how?

KRISTAL: Yes, so we have three main verticals. First of all, we get calls from, say, a commercial building owner that says, "We're interested in renewable energy, but we have tenants, and we don't really want a system that the tenants own because they move out in a few years. So what are your options?" And I say, "Well, you can do community solar, you can leverage the square footage on your roof, and sell the energy not to your local utility, but to your local community members. And that way, you now have a source of revenue." And also at the same time, we can take some of their common areas in the building and subscribe that to their community solar farm, which can act as the anchor financing for us, because banks love to see a strong credit anchor tenant, and that's not necessarily going to be low-income individuals. And then the building is also going green, right? We would build those systems for them and get a development fee. The building owner would own it, and they would save money on their energy bill, and also receive solar credits that would make money through receiving that ongoing cash flow from the community subscribers, because it's their system, and we can put everything together for them and get the development fee.

Another way that our business model works is that we will leverage our brand for new developers who struggle with bridging language, culture, and community barriers, but have really good teams and can move fast and have resources to develop community solar, but just don't have the community connections. And they say, "Listen, this is what you do great. We're building in this part of town, but we know that your name, WeSolar, is very well liked. And so could you come on and be our manager for subscribers and sales?" And so we will get paid for acquiring and managing those sales channels.

And then, last but not least, we are now developing our own projects. And so we receive calls from realtors and owners that don't want to own the system, but would like to get a simple land lease, and we will put the entire deal together: find the buyers, do the financing, and then, they get an ongoing payment for the land lease. And so, the way that WeSolar makes money is that we would actually own the solar asset itself, develop the project, and then also work with the community partners and owners of the land or building, and cut them into the deal that way.

Those are our three main verticals. We also have so many different partnerships. We work with a lot of community organizers and hire nonprofits to do a lot of marketing and events for us. We mostly hire small vendors and work with them. We also get paid to speak and talk with new up-and-coming energy companies who just want to hear our lessons learned.

Me: Would you mind talking a little about your funding strategy, and how you took WeSolar to where it is today?

Kristal: I was one of those daring, crazy entrepreneurs that launched a business in the middle of a pandemic. I primarily bootstrapped for the first two-and-a-half years, and raised a friends and family round of about $150,000. Then this year I did a crowdfunding campaign and raised close to $200,000 with a company called Raise Green, and that allowed me to cover operations and bring on about five consultants. And now we are looking to close our first seed funding round from angel and impact investors because we have to scale. We have had a lot of demand on those three verticals that I mentioned. The hardest part, I'd say, was to bootstrap and to raise a friends and family round. I started off with my own funds: I put in about $30,000 of my own money and $5,000 from an aunt, and then the following year I raised about $150,000 from friends and family, and then $200,000 from crowdfunding. And then right now, we have about $5 million in contracts.

ME: Congratulations!

KRISTAL: Thank you.

ME: So would you mind talking a bit more about your social and environmental mission and how you carry that out?

KRISTAL: So the "why" behind WeSolar really goes back to my early days of organizing in my very first role in the solar energy space, and one of the things that stuck out to me was the lack of representation from all sides of the supply chain, whether it was the financiers, the developers, and at the time, even the subscribers, as well as the traditional renewable energy groups and nonprofits. The intersection was missing between the information and really getting that information to the folks that needed it most, or who were disproportionately impacted by climate change. I felt like, if we're able to save 20 percent off of folks' utility bills, we really need to be offering this to people who have an energy burden. The percentage of people living with energy burden in Baltimore is like 30 percent. So the communities that really needed the information, like women and minorities, were being left out. 80 percent of the solar industry is run by white men. And so the social justice and environmental impact is through and through. It's about being represented in an industry where traditionally we are not. It's also about focusing the resources in the communities where we build, by hiring local people and bringing on contractors that look like myself, and doing the education around that. That's our social justice and our environmental justice impact. It's second nature for us. It's the community that I grew up in, even though I grew up in New York, not Baltimore, but it's the same type of issues.

Being able to work with communities of color and underrepresented groups across the country is how I end up getting calls from fifth graders who say "Oh, I saw you, and didn't know that I could be a solar developer, or that there were Black people in solar. I want to do that." That's social impact. Just being representative. And that's what WeSolar stands for. So if I can reach one youth that thought that they had to do something else because they didn't have this exposure, I'll have influenced someone who wouldn't have had this opportunity before. So it's all about exposure to the younger generation as well.

ME: You mentioned that you don't really have to think about how you're carrying out your mission because it's so central to what you do, and who you are. I wonder, though, if you've ever faced times where you had to choose between the mission of your business and the financial goals of your business? I'm writing about tools and methodologies for figuring out what to do when the monetary goals and mission of your business compete. How do you choose between them? Has that ever happened with your business?

KRISTAL: Yeah, for sure. I mean, solar is hard. Development is not for the faint of heart. Solar is up 25 percent as it relates to inverters, panels, land, capital, and interest rates. Everything is higher than it was a year ago. And when you're serving a community and you are still working with very thin margins, you're like, "Okay, I want to sell my energy at a discount. But for me to even build, I'm paying a certain price." So the question is like, how do you do this? And in some cases, you're not able to give the 20 percent discount you want to give. You might only be able to give a 5 percent discount just to get the doggone projects done, right? And the cost of the financing is more expensive too. Even a year ago, my models showed that my project would have been able to accommodate a 20 percent discount for low-income families, but that's not the case anymore.

So I would say that you use what you can, right? You negotiate. You have lenders that have to make a return because they have investors that are investing in them. You go with the times and the resiliency of your leaders. The people understand what's happening. And they want to see you succeed. There might be a point in time when the energy rates go down, and I am able to offer that 20 percent discount. Or I have a corporate sponsor that says, "Hey, you know we want to buy some renewable energy credits," and I'm like, "Well, you can offset my existing low-income families' bills. Now they receive a 5 percent discount, but I really want to get to 15 or 20 percent. And you can write that off." So, you just have to be creative. You have to embrace resiliency and remember that there's power in change.

There's always going to be the unknown and stuff that happens that you cannot account for. And I think that just having a strong team of advisors, mentors, other business colleagues, and peer-to-peer mentorship helps a lot. That's one of the practices we use. When there's a policy change that puts a halt to everything, I know that it's not just impacting me and our business, it's impacting my colleagues too. And so having enough brain capital around you, and having other people in your space to talk to, can help offset some of that anxiety you get when you're putting out fires. I like to surround myself with really successful and smart people in this space; those who have done it 1,000 times over. It's all about community. For anyone that's looking to jump into a space where they may feel intimidated, building community really helps. In the beginning I did feel siloed, but not anymore. There are dozens of people that I can lean on.

ME: I think that's really important advice. Being an entrepreneur can be a bit of a lonely road, and building that community is really essential to longevity, and being able to navigate issues like that. So, along those lines, what would you say is the biggest challenge you have faced in your business so far?

KRISTAL: I'd say the biggest challenge is . . . you know, I don't really like talking about this . . . it's real, but it's almost like the expected answer. And that's the challenge, right? The challenge is, yes, I am a Black woman in this space. And damned if I do, damned if I don't. So, damned if I do talk about the covert and overt discrimination that I face. I can be the energy expert and still be talked to like a child. I can make a recommendation and have people question it, then I can have my colleague that's white come in and say the exact same thing that I said five minutes ago, and everyone's like "oh, that's a great idea!" It's a problem. But then if I say it's a problem, I'm complaining, or I'm making excuses. And so there's this internal battle. I don't want to be labeled, but the reality is that it's a situation that I have to endure time and time again, and it's just a barrier that I have to face that other colleagues and developers don't. They just get to talk business and do deals. And their knowledge is just taken at face value. Which is not the case for me or WeSolar. We have to be twice, maybe three times as good. So yeah, that's the challenge.

ME: I imagine that's especially true in an industry whose executives are 80 percent white men . . .

KRISTAL: Yeah, absolutely.

ME: Well, what would you say is the most rewarding part of starting and running a business?

KRISTAL: It's super rewarding to serve my community. It's super rewarding to be a part of the transition to renewables and getting away from fossil fuels, and creating opportunities for other young people and minority engineers and HBCU [Historically Black Colleges and Universities] students, who can feel like, at the firm, that they have a voice and a safe space. That's very rewarding to create opportunities that weren't there before your firm. It's like, "Whoa, we're really doing something here, and serving the planet at the same time. And obviously, making folks money too." It's the triple bottom line, to go green, to share with the community, and to save the planet. And I think that's pretty cool.

ME: So do I. Ok, my final question is, what advice would you give to new social entrepreneurs?

KRISTAL: Quiet any type of fear. A lot of people are ruled by fear. Tap into your emotions, however you feel, and see them as energy. Emotions are just energy in motion. Go with your instincts. Listen to it, but don't feed into the fear, and don't give up.

There are going to be nights (and days) where you might question what you're doing. I would say, run from that. Those are your survival mechanisms helping you problem-solve and get through those tough times, but resiliency is a success factor. So definitely be resilient and just keep going. Don't shy away. And if you're feeling a little fearful, that means you're onto something good. And be an empathetic leader, tap into those emotions, it's energy in motion. From *Inc. Magazine* to *Forbes*, they've talked about the empathetic leader and how those leadership skills reign supreme. And then, like I stated, when the hard times arise, resiliency and the experience that comes with it is invaluable. And just keep going. Keep going.

ME: Thank you, Kristal.

Interview #2 with Jordan Phasey

Founder of Phinite, a start-up that turns livestock waste into regenerative fertilizer, located in Clinton, North Carolina

Interview conducted on November 18, 2022
The Phinite company profile can be found on page 79.

ME: Can you tell me in a nutshell what your business does?

JORDAN: Phinite is an ag robotics company that makes fertilizer out of animal manure. We have developed a low-cost, low-energy drying system that makes it profitable to mine and manufacture fertilizer from animal farms.

ME: How is that different than how farmers have been using animal waste as fertilizer in the past?

JORDAN: So, animal manure that is produced by animal farms is typically very wet. And that water adds a lot of bulk and expense to transporting the material from farms—so much so that often the cost of applying the manure is actually more than what the fertilizer is worth. And that makes it challenging to utilize the material efficiently, particularly the phosphorus and potassium in fertilizer.

Manure is not a balanced fertilizer. It has about the same amount of nitrogen, phosphorus, and potassium, and crops need a lot more nitrogen than they need phosphorus and potash. Manure is normally applied at nitrogen rates, which means that phosphorus and potassium tend to be applied to land at rates that exceed what the crops can use. And that leads to a buildup, particularly of phosphorus, in soils which can lead to pollution if not applied agronomically.

So what we do is dry the material using a low-cost, low-energy drying system powered by a robot. The robot handles all of the materials through the process and drives out a lot of the labor costs associated with the fertilizer manufacturing process. And these two things in totality lead to us being able to dry fertilizer for less than what the fertilizer is actually worth. And so we can sell that material, and profit from it. And farmers can actually profit from the sale of this material as well; the cost of production is that low.

We want to turn animal farms into the renewable fertilizer mines of the future. And what is key to doing this is finding a profitable model for farmers to adopt a technology solution, while also generating enough value for a third-party, low-cost technology provider to justify doing this whole thing at all. That's what we do.

ME: Thank you. And could you tell me the story of how you started your business?

JORDAN: So I am a water and wastewater engineer from Australia. In Australia, my work was to do the drinking water treatment for remote Aboriginal communities all spread out across the Northern Territory of Australia, which is where I'm from. The Northern Territory is the most remote part of Australia. It has 260,000 people in an area twice the size of Texas. And these Aboriginal communities are in the most remote parts of the territory, usually about 200 miles by dirt road from the nearest town. And so my work was to develop simple and robust treatment systems to provide safe drinking water in that environment. And it turns out that the engineering challenges of working there are very similar to working on animal farms.

In my spare time, I was interested in finding ways to make money out of treating waste, and I developed two technologies to mine the fertilizer present in sewage, because phosphorus sustainability in particular is very important for global food security. And so once I got into the economics of those processes, I decided to move my work into agriculture, because ag wastewater is more concentrated, and the resource recovery opportunity is larger.

Where I am from in Australia, there are not many animal farms. And so you know, I got on the internet and googled, "how do I find animal farms?" And I came across a technology competition that was being run by the US EPA (Environmental Protection Agency). They had issued a global call for innovations and new technologies to make value-added products out of manure. And I saw this competition, and thought, "Hey, I've got an idea of how to do this! So I'll submit it and see what happens." So the EPA loved it. They thought it was one of the ten best ideas in the world and gave me an award at the White House in 2016.

The EPA had brought together the biggest pork and dairy producers in the country to be judges in this competition. So at the White House, some livestock farmers tapped me on the shoulder and said, "Hey, we love what you're doing, can you come to visit and look at our farms?" What the farmers explained to me was that it turns out that the central problem with sustainability in animal farming is that animal farmers really lack access to a low-cost, low-energy drying system to take the manure that's produced on their farms and dry it to a point that it's transportable, and then allow for the regional redistribution of nutrients.

The farmers we're working with have a particularly acute version of that problem that every animal farmer in the world has to some degree. And so we got to work digging in with the industry to understand what the issue was and worked on developing our first-generation technology, which we brought to market in 2017.

ME: All right, thank you. You have mentioned this a bit already, but can you walk through what exactly the business model of Phinite is? As far as who's making money and how and where?

JORDAN: Okay, sure. Our company provides a technology, which is a distributed fertilizer mining operation that is located on animal farms. Animal farmers purchase the drying system from Phinite, we use subcontractors to install the technology on the farm, and then we operate the drying systems remotely across a whole number of different animal farms.

In our first target geography, there's no market for the fertilizer product locally, so what Phinite does is centralize this resource so that fertilizer comes from all these multiple production systems that have been installed by farmers, and we then centralize that resource and we sell it through offtake agreements with fertilizer distributors on behalf of farmers. And then we split the profits back with farmers to give them a payback on their asset. So farmers themselves receive a profitable model for relieving themselves of the nutrient burden that is present on their farms, while Phinite primarily makes money from the sale of the fertilizer.

ME: Okay, got it. Could you talk a bit about funding strategy, if you've brought on any outside funding, and what that has looked like for you?

JORDAN: We've raised two rounds of funding so far. We raised our pre-seed round in 2018, which supported the construction of our first production system on our trial farm. And then we raised our seed round in 2022 to bring to market our third-generation drying system that has this profitable model that I was describing. We've raised money from both grant sources and from equity investors.

ME: How has that process been for you?

JORDAN: So, fundraising is never easy. The space that we operate in is one where many companies have failed before us trying to build low-cost waste management systems. So it was initially very hard to distinguish us from the pack in that regard. Ultimately, what we did was raised our first close on our seed round from farmers themselves—the ones that had the problem that needed to be solved. That first close was instrumental in raising the remainder of the seed round. We also received investment from a number of early-stage agtech groups: Ag Startup Engine and AgVentures Alliance in Iowa, and AgLaunch in Tennessee. The support of these groups has been very important to us to build the credibility in the business that we have. Those groups have been great.

ME: Can you talk a bit more about the social and environmental mission of what you do?

JORDAN: Okay, so half the world's population relies upon synthetic fertilizer for survival now, and fertilizer is a very unsustainably produced product. Nitrogen fertilizer is currently made directly out of fossil fuels, while phosphorus and potassium fertilizers are both mined from finite resources that are present in the ground.

So Phinite was born out of a desire to improve global food security by recycling phosphorus in particular, which is where our name comes from. Phosphorus is a finite resource, and we exist to make it renewable. There are a lot of opportunities to improve the environmental footprint of fertilizer use within agriculture. Nitrogen fertilizer, being made from natural gas, is pretty challenging to make sustainably. There are ways to make nitrogen fertilizer more sustainably, but at the moment, those technologies are still not cost-effective. They probably are more cost-competitive if the carbon emissions from the manufacturing are included within the cost of the product, but separately, nitrogen fertilizer use and phosphorus fertilizer use both can lead to environmental pollution through the way they are used.

Nitrogen fertilizer leads to a lot of greenhouse gas emissions both in soils and in waterways if the fertilizer is washed off fields, and phosphorus has the same issue. Phosphorus often leads to algal blooms, while nitrogen fertilizer leaching is the cause of the dead zone in the Gulf of Mexico due to the enormous quantities that run off from fields every day.

Manure-based fertilizer has been around forever. The big advantage of manure-based products relative to conventional synthetics products is that they are by nature very slow-release. That means there are fewer opportunities for that manure product, if it's used agronomically, to enter the environment. And that's the goal for us. So when farmers purchase the product, they purchase it based upon the agronomic value of the material in totality, as opposed to just the nitrogen, which is how manure-based fertilizers are used now, and that means that farmers will manage the use of that material appropriately and prevent it from running off to waterways.

There is a substantial greenhouse gas emission reduction that occurs by using a product like ours, because it does not require natural gas in order to manufacture, and it's totally renewable. And the phosphorus present is literally being recycled. The product creates this sustainable loop for natural resources and agriculture.

ME: Awesome. And have the social and environmental mission of your business and your monetary goals for your business ever come into conflict?

JORDAN: I would say not yet. The beauty of what Phinite does is that our environmental and economic interests are very aligned. We make fertilizer, we sell fertilizer, we make money from it. And guess what, we offset lots of greenhouse gas and environmental issues associated with the product that is no longer being used due to the use of our product.

ME: How about on the social side? Has figuring out how much to charge for the fertilizer, for example, been a challenge at all?

JORDAN: That's a good question. We charge market rates for the services that we provide. Those market rates are competitive and particularly competitive at the moment, given what global fertilizer prices are like. So at the moment, it hasn't been an issue. I can understand how that could be a conflict. But it hasn't been a challenge for us yet.

ME: Good. Okay. What would you say are the biggest challenges that you have faced in your business so far?

JORDAN: Well, the world is a pretty big place. And it was particularly hard to dig a hole straight through the middle of it, to get from Australia to the United States (laughs). So overcoming that challenge was a pretty difficult thing to do. And I would say that we have had all of the normal challenges that any early-stage company has. People don't know who you are, people don't know why they should believe that what you're doing is real. You don't have any money. Yeah, all the normal things.

We are also a hardware company. And hardware start-ups are much harder to build than software start-ups. Thankfully, we're making it work, despite those challenges, but I would say that we are lucky that the environmental and social effects of what we do are baked into operating a normal business just by the fact that our business works the way it does, and so we are able to just be a normal business and achieve massive global impact as a result of that. The two things are not opposed to each other at the moment.

ME: Would you mind talking about your decision to take the plunge and dig a hole through the world to move from Australia to America?

JORDAN: Well, for me, there were really two reasons that coincided to make this a reality. First and foremost, sustainability is going to be the issue at the center of the lives of every person that is alive on the planet right now. We are at a point where the carrying capacity of the planet cannot sustain this business as usual going forward. For me, in the scope of the technical experience I have, the major opportunity that exists is around nutrient redistribution, and particularly phosphorus security. So the world is running out of high-quality, easy to obtain phosphorus resources; and as we said before, half the world's population relies upon this material to survive. The fact that there is less of that available than there used to be means prices are going to rise, and that is an enormous problem facing the planet now.

I am really afraid of what happens when fertilizer prices rise as a result of this. We've really seen it in the last twelve months. The Covid crisis and then the war in Ukraine have stressed global fertilizer markets enormously. And we are only now just beginning to see the pain that can happen once food becomes more expensive. There's still a large amount of the world's population that is very food insecure. The driving purpose behind founding Phinite was to save lives by feeding people from a resource that currently is not being utilized. For me, I can't think of a purpose or mission that could be more important than that. And servicing that mission is worthy of making big sacrifices to do it, and that's why a seemingly crazy venture from the outside could actually happen. So that's sort of reasonable.

Reason number two was the opportunity presented by having basically had livestock farmers offer me a multi-billion-dollar opportunity that it didn't seem like anyone was working on—it was really like a once-in-a-lifetime thing. And to an ambitious person, you really have to grab those opportunities when they come, because the alternative is that you look back on your life and wonder what you did with the chances that you had. And so for me that was the motivating factor.

ME: So we've discussed the biggest challenges you've faced. What would you say are the most rewarding parts of starting this business?

JORDAN: Seeing the vision come to life, and seeing people come to believe that it's possible to do something that up until now has been impossible to do. We have some really important investors that are members of industry that have seen ventures like this try and fail before. And so seeing them believe that there is something possible here that has never been done before is very rewarding.

ME: What advice do you have to give to other social entrepreneurs or mission-based entrepreneurs?

JORDAN: You need to have a very convincing understanding of the social-environmental impact that what you're doing has on the world. That conviction is necessary to get through all of the hard periods that happen at the beginning. And in some ways that conviction can be a superpower compared to other businesses. Because if we were just inventing another widget for people to buy, this company would have failed a long time ago, because it just isn't that important to the world. But being able to really get to the marrow of the opportunity that exists to yourself is necessary, I think, to deal with the hard knocks that come from starting any start-up. But once you do that, you really do have to operate your business like a business and allow normal economic criteria, decisions, and practices to weigh things, because that's why business works.

We've iterated a lot of times on what we do before we got to something that worked. And it took an awful long time of being unpaid to do it. But becoming an expert in your domain and really understanding the knowledge base backwards and forwards is critical to getting the pieces of the puzzle right. Because if you are serious about having social impact, then the conflict between economic requirements and social requirements will happen, and the better you have built the puzzle at the beginning, the easier it will be to deal with that conflict.

ME: Thank you. Is there anything else that you would like to share? Either about your story or business or being a founder in the space?

JORDAN: No, no I don't think so. Phinite's gonna change the world! (Laughs) Thank you for listening.

ME: Great. Thank you so much.

Interview #3 with Michaela Barnett

Founder of KnoxFill, a zero-waste store located in Knoxville, Tennessee

The KnoxFill company profile can be found on page 152.
Interview conducted on October 18, 2022.

ME: Can you tell me in a nutshell what your business does?

MICHAELA: My business is a zero-waste refillery. We provide personal care and household goods in refillable, reusable containers, to completely prevent the need for disposable packaging.

ME: Great, could you please tell me the story of how you started KnoxFill?

MICHAELA: I'm a sustainability scientist and a behavioral scientist, and I was getting my PhD at the University of Virginia studying problems with our waste system, and I was learning about all of the issues with plastic pollution, particularly all of the human factors of the waste system, and finding how many problems that system contributes to. It's a system that relies on people at every stage, and if you have human error, the system can get messed up really quickly. Waste is not something like energy or water that really good design can fix, at least not right now.

So I was studying all of these problems every day, and reading these statistics, and meanwhile, finding that the timeframe of impact in academia takes so frickin' long! You're like, okay, I'm going to spend two years working on this paper and then go through however long the review process takes, get it published, and then maybe it gets noticed and is picked up. And then I just hope someone does something with that. That's like, honestly, the theory of change in academia. So, I was feeling very disillusioned. I always knew I didn't want to go into academia, but I went in to learn that last piece of the sustainability puzzle that had always eluded me, which was the human behavioral component.

To make a long story a little bit shorter, I was selected to be part of a development challenge called the Nudge Global Impact Challenge based out of the Netherlands. The project that I had pitched them on to get into this challenge was a "take back your trash" movement. My plan was to create a social movement wherein we would provide people with prepaid postage to send corporations' trash, found in the wild, to the board members and CEO and senior leadership to really emphasize that this is something that's so often framed as a consumer problem, but it's really a corporation problem, and this is not our waste, it's their waste. I still think it's a great idea.

ME: So do I!

MICHAELA: Thank you, maybe I'll do it someday. But during this challenge I wasn't sure how I would figure out the legal challenges of it, and I wanted to do something where I could make an impact somewhat quickly, and in my local community. Honestly, I also really wanted a refillery in our area. And I felt like I kept waiting on someone to start it. So during this challenge, which was over the period of eight months, I began to work through the idea of what would become KnoxFill, and then launched the business during the challenge. At the end of the eight-month period there was a competition, and I was one of the people chosen to present at it. I also received some money for KnoxFill, which was helpful.

So KnoxFill really came out of an academic frustration and a desire to make change on the problems I was studying. And finally, just the thought that I would like to patronize one of these stores. I would like one here and I'm going to start it, I guess. So that's the story of KnoxFill!

ME: Thanks, I didn't know all of those details. Would you mind walking me through the business model of KnoxFill?

MICHAELA: Right now, I honestly feel like I'm creating three businesses. Currently, our meat and potatoes is our delivery program. We run a weekly delivery and pickup that works like the milkman. We pre-fill containers. When folks order, we either deliver the items to their house, or we take them to our pickup partners, of which we have four, so that people can pick them up. They return their empties, and they get a slight discount when they're refilling versus when they're purchasing for the first time. That's about 80 percent of our business right now. Then we have markets and pop-ups for people to refill in person. That's a very popular model right now. We're working on finishing our mobile refillery trailer, which is going to be a game changer. But the pop-ups are very time consuming. Even though they can be lucrative, they can also be very hit-or-miss.

And then, finally, the last part of this is that we just recently started supplying to businesses. We just launched our business program and are now looking further upstream in the chain. We are supplying cleaning products, house soap, and so on for local businesses around town as well.

ME: How does that work? Do the customers return the containers to the business?

MICHAELA: No. In our pickup model that's what happens, but in our business program we are actually supplying businesses with their hand soap. They get a larger container and can refill their smaller containers. So they'll get, for example, four dispensers and a gallon of hand soap. Then they'll fill their own smaller containers from their larger one. And then they can return their gallon container to us for a refill.

The big priorities for the end of this year are moving into a new fulfillment center and also launching our first of two mobile refilleries. Then the priority for the new year is getting into a brick-and-mortar space. It's really hard to make money selling soap, as you can imagine. We've got a big and loyal customer base, and I'm really grateful with how this business model has been so embraced and even championed by people. But at the end of the day, you either have to sell a lot of soap, or your margins have to be really good.

Right now, there are a few companies that supply refilleries across the country with closed-loop supply chains, so you're sending the large containers back to them to be cleaned, refilled, and sent back out. Then we also have the ingredients that our customer base cares about and are competing on price levels. It's really important for me to make this something that's accessible for folks. But right now our margins are tighter than they should be, so I'm actually working with the owner of Sage Refill Market in Nashville to talk with different cosmetic manufacturers about doing custom formulations for our two businesses in bulk. Then we might actually start wholesaling to other refilleries, because there is currently a gap in the market right now. That's something that will hopefully be really useful in the new year.

Right now we're still definitely at the growth and grind stage of things. I'm still not paying myself. The business right now is self-sustaining, we pay for supplies and employee labor through our revenue, and have some money set aside for growth, but we're still not paying me, which, as of now, would be the business's biggest expense.

It's funny, they always say that it can take like three years for a business to start really making money. I am someone with a lot of confidence. I'm a very executive decision-maker, and if I set my mind to things, I do them. And I really thought I was going to be the exception to that rule! I really thought I was going to be cash-positive way sooner and paying myself that money! (Laughs.) So it's been a bit of a reality check.

Since I graduated, I've also been doing some sustainability consulting on the side, which helps pay the bills. It makes me see the appeal of being employed by another company, like whoa, you would pay me a regular paycheck?

ME: One more question on the business model, do your customers pay on a subscription basis? Or per order?

MICHAELA: Most of them are paying per order, through a mix of in-person and online. I will say, I do think that those ratios will shift with some of the changes that we're making. And I think that's going to be also really good for the business and for me.

ME: As far as financing strategy, did you have to seek any outside funding to get to where you are right now?

MICHAELA: So far, it's all been bootstrapping. Although I do have a prospective investor who I'm going to have lunch with next month. We're going to see what that could look like. She's actually a customer of mine.

I started Knoxville with $10,000 in savings. And did that while pursuing a PhD full-time and getting paid for the PhD. Also, I'm pretty lucky that my husband has helped support us. Also, as I mentioned, I won that competition, which gave me a few thousand euros to get going. When I first moved to Knoxville, I purchased a house in North Knox and we sold that this summer, so that's provided a good cash padding all around. Selling a previous investment of mine has allowed me to go without a salary for the time being and has made this all feel possible. That, and the loyal customers that buy from us every month.

ME: Well, revenue is definitely the best kind of funding! Could you tell me about the social and environmental mission of your business and how you carry that out?

MICHAELA: Absolutely. Sustainability is at the core of my business. I think about that in social, environmental, and economic terms. The economic part is the one we're still tinkering with.

Starting with environmental, we're in a crisis of overproduction and overconsumption generally, and with fast-moving consumer goods specifically. A lot of the environmental scientists and climate scientists that I've worked with can be really dismissive of working on the plastic waste problem, because it's almost too mainstream and can seem a little naive to some people. And to be fair, some of the efforts around reducing plastic have been very small and short-sighted. But especially in the last few years, what we've seen is the way that this crisis connects with our greater climate crisis, and issues of environmental justice as well, which will only get worse in the coming years because plastic production is anticipated to ramp up as we move away from oil for energy. Plastic production is what fossil fuel manufacturers are really looking towards as a new business model while continuing to foist ineffective recycling upon us as consumers.

Then if we look at the lifecycle of the production, transportation, use, and disposal of these products, we can see this isn't just a microplastics problem. This is a greenhouse gas emissions problem. So for me, the two are inextricably combined. With microplastics, we really don't know what we don't know. I understand why it's such a popular issue. It's scary. And it hits really close to home. There was a study by the University of Tennessee that found that the Tennessee River is one of the most plastic-polluted rivers in the world, based on the amount of microplastics found in the water. Microplastics have been found in our placentas, in our blood, our bodies, everywhere. At this point, we don't totally know what health impact that's going to have. So, as a scientist, I want to stick really close to what we do know, which is that from an ecological systems perspective, this is harming our ecosystems, even if we don't yet know the

direct impact on human health. Then if we look at the end destination for these products, the majority are being landfilled,
incinerated, or ending up in the natural environment. When
they go to landfill, they're being placed in the most vulnerable
communities that are seeing resulting health impacts. So, if
we talk about the environmental impact of the business, that's
really one of the driving factors in the decision-making framework for me. That piece has to be with every business decision
that I'm making.

In terms of social sustainability, there are a lot of different pieces to my strategy. I've seen a lot of the ways that we've
communicated about sustainability to be really ineffective, and
they either make people feel very overwhelmed, very guilty, or
nihilistic—basically, a lot of things that promote inaction instead
of action. A lot of efforts also promote myopic action instead of
system-changing action.

At KnoxFill, we work really hard to be intentional in our communication about what sustainability actions customers can take.
We want to be clear that purchasing from KnoxFill is not going
to be the ultimate sustainability solution. We are very focused on
systems change efforts, and on empowering people to be imper-
fect. We want to help environmentalists take action and turn that
action into a rolling snowball that accumulates, rather than feeling like you have to do everything perfectly at once, or nothing at
all. It's also very easy to feel that as individuals, our actions don't
matter that much. But by creating a community around sustainability and empowering people to live out their environmental
values, and using our platform to say "Hey, all those things that
we're doing on an individual level, those are good. What if we
did individual actions that changed systems instead? What if we
focused on collective action and impact?" In all of the messaging and education we do around these issues, we work hard to
encourage a holistic approach. So, that's why it sometimes feels
like I'm running twenty businesses!

ME: A lot of moving pieces! So, I think this next question flows
well with what you were just talking about—do the mission and

monetary goals of your business ever conflict? And if so, how do you handle that? What is your decision-making process?

MICHAELA: You know, just in the past two weeks I've been working on coming back to my core, and thinking, "Okay, I need to bump the money aspect of all this up a little higher on the priorities list." I worked at this farm in college, it's a small, sustainable place in upstate South Carolina, and the farmers I worked with always said, if we're not sustainable economically, we can't do the environmentally sustainable work that we're doing. And that really resonated with me. I went into this business shooting for that. And I've been lucky because I've been able to do a lot with savings, and I live in a dual income household with no kids. And with the cash influx from the sale of our property, it's been a lot less stressful and I've been able to give it time. But now that I've finished my PhD, I'm like, "Okay, I need to make money!" I would like to be paid what I'm worth, and I think it's going to be awhile before KnoxFill can do that. I also think there will likely be some future divergence where KnoxFill starts running more autonomously through employees, and I can focus more on my consulting work.

The economics are challenging because I want our products to be accessible and competitive. I definitely was not charging enough in the beginning. That piece is still a bit hard, because I look at some of the alternatives that you can get from the big box stores, and I want our products to be an option for people. It can also be difficult to get pricing right when people bring their own containers. Some of our products people buy and remark on how cheap they are, and other times, someone will bring a really large container to buy dishwasher detergent and I'm watching it tally up and am about to have a panic attack because this person is about to spend forty dollars on dishwasher detergent!

A lot of these hard decisions I haven't had to make yet, but I think I will in the next six months to a year. A lot of refilleries have been closing lately. I'm part of a lot of those online communities. I'm really lucky that KnoxFill is doing well and thriving and I think there's a lot of opportunity for growth. We're getting customers every week, which is great. But also, this movement is beginning to be embraced by the Unilevers and Procter & Gambles and the big guys because they know they need to do this. And I think that's really wonderful, but we're going to have to see what that looks like for those of us who are much smaller and were out front surfing the wave.

ME: So we've touched on this a little, but what would you say are the biggest challenges you've faced in your business? And what have been the most rewarding parts?

MICHAELA: The hardest thing about my business, which has been pretty unexpected, is that it has actually brought a lot of conflict and tension in my personal life, even in my relationship with my partner. Creating boundaries around this business has revealed a lot of the ways in which we're really different. He has contributed economically, and is a very supportive partner, but I think the business has brought more conflict into our relationship than anything else has. It's been hard to have something that has been so life-giving and beautiful and has given me a lot of really wonderful things but has also brought conflict and tension into my relationship. I believe that part of it has been that boundary-keeping. We have very different levels of risk tolerance and different backgrounds and that has been hard to disentangle.

We live in a patriarchal society, and sometimes I feel like what I am doing is seen as "women's work" even from friends and family that are not misogynistic. The work I am doing is very hard, and it's very draining. And a lot of it is very small. So much of the work is the day-to-day operations of growing this thing, so that eventually, I won't have to do so much of the day-to-day operations. But I don't know that this work is always seen and valued in some of the patriarchal systems of which I am embedded in. Status and ego are part of it as well, of course. I'm very ready to be at the next stage of this, and there's a big ego part to that too. I don't want to be someone selling soap at markets anymore, you know? I want to have my own space, doing this change on a much bigger scale in a way that feels much bigger and more established than this small business that I'm creating and running.

ME: It feels like entrepreneurs get a weird mix of being glorified one moment, getting asked to speak at events and be interviewed, and doing the real invisible drudgery the next.

MICHAELA: Yeah, you're totally right. It is interesting. It feels like 90 percent of what I do is invisible. But there are also so many parts that are incredibly rewarding. So to get to the second part of your question: the best parts. It's hard to focus on just one. Before I started this business, my default was pessimism about our environment; pessimism and a bit of nihilism. I also felt way too responsible for all of it. And now, working in this business and encountering all of my customers, my KnoxFillers, I feel like, "Okay, a lot of us are doing our part, we're all working towards this shared goal," and it's given me a lot more hope that we will find our way out of this. That's been really nice. I've become more of a circularity optimist and more of an environmental optimist than I ever have been.

I also think the entrepreneurial community in Knoxville is really special. I never felt very rooted here until I started a business. I don't think I had a very developed community here. I felt like I was floating a bit. And then starting a business has helped me tap into the cool things a lot of people are doing around town. It feels like peeking under a rock seeing all of the worms and centipedes, and being like "What? This whole world is here?" That's what it felt like starting a business. "You guys are all doing all of this, and I had no freaking idea." So that's been really neat.

I also have really amazing customers. It feels weird to call them customers because that sounds very transactional, which part of it is, you know, but they are just really grateful and really loyal, and really kind. Customers give me home-brewed apple cider vinegar, or milk in a glass bottle that they found in a special grocery store that they knew I would like, so they bought it and brought it to me at a pop-up. Or, one customer's daughter who drew me a picture of the earth after she saw me upset on social media about the war in Ukraine. She asked her mom "What does she love?" and her mom said, "Well, she really loves the earth." And this little girl drew me a picture of the earth that hangs on the storeroom wall.

I just feel like I'm in the fight. And I didn't feel like that before. And I feel like I'm in the fight with other people. And that has been so beautiful, nourishing, and life-giving. And so, on days when I'm about to pull my hair out, because I spent four hours processing containers, then started another hour of doing inventory management, and then I have to go and figure out our market schedule and spend ten hours packing up and tearing down while building a mobile refillery and all those things, and am like "Man, I'm tired," I can come back to that core. These things don't level out, they're not equivalent, but I have to come back and be like, "Okay, let me just rest in this space for a little bit. Just snuggle in here." And that feels really, really nice.

ME: All right. So then my final question is, what advice would you give to new social entrepreneurs? What would you say to people who may not necessarily be doing the same thing as you, but that want to start a business that is making a positive impact on the world? What are some things you wish that you'd known earlier, or that you wish someone had said to you?

MICHAELA: You know, I think a lot of it you just have to do. I can give whatever advice that people could have given me, and did give to me, but you also have to honor that spark within you that's telling you to do this thing. And you're going to figure it out on the way. One thing I do wish, and this isn't really advice, it's more like a yearning, I wish I were doing this in partnership. Entrepreneurship on your own can be really lonely and it can be really hard during the times when you're like, "I really wish someone else could do some of these things." Right now I have to train and delegate and pay for help, and partnership would go a really long way.

Also, as I mentioned, I was not totally prepared for the ripples in my personal life. So you have to be ready for this and know that it can shake some things up. I've learned a lot about how important boundary-keeping is as an entrepreneur, and boundary-keeping with your spouse and family, and your time, and how to prepare yourself for that. You have to realize that not everyone's going to have your vision, and not everyone's going to have the confidence in your business that you have. And asking them to hold all of that confidence for you, isn't always where people are. On the flip side, sometimes you need other people to be the confidence-holders, so that you can have the space to have your own fears and concerns and worries and doubts. So that's the dance.

ME: Any final words you'd like to include? Or questions I should have asked?

MICHAELA: I'm in an intense moment right now. I think if we'd spoken three months ago or six months from now, the conversation would be very different. But one thing I've been thinking about is what makes any entrepreneur and what type of people are entrepreneurs? Because there are some people that just want to be entrepreneurs and that the "what" of what they're doing matters less than just being an entrepreneur. For me, entrepreneurship was the path to the most and quickest impact. Don't get me wrong, I'm not interested in having a boss other than myself right now, but I have been thinking about how being an entrepreneur for the sake of being an entrepreneur is different. You know there are people whose drive is to create and sell and create and sell. Versus me being like, "Okay, this is just the vessel and the vehicle for my larger life, mission, and purpose." And because of that, I think I've got to make my business work for me in a different way than maybe a serial entrepreneur would.

ME: That's an interesting point. I think there are probably more social entrepreneurs who fit into that category than other types of entrepreneurs.

MICHAELA: You're totally right. Which makes me think, what is it? How is this a different journey? Should there be different advice for this class of people versus others? Which is what's exciting about the thinking you are doing here.

ME: Well, thank you so much. This has been great.

MICHAELA: My pleasure.

Interview #4 with Tinia Pina

Founder of Re-Nuble, a startup that turns food waste into plant nutrients for indoor farms, located in Rochester, NY

The Re-Nuble company profile can be found on page 31.
Interview conducted on December 12, 2022.

ME: To start off, can you please tell me in a nutshell what your business does?

TINIA: Sure, Re-Nuble uses vegetative waste to create a platform of sustainable technologies for use in controlled environment agriculture. Essentially, we're focused on creating a positive financial and climate effect for indoor growers.

ME: Okay, let me restate that to make sure I understand. You take food waste, run it through a proprietary process which involves some fermentation, and turns the waste into plant nutrients or fertilizer that can be used in indoor farms, or hydroponic systems. Is that right?

TINIA: You're exactly right. So we can say plant nutrients or fertilizer. We also make grow media, which is an alternative for soil.

ME: Gotcha. Okay, cool. And then I think I saw that you also do closed nutrient systems for indoor agriculture?

TINIA: That's correct. That's not a major service for us right now, but we are working with one farm. The focus is on how to take different kinds of by-products—for example, fluid from a lagoon, or waste from a cidery—and help them close the loop for reincorporation either into value-added products for soil use or just within the food production system that they're already running. The reason we offer that service is that we've been in the industry for almost eight years now, and we've had a chance to see so many different technologies and processes to take one by-product and turn it into a different type of product and use or application. So, we don't have one specific type of system or process that Re-Nuble is trying to commercialize. It's more of a consultative approach.

ME: Ok, got it. And you said that's a pretty small piece of what you all are doing right now?

TINIA: That's correct.

ME: All right. Can you please tell me the story of how you started your business?

TINIA: Yeah, absolutely. I actually majored in information technology at Virginia Tech. So I didn't go to school for plant biology, or plant science, or anything along the agricultural spectrum. I took my undergraduate degree and worked in financial services within Ernst & Young, and at an investment management firm for about seven years. And during that time, I did a lot of pro bono volunteer work. I was involved in some urban farms, I was also a prep SAT teacher in Harlem after my nine-to-five. And during that time I really saw what the kids were bringing for lunch options and how that immediately impacted their attention levels, which ultimately impacted their ability to retain information. It comes down to nutrition and the type of food that we're eating. So the heavily processed foods, not the most nutritionally dense foods, are often found in areas that are food insecure, which was the case with that particular high school. With me being a vegetarian, I felt very aware of the drop-off in attention levels I witnessed. Or, for those fortunate enough to eat more nutritionally dense foods, the retained alertness, and ability to be at your optimal performance.

Around this time, I learned how much New York City was spending to deal with their food waste. In 2012, we were spending $77 million to export food waste to places like China, Pennsylvania, and Virginia because New York State didn't have the composting infrastructure to manage it at a local level.

So, when you look at those two very different problems, one is at the human level, and another is at a systems and structural level, I always felt like, well, if we could take the food waste, which there seems to be a growing abundance of, especially in urban or metropolitan areas, and use it as nutrients for more indoor farms? I felt even back then there was going to be a trend towards indoor farms because the efficiency of hydroponic or soilless systems is far higher than open field, and the need to have more locally produced and distributed food would continue to increase, especially with the trends of more densely populated urban areas. I always felt that to help those growers grow using either less chemically laden inputs or zero chemicals would have a huge impact.

As you probably know, compost has amazing benefits and amazing properties for soil. Why can't we recreate that for soilless, or hydroponic systems? The reason why that problem is so challenging is because in a hydroponic system, anytime you add something that's biologically rich, let's say fish fertilizer, which is great as a soil drench, or even with newer base fertilizers like bat guano in a hydroponic system, bacteria wants to immediately consume sugars and wants to compromise your air source. So it leads to a very disruptive, unpredictable, though natural environment, that doesn't see the same benefits that compost has for soil or open field or regenerative agriculture. So the focus has always been on replacing those nutrients with synthetic inputs, which are especially emissions-intensive inputs, in CEA or Controlled Environment Agriculture, specifically for greenhouses, vertical farms, and any controlled environment, which also includes hoop houses. So, I wanted to see if I could use this food waste stream to create replacements for some of those products. We were in R&D [research and development] for roughly seven years, so a large amount of time, because there wasn't really a precedent to work from. And that's what has helped me be really driven and focused on this problem.

ME: Awesome. Also, I'm curious, how did you initially become interested in food and agriculture? You mentioned that you were volunteering at an urban farm at an early point. In my experience, especially when I was living in New York, it felt like there tends to be a bit of a disconnect between food and the actual growing process, and how it comes into being, because agriculture is so removed from daily life in the city. I'm curious how you became interested in that?

TINIA: Yeah, you know, even back when I was in finance, I was volunteering for Red Hook Farms. I have always had this curiosity around it, and I've always had a green thumb, so naturally, I've had a desire to work with plants and enjoyed learning about biology. I didn't realize for a long time that that's where my heart and soul is—working with plants and food.

I've also always just had this voracious curiosity around—well, now we call it circularity, but there is this one theory called "urban metabolism;" it was the idea of achieving material balance in a discipline within engineering, looking at the inputs in a city and then balancing the outputs and trying to make it so that the usage and consumption of materials are balanced so that you're not offsetting inputs or the outputs, and more importantly, the emissions to sustain such an intensive system.[1]

That type of thinking always interested me. I was volunteering with a number of different organizations, from City Harvest, helping to distribute food, I mentioned the SAT prep program I was doing in Harlem, and then the urban farms; it all connected to food. I eventually realized that this is going to be my professional path. As someone who is a vegetarian and believes strongly in holistic medicine, my professional path became very much aligned with my personal path. And, I don't know how to say it, but when you're aligned, things kind of gratuitously fall into place for you.

ME: You see it all sort of connecting.

TINIA: Yeah, that's right.

ME: Will you walk me through how it went from this idea to forming an actual business? What were your steps there?

TINIA: I was still working full-time at first. I didn't leave New York until 2012, when I took the business idea and moved back home to reduce my cost of living and live with my family for a brief time. And then, even after I left my full-time job, I did a number of different gigs and hustling, including consulting on several different projects, and even dog walking. I always had some type of money coming in while we were still trying to figure out exactly what our focus was, developing a product, and making sure there was customer / market fit.

So, I was moonlighting, working on the business full-time, and literally working around the clock. And as I was doing that, I started pitching for these business plan competitions. I would pitch for $25,000 or $5,000 or $10,000, here and there just at the business idea level, and that allowed us to bring in the early money to get customer / market fit, along with doing an Indiegogo crowdfunding campaign. Those initial steps secured our ability to raise our first institutional money which was from SOS Ventures through the Food X Accelerator back in 2015.

The Indiegogo campaign helped us solidify customer / market fit, so then we focused on putting a business model around it and getting venture funded. There's a sizeable market around this, and there is a large unmet need for solving this problem. It's something that is a real problem, not a feature or a "nice-to-have." So, I felt that there was a good case for it to be venture-funded, and SOS Ventures confirmed that for us. From that point on, we largely bootstrapped our R&D, because there were still things about the product and the formulation and the science of it that we still needed to master.

I put in a fair amount of money myself in the form of debt, my savings, and some of my 401(k). We had a small round of family and friends funding, and then from then on, as we were able to raise money from others and made milestones showing that there were sizeable customers interested in paying for this, then we were able to raise more diluted money. At the same time, we were also raising non-dilutive [grants], so in total, we raised $600,00 from non-dilutive money and have raised in total $3 million in dilutive funding.

ME: Congratulations!

TINIA: Thanks, it's been a long hustle.

ME: When you were first starting up, did you have a co-founder, or did you have people you were collaborating with at an early stage?

TINIA: I did not. When we first started, it was me as a solo founder. It was really hard to find someone who was really 100 percent or more into this, and not driven by headlines. I had a number of different co-founder interviews, but it was just not a good alignment. So, that probably also contributed to how long it took us to get here. But I also feel that I avoided a lot of the common co-founder issues that can cause a company to fall apart.

ME: Yeah, totally. Bringing on the wrong person can cause all sorts of problems. My next question is around the business model, meaning, how are you making money, and from whom and where?

TINIA: Our facility is located in Rochester, New York, and we basically receive vegetative waste for free, and if not for free, for a very cheap price point. Food manufacturers and food processors often have waste that can't be easily or quickly given to a farm because of the logistics. Often a farmer is unable to meet them in time for them to move the waste outside of the processor's back of house. That's where we come in. We are often much closer to these food processors or manufacturers. We can pick it up, they pay for transportation, and we essentially turn it into a product and ultimately the value that we provide for them is reliable quick service as an offtaker. We're able to turn their waste into a value-elevated product intended for agricultural use and close the loop for them in a way that is often less emissions-intensive, because we're not as far away as a farm or composting facility.

So, we receive the vegetative waste and we turn it into two product types that we talked about earlier, plant nutrients and grow medium. Both products are consumables for indoor agriculture. We are a B2B2C model, so that means we sell to commercial farms, but we also sell to customers like ScottsMiracle-Gro, where they use a nutrient like ours, and it's sold within their indoor garden. That's our core focus, selling within the indoor gardening or indoor commercial growing space.

ME: Great. Okay, could you tell me a little bit about the social-environmental mission?

TINIA: The social and environmental mission for us is to be able to make zero or minimal carbon-footprint products or consumables for indoor growers using food waste, with zero or very little adverse impact to the environment. We do that by focusing on our entire process. We have less than 1 percent of actual waste that cannot be recycled or reclaimed. And when I say reclaimed, that also means for use in creating a product. A good example is water usage. All the water that we use comes from the municipal water line and is incorporated into our product. If there's any residual wastewater, for example, from the food waste itself, we reincorporate it through reverse osmosis. So our entire process is designed to have very little, if not zero, or negative emissions. And that's just through the manufacturing process. The reason I speak with vagueness around whether we're either zero, or minimal, or negative, is because we are currently conducting our own lifecycle assessment. We're very confident in our manufacturing, but now we need to look at our Scope 3 emissions impact from the transportation or bringing raw material to our place, and so on.

From a social side, especially given the fact that we've raised money from impact investors, we focus on ensuring that there are long-term, high-impact jobs being created from our work, with living wages in underserved areas.

There's so much more that I would love for us to be able to do. We're not at the stage yet to be able to do it all yet, but our company is a social enterprise. We're not profitable yet, but when we do hit that profitability milestone, we want to make sure that a percentage of our profits goes back to nonprofits that actually impact the kind of kids that I was teaching at one point, to help them understand how to grow food on their own and to make those behavioral decisions that will change their eating patterns and eating behavior so that they are eating more nutritious foods. And finally, providing on-the-ground education is part of our mission. We've helped nonprofits such as Teens for Food Justice and New York Sun Works engage youth in growing. That's something we can do right now, before we are profitable.

ME: And do the mission and monetary goals of your business ever conflict? I realize that the core business model is aligned with your mission, but when you think of things like making sure the manufacturing process is a sustainable process, or that you're paying living wages, things of that nature, have you had moments where you feel like the goals of mission and money conflict?

TINIA: I don't think so right now. So far, we have had ownership of our supply chain, production, and packaging of all of our products. In the future, when profitability is there, I can imagine it being a challenge to ensure that all of our investors on our cap table are aligned with our mission to drive back a percentage of our profits to nonprofits, and wanting to use impact as a marketing effort or campaign. It may be a challenge to make sure that our investors understand that we want to remain firm in that commitment.

ME: So my next question was going to be, how do you handle the situation when it arises? But it sounds like maybe it's not something you're dealing with yet?

TINIA: Yeah, I think the only other challenge we could speak to regarding that is a question we get asked often about the emissions from shipping our product. It's emissions-intensive to be shipping product from our single facility in Rochester. So we often get asked what our plan is to reduce that, especially as a green company that's focused on reducing the carbon footprint of the food supply chain. And the way we approach that is to explain that there are four other states we want to have a facility in: California, Texas, Florida, and Illinois. The goal behind that is to obviously reduce shipping costs and distribution costs, but also to ensure that that regional production model, or what we call distributed manufacturing, is being agile to the needs of the market, and also being really conscious of the emissions impact at that kind of regional level as well.

ME: So you think of it as necessary for making your business work at this point, but you have a plan to improve that in the future?

TINIA: Yeah, that's correct.

ME: So what is the biggest challenge you'd say you have faced in starting a business so far?

TINIA: Maybe you can agree with this also, but food waste wasn't popular until there was a headline about food waste being a $3 trillion opportunity. And before that point, at a time when food was very cheap, I'd be in meetings with some investors, and one in particular that was like, "You know, why don't you just buy the food from supermarkets and use that as your raw material?" So education was the biggest challenge. And now others have done the work to help the market realize that there are a lot more solutions that aren't just software-based or an app to help make efficiencies greater in food waste handling and recovery and all that. But even so, I think the biggest challenge may still be showing that. Not just for Re-Nuble, but hopefully for others too. For other companies that are taking a waste stream and turning it into a product, that there will be more investors willing to invest in those types of business models, and not just software, because there may be more risk in those opportunities, but also a larger opportunity. So, I hope that we can show that this is viable and scalable, just as much as software. But that still remains to be proven.

ME: What about on the personal side of being an entrepreneur? From your story it's clear that you've put a lot of personal assets and time into the business. And that's not an easy thing. From the personal side, through the lens of talking to other up and coming social entrepreneurs, what would you say has been the most difficult part? Anything that you didn't anticipate to be so difficult?

TINIA: Yeah, I think a lot of people in this space need to put up a higher bar in terms of who they work with, because there's just so much noise out there, and you really have to be discerning of people's intentions. And so for me, I really go with my gut often, and that helps me understand, is this person speaking with me with the right intentions? Do they want to be on the team for the long-term? Re-Nuble was never really positioned as something that would be a quick flip— I'm not trying to quickly exit this company. And so, I'd really encourage people to talk about what they're doing early, as soon as they have a really clear idea of what they're doing and who they're serving in their product, and then to really be open to everyone's feedback and to what they want to share with you. But at the end of the day, you really need to check in with yourself and be discerning because not everyone's energy is deserving of yours.

ME: Yeah, definitely. Okay, for a more fun question, what is the most rewarding part of starting and running your own business?

TINIA: I think it's being able to help other people realize that they can do this too—it's within their reach—and seeing that kind of realization on their face. Being able to contribute to that inspiration, whether it's a milestone of writing and publishing your own book, or starting a company, young people often don't have that tangible example. They may see it on TV or read it in a book or something, but I think showing that the model can be relatable or that the thing they also want to do can be very attainable, is what is really rewarding to me. So I try to mentor a lot, as much as possible, so that people can see that they can also do this.

ME: Okay, so one final question. Do you have any other advice you would give to new social entrepreneurs?

TINIA: As I mentioned earlier, be sure to talk to as many people as possible. And also always be thinking of the cheapest, easiest, and quickest way for you to reach that prototype, or reach whatever indicator is going to help you know that it's even worth your time to pursue this new business idea. I think a lot of people develop a business in an echo chamber, and they put all these resources in and then, it's not too late, but it's much later than it ever should have gotten to before you realize you're on the wrong track. We need to hear that raw feedback sooner and more quickly and cheaply. Create that raw, crazy-looking prototype in order to get that confirmation sooner, while you still have a full-time job.

ME: Right, find out if you're actually onto something. And would you have any different advice for social entrepreneurs as opposed to other kinds of entrepreneurs?

TINIA: I think the point about the MVP [minimum viable product] is especially relevant for social entrepreneurs, but also, there are a lot of "me toos," and I think because everyone's trying to focus on the same large mission, it's important to partner with others and provide a unique service or product to a niche. I see that there are a lot of redundancies, especially on the social entrepreneurship and nonprofit side. And it's really hard, especially in a very noisy environment, to be differentiated. And the more you can have a differentiated brand, the easier it is for you to sell and find your audience and find your customers. I would really prioritize that first.

ME: Differentiation and partnering where you can.

TINIA: That's right.

ME: All right. Well, thank you so much for taking the time, I really appreciate it.

Insights from Successful Social Enterprises

While speaking to and learning about dozens of social entrepreneurs and their unique strategies, approaches, and lessons learned, there are a few learnings that stood out. Below are eight trends from successful social entrepreneurs to help you on your way.

- *Test before you build.* Test your idea before jumping all in. The founders of KnoxFill, White Dog Cafe, and New Belgium Brewery all started their businesses out of their homes; Patagonia started out of the back of a car ... you get the idea. All of these businesses started slowly, testing their ideas and expanding as their businesses generated the income to do so. Identify the core questions that will make or break your business, and then find ways to test them while you still have the nimbleness and flexibility to pivot and iterate if needed.

- *Pivot on your product, pivot on your business model, but don't pivot on your mission.* Successful entrepreneurs know that their initial hunch about their product, their market, or their business model may be incorrect. Once you run tests on your product, learn more about your customers, or run a pilot with your business model, you may learn that you got a lot of things wrong on the first try. Customers may not interact with the product in the way that you thought they would or want to pay for it through the model you designed. That's okay. Every pivot gets you closer to finding product / market fit and designing a successful business. Successful entrepreneurs take these temporary setbacks in stride and see them as learning opportunities rather than failures. What you should not pivot on, however, is your mission. If you lose track of the reason you are doing this in the first place, or try to shape your mission to fit the product you have developed, it can be easy to get lost or even give up. Entrepreneurship is hard. If you take away your source of fuel (your mission) that keeps you at it when the going gets tough, you may also take away your best chance of success.

Take a look at the business TruePani, profiled on page 53. Their mission was to provide clean drinking water to those that needed it. They started out with a physical product that would kill microbes in drinking water in India. After testing, running pilots, learning more about their customers and market, they eventually landed on a service business model (rather than a product) to test for lead and remediate water systems in the United States. Their business offering and market completely changed, but their mission remains intact.

- *Build multiple income streams into your business.* Many of the most successful social enterprises operate with complex business models. If you study the business model sketches of the businesses profiled in this book, you'll notice that many of them have multiple arrows labeled with dollar signs pointing back to their business. Don't be content with figuring out one element of your business that can generate income. How else can you monetize the core value you are creating?

- *Partner with competitors.* The successful social enterprise looks for win/wins. They find ways to partner with would-be competitors, provide benefit, and profit from the partnership. Look at the way thredUP (profile on page 108) is partnering with large clothes retailers to provide a platform for customers to purchase secondhand items from a specific brand; Greyston Bakery consults with other businesses to help them develop their own inclusive hiring models.

- *Sometimes the mission comes later.* If you currently run a business that you don't consider to be a social enterprise, but you are interested in implementing some of the impact strategies outlined in this book, don't worry—you didn't miss the boat. It's never too late to integrate social and environmental impact into a business. In fact, many companies that are viewed as leaders in this space, such as Ben & Jerry's, Interface, and thredUP, integrated their social and environmental mission into their business after being in operation for many years. The tricky thing is that it can be harder to shift your brand and messaging to integrate your mission when you're already a ways down the road as a business. On the other hand, if you already have revenue, it can be easier to implement and self-fund some of your mission-oriented initiatives to get them off the ground.

- *Everything takes longer than you think it will.* This is really one of those irritating facts about life in general, not just entrepreneurship, but it holds true for entrepreneurship as well (fun fact: this is also true for writing a book!). Whether it's technology development, getting regulatory approvals, closing a fundraising round, or path to profitability, you can bet that it will end up taking a lot longer than it feels like it should. When that happens, remember that this is true for almost everyone, no matter how qualified or successful they are, and that just because it hasn't happened in the time period you think that it should, it doesn't mean that it *won't* happen.

- *Build a community and brain trust.* Being an entrepreneur, especially as a solo founder, can be a lonely expedition. Even when you start to build a team around you, there is still a limit to how much you may feel like you can confide in and get advice from your colleagues. How do you tell your employees that sometimes you feel like *you have no idea what you're doing*? As Kristal Hansley pointed out in her interview on page 249, it's important to build or tap into a community of other entrepreneurs and/or people in your industry. Whether you do this through a co-working space, your local entrepreneur center, or other industry-focused networking platforms, a community to commiserate with and bounce ideas off of can be very powerful and helpful to you as an entrepreneur.

- *No one agrees on everything—especially not anything that matters.* As mentioned throughout this book, it's important to seek input, find facts, and test your ideas by talking to others. However, remember that every important idea has had a multitude of both supporters and doubters. So seek facts, seek information and feedback, but remember to treat each conversation as what it is—*one person's opinion*, or one data point. Also keep in mind that some people's opinions are more important than others. The opinion of the CEO at a battery manufacturing facility that you imagine to be a prime potential customer of your business should hold much more weight than your Uncle Charles' opinion, no matter how enthusiastic or dismissive it may be.

20

Opportunities Unique to Social Enterprise

Now that you are nearing the end of the book, there's a chance you may feel a bit overwhelmed. There's no need to sugarcoat it—starting a social enterprise is *hard*. There are so many aspects to consider, from finances, to sourcing, to pricing, to the impact of your business on your community, and even on your own life.

But, that said, I also want to leave you with a reminder that challenging the status quo, finding a way to shape the world in a more positive way, while also making a profitable business, is essential for the future of our world. If you are taking part in this effort, you are acting as an architect of the future, and your work is essential. And while creating a social enterprise can be difficult, it is very, very possible. And not only is it possible, you are also joining this effort at an ideal time. More and more, the world is beginning to understand the need for mission-driven business, and there is more demand today, more resources, and more opportunities for social enterprises than ever before. So let's talk about what some of those opportunities are and how to ride that wave.

Social Enterprise Performance

Many business leaders assume that pursuing ESG (Environmental, Social, and Governance) goals means compromising on financial performance. However, recent studies have found the opposite to be true. Research accumulated by McKinsey found that startups with a strong

ESG proposition correlated with higher equity returns and lower risk for investors and shareholders because of lower loan and credit defaults and higher credit ratings.[1] Investors are noticing these trends. 56 percent of asset managers in North America already use an ESG risk factor framework, and 61 percent offer impact investing strategies; in Europe, these numbers increase to 73 percent and 70 percent, respectively.[2]

At first, it may seem counterintuitive that businesses with a strong positive environmental and social impact would outperform other companies. That is because this intuition is based on the deeply ingrained myth that mission and profit can't go together. We still associate a social mission with nonprofit organizations, which by definition are not focused on profit. However, this myth has not been true for a long time, if it ever was. So why exactly do social enterprises have the potential to outperform other businesses? Ideally, impact metrics will coincide with financial metrics in the following ways:

- Top-line growth: Companies with a strong ESG proposition have the potential to reach a broader base of customers and improve customer loyalty. 62 percent of customers report that they expect companies to take a stand on social and environmental issues; 47 percent stated that they would be willing to walk away from a company that failed to do so.[3]

- Cost reduction: Efficiency and environmental stewardship often go hand in hand. Improved environmental practices, such as decreased energy and water use, result in lower costs. Less waste can result in fewer fees and disposal expenses.

- Regulatory and legal interventions: Improving certain environmental metrics can help companies to access government subsidies or get ahead of government regulations.

- Productivity uplift: A strong social and environmental mission can increase employee productivity and loyalty and give morale a boost. As millennials age, it is becoming more and more common for workers to look for fulfillment in their work and search for positions where they can make a positive social and environmental impact. The Huffington Post reported that 94 percent of millennials are interested in using their skills to make a positive impact in the world.[4]

- The long view: Better social and environmental practices often align with long-term planning, thoughtful investment, and asset optimization.

These business trends are not going unnoticed. The 2020 Global Human Capital Trends survey by Deloitte polled almost 9,000 business and HR leaders around the world; 50 percent of respondents reported that their organization's purpose was "broadening extensively to include all stakeholders, including the communities they serve and society at large." In the 2019 survey, 56 percent of respondents expected social enterprise to be more important to their organization in three years' time than it is today. The report went on to describe the social enterprise as "a profound shift facing business leaders worldwide."[5] So when you're looking enviously at those large, established companies that seem to have it so easy, remember that those companies are also looking at you, and trying to learn from the new wave of social enterprises that are changing business.

Funding

Okay, so impact-driven business may sound like a great idea, but how do we actually get these operations off the ground? Often (although not always), starting a business requires outside funding, particularly if the business is capital-intensive, meaning that it needs a lot of money, equipment, or other investment to begin, or if it requires a lot of scientific research and development before actually getting to a product.

There are some ways in which social enterprises are more difficult to fund than other kinds of businesses, particularly if the expected financial returns are not initially as high as their traditional business counterparts (although, as discussed in the last section, this is not necessarily the case); however, there are also a whole suite of other funding opportunities that are available to social enterprises that are not an option for standard businesses. More opportunities are popping up all the time as financial institutions realize the benefits of impact investing and nonprofits and government entities recognize the benefits of making socially driven investments rather than traditional grants. To begin, let's take a look at the different kinds of funding options that are available to businesses and where there are some unique opportunities specifically for social enterprises:

Bootstrapping

While not technically a form of fundraising, bootstrapping is important to mention because businesses don't *have* to raise outside capital, and if forgoing fundraising is an option for a startup, that can often be the best strategic play for a business. "Bootstrapping" is a term used to refer to a business that grows organically rather than taking outside money. If a business has the capacity to self-fund and grow slowly (perhaps while a founder works at another job) and gradually build revenue, this can be an effective business strategy. Companies that bootstrap retain full ownership of their business, have the freedom to pivot and make strategic business decisions with fewer outside stakeholders involved, and can remain debt-free.

Businesses that are most suited for bootstrapping are those that are not capital-intensive (meaning that they don't require expensive equipment, buildings, or land), and are able to begin producing a product or service soon and can begin earning revenue quickly. Companies that bootstrap may not grow as quickly as those that take on outside capital, but they may also have the advantage of growing more strategically, because they are able to move slowly, testing and making pivots as they expand.

Grants

Grants are most commonly thought of as resources for nonprofit organizations, but businesses can access grants, too, and there are an even greater number of grant opportunities available to social enterprises. Unlike grants for nonprofits, which can sometimes be used to support ongoing operations, grants for businesses are generally intended to fill a specific gap that will help a business to grow or reach financial sustainability more quickly. Common grants for businesses offer funding for purposes such as:

- **Research and development (R&D):** As mentioned previously, companies working in advanced technology often require long periods of research and development before they have a product that is anywhere close to ready for the market. SBIR (Small Business Innovation and Research) and STTR (Small Business Technology Transfer) grants are offered by government agencies such as the National Science Foundation (NSF), the National Institutes of Health (NIH), and the United States Department of Agriculture (USDA) for businesses to complete technical or scientific research. Some agencies offer funding for very specific research initiatives while others fund more broadly.

- **Equipment purchases:** Another thing that businesses can sometimes access grant funding for is equipment purchases that will allow a business to operate more efficiently or sustainably, serve new markets, or significantly increase revenue.

- **Technical assistance:** Some nonprofits and government agencies will provide funding to businesses for specific training or technical assistance, such as the Small Business Administration's 7(j) Management and Technical Assistance program, which provides technical assistance to help businesses compete for state and federal contracts, or the USDA Value-Added Producer Grants available to farmers to produce and market value-added products to increase income (such as making berries into jam or milk into cheese).

- **New sustainability initiatives or practices:** Finally, businesses can sometimes receive grant funding to help support the implementation of new equipment or practices that will improve a business's environmental footprint. For example, the USDA Rural Energy for America Program provides loans and grants to rural small businesses and agricultural producers for renewable energy systems and energy efficiency improvements.[6] Similarly, the EPA provides Pollution Prevention grants to help businesses reduce pollution.[7]

In addition to the direct grant opportunities described above, governments also provide funding to nonprofits and small business support organizations with the goal of providing services and funding directly to business, so keep an eye out for local opportunities in your area or industry. A lot of these opportunities come through business plan or pitch competitions. While these may feel like a waste of time when you have a business to build, pitching can be a valuable skill; a strong pitch can open a lot of doors to you, not to mention prizes, grants, and exposure. Re-Nuble (company profile on page 31 and interview on page 278) used money from pitch competitions to fund initial operations and take the company to the point where it could secure venture capital funding.

And finally, there are many nonprofit organizations and accelerators that provide funding and resources specifically to startups working in social entrepreneurship or cleantech (see the section on support organizations below). The Social Enterprise Alliance, a network that supports social entrepreneurs around the world, offers a database of funding opportunities for social enterprises to its members.[8]

Loans

Loans are another common type of funding available to social enterprises. While grants may be considered "free money" (if you don't count the amount of time and energy spent completing grant deliverables and reporting), loans represent borrowed money that a business is permitted to use for a certain amount of time with the expectation that they will leverage that funding into enough additional revenue to repay the loan, plus interest.

- **Loans for those that fall through the cracks:** When you think of loans, you probably think of banks. But, while banks certainly make loans to businesses, it can often be more difficult for small, early-stage startups to acquire loans from a bank. To receive debt funding from a traditional source like a bank, you generally need to be able to show substantial revenue, have an exceptionally strong business plan with letters of commitment from customers, or have significant assets to leverage, like land, buildings, or equipment. Luckily, this is a known gap, and there are entities and government programs that are working to develop offerings to help small businesses and early-stage startups acquire loans. The Small Business Administration (SBA) offers programs to sometimes guarantee loans, meaning that if the borrower defaults on the loan, the SBA will assume the debt—this effectively decreases the risk for lenders and makes them more willing to work with borrowers they might have ordinarily turned down.[9] The SBA doesn't offer this service to all lenders; they have a database of approved lenders and will match borrowers with lenders that may be a fit for them through the lender match portal offered on the SBA website.[10]

There are also funders, such as the B:Side Fund, whose mission is to lend to small businesses that may ordinarily fall into the lending gap I described. The government also provides funding to businesses via mission-driven, private-sector financial intermediaries called Community Development Financial Institutions (CDFIs) located throughout the country that focus on community development. CDFIs are often willing to take on loans that traditional lenders would not, and they will generally offer more affordable rates.[11] Some CDFIs, such as the Mountain Association, located in Berea, Kentucky, also offer business support and consulting alongside funding.[12]

- **Impact lending:** Finally, there are some organizations that specifically make loans to empower social enterprises. GroFin, located in the African country of Mauritius, is an impact-driven fund that provides loans specifically to Small and Mid-Size Enterprises (SMEs) that have the potential to create sustainable jobs.[13] Invest Appalachia is a social impact fund that provides a combination of loans, investments, and grants to organizations working across Central Appalachia in community health, clean energy, creative placemaking, and food and agriculture.[14] RSF Social Finance offers a platform for individual investors to operate as a collective and provide loans to social enterprises.[15] See the section on crowdfunding in this chapter for other loan and investment structures designed with a similar mission.

Equity investment

Another common form of funding for startups is equity investment. Unlike a loan, a startup is not required to pay back the funding they receive through an equity investment. Instead, an investor receives an ownership stake in a company's equity, meaning that the investor will own a piece of the company and will receive a percentage of the money generated when a company is eventually acquired or goes public. An equity investment is a gamble for an investor, because they may never see their money back, but these investments have the potential to generate a future payoff that is much larger than the return a funder would see on a loan.

For a startup, there are pluses and minuses to equity investment. The major plus, of course, is that a startup will receive funds to help get their business off the ground and won't have to worry about regular debt payments. The downside of equity investment is that entrepreneurs may lose some control over their company, may decrease their own ownership stake, and can sometimes lose decision-making power, particularly if investors take a seat on the board. In certain cases, investors can even boot a CEO out if they don't think he or she is steering the business in a good direction. However, on the flip side of this, another benefit of bringing on equity investors (in addition to money) is that you have a group of people committed to the success of your company, with skin in the game. If you choose your investors carefully, this support can be a powerful thing. "Strategic investor" is a term used to describe an investor that brings more than money to the table, such as industry connections, resources, and strategic guidance.

Equity investment is usually categorized in stages that align with the size of the investment, the stage of the company, and the type of investor, although there are no hard lines delineating the different stages:

- Friends and Family: Early-stage funding raised from a founder's friends and family

- Angel Funding: Funding from high net worth individual investors, usually at an early stage. These can be one-time investments or periodic investments over time as part of future funding rounds.

- Venture Capital: Venture capital (VC) firms invest in companies at a range of stages, from very early (called a pre-seed or seed investment) to later stage expansions (called Series A, B,

C, D . . . and so on). Funding rounds usually increase in size as the letters go on. Companies are expected to advance in stage and profitability in each round. Different venture capital firms usually specialize in particular industries and stages.

Impact investing

Impact investing is a form of investment that seeks to earn a financial return by making a positive social or environmental impact in the world. Impact investing can be found throughout the full spectrum of investment types, from your 401(k) to startup venture funding. In this section, we'll be talking about impact investing as an opportunity for entrepreneurs.

While still relatively new, the field of impact investing is growing rapidly. In 2020, a study found that one-third of professionally managed assets in the United States were being invested in socially responsible investments.[16] Impact investing can be a good funding opportunity for social enterprises looking to raise debt or equity investment. Some common questions about impact investing include:

- *What do impact investors look for?* Although every investor has their own investment strategy, in a nutshell, impact investors look for four primary things:

  - A financial return: You might expect this to come lower on the list for impact investors, but impact investors are generally still looking for a financial return just as much as any other investor is; impact investors just have other factors they consider as well. No matter how compelling an entrepreneur's impact story is, they still must have a strong business case to attract the attention of an impact investor.

  - A social or environmental impact: As mentioned previously, impact investors want their money to do *more* than just generate a financial return; they also want to fund something that will make a positive impact in the world. Investors judge and define impact in different ways, but many use an impact framework like the ones described in the Measuring Impact chapter on page 241.

○ <u>A founding team they believe in</u>: When an investor decides whether or not to invest in a company, one of the things they look most closely at is the team. Can the team pull it off? Will they stick with it? Can they do what they say they will? And finally, do I want to work with them? An investor–investee relationship is a partnership, not a transaction, and both sides should carefully consider whether they would like working together.

○ <u>A company operating in their wheelhouse</u>: Finally, as I mentioned previously in this chapter, investors usually have a particular stage and type of company they prefer to work with and are most familiar with. This is also true for impact investors. In addition to company stage and preferred industries, impact investors may have specific areas of impact they are most interested in, such as public health, climate change mitigation, or poverty alleviation.

• *Do impact investors offer better terms than traditional investors?* Not necessarily. As I mentioned previously, impact investors are often looking for just as much of a return as any other investor and may offer very similar investment terms. However, this is certainly not a hard rule. Some impact investors will make a concentrated effort to offer business-friendly terms—some funders such as Common Future exist entirely for this purpose.[17] Some impact investors will also be open to more creative forms of investment, such as revenue sharing.

• *Who are impact investors?* Impact investors don't fit neatly into a nice little box. They are an incredibly diverse group. From individual angel investors to corporate investment arms to venture capital firms, impact investors exist all along the investment spectrum. Even nonprofits are getting into the game. Nonprofits such as the Surdna Foundation, the Bill and Melinda Gates Foundation, and the Nature Conservancy all have their own impact investing arm.

• *Where do you find impact investors?* Finding an investor that is the right fit for you can be a challenge. You can find lists of impact investors in networks such as the Global Impact Investing Network (GIIN), but, as with anything, a warm introduction or a personal connection always works best. Attending social enterprise or impact investing conferences can be a good strategy, as can joining networks such as the Social Enterprise Alliance. Participating in accelerator programs, incubators, or pitch competitions (described in more detail in the Supporting Organizations section) can also be a good opportunity to get exposure and warm introductions.

Crowdfunding

Finally, another avenue for social entrepreneurs to raise funds that can't be ignored is crowdfunding. Crowdfunding is a way to fund a company or project through lots of small investments from different contributors. Software platforms such as Kickstarter and Indiegogo have made this form of fundraising both more possible and more well-known.

Kickstarter and Indiegogo are basically a means of pre-ordering a product to help pay the entrepreneur to develop it. Depending on the offering, there are usually different levels of contributions a customer can make and different associated benefits provided by the creator. The platforms not only enable entrepreneurs to have essential startup up cash to develop a product, but they also allow the customer to be part of the development process. Of course, with any kind of investment, sometimes the project goes south and the customer never receives the end product, so the backer has to know they're entering into a bit of a gamble as an early supporter.

As with any type of fundraising, there are some things to be cautious of with these kinds of platforms from the entrepreneur side as well. Since a product is generally in prototype phase when it gets funded, this means that an entrepreneur may misjudge how long the product development is going to take (thus resulting in an angry customer base), or misjudge how much money the product development and small-scale manufacturing will cost and undercharge their backers, meaning that the creator may actually end up in the red after fulfilling their crowdfunded orders. Finally, if you're not a company making some sort of innovative B2C product or art piece, crowdfunding platforms like Kickstarter and Indiegogo might not serve you well.

Fortunately, there are other platforms that have figured out different ways of utilizing crowdfunding and peer-to-peer funding to support entrepreneurs. WeFunder, for example, is an "equity crowdfunding" platform that allows individuals to make small equity investments, as low as $100, into a startup. Ordinarily, if a startup were going to accept thousands of equity investments of $100, keeping up with these investments and ownership stakes would be a complete nightmare. But WeFunder's platform offers the service of organizing these many small investments into one line on an entrepreneur's cap table.[18] WeFunder touts that it supports everything from coffee shops to flying cars, and it has enabled startups to collectively raise $567 million on their platform as of 2022.[19]

There are other crowdfunding platforms that have been created with a social mission or designed specifically to benefit social entrepreneurs. Raise Green operates similarly to WeFunder, but it is specifically geared toward climate tech startups and clean energy developers.[20] Kiva is a platform well-known for providing zero percent interest, peer-to-peer, small loans (or "microloans") to entrepreneurs. Although you may think primarily of small international companies when you hear of Kiva, the platform can also be used by entrepreneurs based in the United States to access zero percent interest loans of up to $15,000.[21] StartSomeGood is a crowdfunding platform that provides project, recurring, and debt financing to social enterprises. Other crowdfunding sites such as GoFundMe and Fundly are designed to be used as fundraising platforms for individuals and nonprofits.

Support Organizations

If you are currently a social entrepreneur, or aspiring to be one, you're in luck. This is a good time to be in the impact business. In addition to all the opportunities described in this chapter so far, there are dozens of organizations, accelerators, competitions, and fellowships whose entire purpose is to support, fund, and mentor social enterprises and to help them refine their business strategy and better navigate the multitude of opportunities and resources that exist in the world. While I won't attempt to list them all here, I'll name enough to get you started and to give an example of the kind of resources that are out there.

The organization Ashoka offers fellowships including living stipends for social entrepreneurs for up to three years to enable them to focus on building their business.[22] Echoing Green provides a similar offering over eighteen months. Accelerators like Flywheel in Cincinnati offer business coaching, resources, and sometimes funding for social entrepreneurs.

For science and tech-based innovators, Innovation Crossroads and Activate.org offer business coaching, living stipends, and opportunities to collaborate with national labs across the country. For cleantech and climatetech innovators, there are organizations such as the Urban Future Lab in Brooklyn, New York, Cleantech Open across the country, the Spark Cleantech Accelerator and Incubator in Knoxville, Tennessee, Greentown Labs in Boston, Massachusetts, and Houston, Texas, and LACI in Los Angeles, California, that provide a variety of resources, such as business coaching, mentorship, connections, and exposure, as well as funding or stipends, and lab or work space.

For agtech and food innovations, AgLaunch offers business coaching, mentorships, and guided on-farm trials. The Yield Lab and Thrive provide accelerator services and investment. Competitions like Grow-NY and the American Farm Bureau Ag Innovation Challenge provide funding and exposure for new ag innovations.

No matter what industry you are focused on, or where you are located, there are dozens of entrepreneurial support programs, accelerators, and mentorship programs to help startups find their way. As the world recognizes the need for social innovators and entrepreneurs, more and more support organizations are springing up. While these programs are a great opportunity to broaden your network and get connected to funding, resources, and advice, entrepreneurs must also be conscious of the amount of time and energy they commit to accelerators and competitions. With so many opportunities available, it can be tempting to jump from program to program without ever standing on your own as a business. However, these offerings are generally most effective if they are treated as a springboard to get your business off the ground, or as an extra burst of energy, insight, and resources to get you through a tight spot. Founders should also keep in mind that not all accelerator and fellowship programs are created equal. Entrepreneurs should do their due diligence on a program before joining, particularly if they are committing substantial amounts of time, energy, money, or equity to participate.

21

Eight Industries Ripe for
Social Innovation

If you started reading this book with an interest in social enterprise but no existing business or business plan, never fear! There are plenty of problems to go around and profitable solutions to be found for those bold and creative enough to build them. In this chapter, I highlight eight industries that are particularly ripe for social innovation. By ripe, I mean that there are pressing, unsolved problems, and businesses waiting to be built. For each industry, I will also provide some examples of companies working in this space that new innovators can learn from.

Opportunity #1: Circular Economy

As I've mentioned several times in this book, the world is naturally a circular system. In natural systems, nutrients and resources are continuously cycled to be used again and again so that populations and ecosystems can sustain over generations. Our human-made systems, on the other hand, have been built on a linear path. This means that resources are extracted from the earth, used, eaten, made into consumer goods, and then thrown into the trash and into the landfill, where the usable nutrients, minerals, and materials proceed to sit untouched for generations.

While there were still plenty of virgin resources to go around, this linear system wasn't that pressing of a problem. However, now that our population has officially reached eight billion people, and everything from fuel to fertilizer to clean water has become more scarce and costly, we've got to start thinking of some alternative solutions and systems. There are three primary approaches that businesses interested in this problem can take:

1. <u>Waste reduction</u>: Companies in this category find ways to iterate on current products and systems to decrease the amount of waste produced to begin with. Depending on the business, they could earn income by saving companies money through material and waste reduction, or by depending on environmentally conscious businesses or individuals to pay more for a low-waste product. Examples of companies working on waste reduction include KnoxFill (profile on page 152), which helps to eliminate packaging on common household products, and Searo, a startup that is attempting to replace plastic with seaweed.

2. <u>Waste Mining</u>: I call this one "waste mining" because waste streams are indeed veritable mines of valuable materials and resources that are not being captured. Startups in this camp find innovative ways to extract value from existing waste streams or to divert these waste streams from the landfill to capture materials that they can recycle or resell for profit. Examples of companies in this category include thredUP (profile on page 108), which collects and resells used clothing; Phinite (profile on page 79) and Re-Nuble (profile on page 31), which both capture nutrients in waste streams and make them into fertilizer; and Revivn (profile on page 205), which collects and refurbishes used electronics.

3. <u>Circular Business</u>: While the first two categories focus on helping existing businesses or systems develop circular waste management, the third category involves developing a new closed-loop business. This means creating a new product or service (or replacing an existing one) in a way that is designed from the beginning to be a closed loop. An example of a company in this category would be Interface (profile on page 93), which creates and sells carpet and has a system built into their business model for collecting and recycling used carpet.

Opportunity #2: Agriculture

Once again, the issue of our growing population, now boasting over eight billion people, crops up. With this many mouths to feed, it's important that we produce food more efficiently than ever. However, we've got a few things working against us. Industrial agriculture, which has helped us grow food on a massive scale and meet the needs of our growing population, is now starting to catch up to us. Practices such as intensive tilling, monocropping, heavy use of synthetic fertilizer and pesticides, and soil compaction (due to heavy equipment) have had the unintended result of making soil less healthy and productive. On top of that, climate change is making weather patterns more unpredictable, with massive storms, droughts, and heat waves adding to the difficulties farmers must contend with. Maybe unsurprisingly, after thinking about all that, farmers are also aging as a population with fewer young people entering the industry. In 2019, the US Census of Agriculture found the average age of the American farmer to be 57.5 years old.[1] Labor shortages on farms are another pressing problem farmers face today.

The thing about agriculture is that these problems must be figured out, since we won't be moving on from food any time soon. I'm not the only one to notice these problems. Investment in agtech is booming. Between the last quarter of 2020 and the first quarter of 2022, agtech fundraising has seen year-over-year growth of 45.9 percent.[2] Some key business opportunities in agriculture can be found in the following categories:

1. Increasing on-farm efficiency: Businesses that fall in this category would be any kind of product or service that would help a farm to get greater output with fewer inputs. One example of a business in this category is a drone company called Rantizo. Rantizo is a "precision ag" company that uses drones to spray crops, which can result in increased precision, less waste and runoff, and improved efficiency.

2. Value Chain: Startups serving the agricultural value chain may refer to anything along the agricultural supply chain, from inputs like seeds and fertilizers to processing and delivering food

products. It became particularly apparent during the pandemic that our agricultural supply chain is vulnerable and that we need to develop new products and services to strengthen it. Companies working to address problems in this category include Secure Food Solutions, a startup that is developing rapid microbial tests to more quickly detect dangerous pathogens in food processing facilities.[3] Good'R is a company that uses advanced logistics and tech solutions to streamline food waste management and get food that would otherwise be wasted to people that need it.[4] Re-Nuble (profile on page 31) would also fit into this category by capturing food waste and turning it into plant nutrients for indoor farms.[5]

3. <u>Regenerative Agriculture:</u> Regenerative agriculture is a suite of agricultural practices that serves to regenerate soil rather than deplete it over time. If implemented successfully, regenerative agricultural practices can lead to healthier, more productive soil with fewer agricultural inputs needed. Technologies, services, and practices that help enable regenerative agriculture are companies that would fall in this category. Phinite (profile on page 79) produces regenerative fertilizer made from animal waste.[6] Another example of a company in this field (pun intended) is Nori, a carbon removal marketplace that allows businesses to purchase carbon credits or carbon offsets by paying farmers to adopt regenerative agricultural practices that sequester carbon. As of 2022, Nori states that they have removed 123,000 metric tons of carbon from the atmosphere and paid $1.8 million to farmers.[7]

Opportunity #3: The Sharing Economy

We live in a culture where individual ownership is the norm. While sharing resources is still common in some communities and parts of the world, in most industrialized nations individual ownership is the default. If we want something, our first instinct is generally to buy it, not to see if we can borrow it. However, how many things do you own that go unutilized for most of the year? In my household we have two electric saws and numerous tools in the basement that only see action a handful of times a year, two cars rarely used at the same time, and a number of dresses purchased for special occasions that hang accumulating dust in the closet. I know I'm not alone in these somewhat shameful confessions, but the proper business models and infrastructure have not yet been developed on a wide enough scale to make sharing resources easy, efficient, and worry-free.

The "sharing economy" is a term used to describe businesses that facilitate the easy sharing of products and resources. This is still a rising industry, and unfortunately, the companies that have been most successful in it have ballooned out of the original vision. Airbnb and Uber both originated within the sharing economy model, allowing people to rent unused rooms in their homes and offer rides to others in their personal cars for a fee. Today, many lodgings offered on Airbnb have been purchased and maintained for the sole purpose of renting them on Airbnb, and as many Uber cars are driven specifically for the purpose of providing rides via the app, the platform has most likely resulted in an increased number of vehicles on the road rather than a decrease. Still, these two popular apps have contributed in at least one significant way to the sharing economy: they have proven that it can work. In the infancy of these two companies, people were skeptical that customers would ever be trusting enough to stay in a stranger's house or enter an unknown car. However, the success and popularity of these two businesses have certainly proven otherwise.

Companies that operate in the sharing economy exist in two general buckets:

1. Resource owners: Companies in this boat own resources that they make available for shared use (for a fee, of course). Think of makerspaces, for example: places that have expensive tools like metal- and woodworking equipment, and 3D printers, and let artisans and creatives use them for the cost of a day pass or membership fee. Another example of a business in this category is Lime, a company that offers a fleet of electric scooters and bicycles that can be driven within a city on a pay-per-ride basis.

2. Software platforms: The alternate model to resource ownership is to run a software platform that enables other people to easily and safely share resources. Generally in this business model, the

business itself does not own any of the shared resources, which has the benefit of lower start-up costs and less ongoing maintenance. Instead, these companies offer the logistics, connection, and infrastructure needed to empower others to share. The challenge with this model is that it is subject to "network effects," meaning that the platform becomes more useful and valuable the more people use it. Business models that are subject to network effects have some pluses and minuses; they are harder to get off the ground initially, but they are also difficult for other businesses to replicate once they get going. An example of a business that operates in this category includes Tulerie, a digital platform that allows strangers to borrow clothes from one another, and Sparetoolz, which operates with a similar model to Tulerie, enabling the sharing of tools and equipment.

Opportunity #4: Public Health

An industry that touches all of us in different ways throughout our lives is public health. This industry, as giant as it is, is also riddled with unsolved problems. Both the pandemic and the mental health crisis that followed quickly in its footsteps are examples of public health issues in need of creative and compassionate solutions. Health issues surrounding water quality, air quality, food, sexual and reproductive health, and so much more would also fall into this category. While full of unsolved problems begging for new solutions, this industry is tricky to work in because it can be hard to determine the morality around pricing. Businesses looking to both do a service and make a profit in this industry have to be very careful not to unintentionally exploit a vulnerable population. See the section on B2C business models on page 13 and the pricing chapter on page 235 for more discussion of this topic. Startups working within public health often operate within three different buckets:

1. <u>Working with healthcare professionals:</u> This can mean that a business is directly creating solutions for healthcare professionals, such as improved tools, equipment, systems, or services. It can refer to companies that develop offerings to help healthcare professionals better connect with or serve their patients. There's

a lot of money here and also a lot of opportunity to do good. However, depending on the business model, there may also be a lot of red tape, regulation, and complicated systems to navigate, which can at best be frustrating and slow-moving, and at worst, can choke out a small, early-stage business. An example of a startup working in this category is CQ Insights, a company that provides data science tools to help healthcare providers better understand clinical data and serve patients.[8]

2. Working with individuals: More and more startups today are working directly with individuals to provide health and wellness products. Many of these products are developed in response to the difficulties and frustrations faced by patients trying to navigate the healthcare system, or in an effort to help rectify the disparities between the different levels of care that is received by different populations. Mae, for example, is a digital health platform focused exclusively on providing health and wellness services for Black women, particularly Black mothers, responding to the fact that Black women are three times more likely to experience a pregnancy-related death than white women and twice as likely to experience a pregnancy-related complication.[9]

3. Working with institutions and government: Finally, startups in the public health space may choose to work with government or other healthcare institutions. Startups in this space may base their business model on funding opportunities provided by the government or international organizations that enable the business to provide resources and services to populations that would otherwise not be able to pay for them. TruePani (company profile on page 53) is an example of a startup in this category. They use funding provided by the government to test for and remediate instances of lead in water sources at schools and daycares around the country.

Opportunity #5: Energy

An industry that is still urgently in need of impact-driven solutions is energy. How we source and use energy affects public health, our ecosystem, our atmosphere, our economy, and ultimately, our future.

As our collective understanding of the threats of climate change grow, more urgency and resources are being committed to reshaping our energy economy to be cleaner, more just, and more accessible. The Inflation Reduction Act of 2022, for instance, committed unprecedented amounts of funding to clean energy sourcing and infrastructure. Startups working in the energy space generally focus on one of three categories:

1. <u>Energy generation</u>: While we still depend on fossil fuels for the majority of our energy needs, there is ample space for innovation within clean energy generation. Simply put, we still need *more* access to clean energy sources. These energy sources can either be fed into the utility grid or sourced directly to a home or business. Farm to Flame Energy is an example of a startup operating within this space. They use a patented combustion process to burn biomass from various waste streams and generate energy on-site with no smoke or odor.[10]

2. <u>Energy management</u>: In addition to sourcing clean energy, one of the greatest challenges facing the energy industry and inhibiting the accessibility of clean energy is energy management. Energy management refers primarily to transporting and storing renewable energy and making it more accessible to more people. There are some inherent challenges in switching energy infrastructure designed for fossil fuels over to infrastructure that can manage renewable energy. While fossil fuels can be burned continuously, most clean energy is only generated at particular times of day (like when it's sunny or windy outside), which means that we need energy storage systems that are able to capture and store these energy sources for future use. Similarly, many electric grids are designed to be "one-way" and generate and transport energy on-demand. With distributed sources of wind and solar energy that may be located all over a city, grids need to be able to accept, transport, and transfer energy from multiple directions. Finally, innovative business models are needed to make renewable energy more accessible to more people.

An example of a company addressing this ladder need is We-Solar (profile on page 181), a community solar platform that handles the customer sign ups and billing allocations for a customer to subscribe to a solar array that is located somewhere other than their home. A company working to address the storage challenges of renewable energy is EarthEn, a startup that is developing a thermo-mechanical energy storage solution using carbon dioxide to help empower a grid based on renewable energy.[11]

3. <u>Energy Efficiency</u>: What's even better than using clean energy? Using *less* energy. Even as we refine and improve energy generation and management, there are still huge strides to be made in energy efficiency. There is some fat, ripe, low-hanging fruit to be captured in this market because there is already a lot known about energy efficiency, and there are often direct savings to be had by investing in it. While it might be a less sexy aspect of the energy industry because it often includes activities like installing insulation and sealing windows, rather than capturing energy from the sun and developing batteries out of new materials, it is still an essential part of the energy puzzle. There is also still ample room for innovation in this industry. Sealed (company profile on page 41), for example, uses an innovative business model and approach to financing in order to make home energy retrofits and upgrades accessible and more affordable to a broader population.

Opportunity #6: Rethinking Finance

An industry that has perhaps received more buzz and funding for impact potential than any other is the finance and finance technology (fintech) industry. Like many industries, the finance industry has traditionally focused primarily on serving the wealthy. However, for the creative and socially minded innovator, fintech has great potential to serve under-resourced and traditionally overlooked communities, and to help alleviate poverty while still generating a profit. This opportunity has not gone unnoticed by impact investors. Fintech currently receives approximately one-quarter of impact investment funds.[12]

Fintech social enterprises primarily focus on one or both of the categories described below:

1. <u>Financial Inclusion</u>: As mentioned above, financial tools and services have been traditionally focused on one customer segment: those that have money, and preferably lots of it. But in today's society, an exclusion from basic financial tools such as a bank account or line of credit can be crippling, and effectively keep the poor poorer while helping the rich get richer. However, this isn't an insurmountable problem. There are many companies innovating within the finance industry today specifically with the goal of designing products for underserved communities. CapWay is a fintech company that designs its products with underserved communities in mind, offering the benefits of mobile banking with no overdraft fees and cashless transactions alongside financial education modules. Sealed (company profile on page 41) uses an innovative financing module to allow a broader customer base to afford energy-efficiency home improvements.

2. <u>Financial Health</u>: Rather than prey on those in hard times that are susceptible to debt traps, like some finance companies do, companies that focus on promoting financial health do the opposite. These companies try to help individuals and businesses achieve financial health based on the theory that those that are in good financial health make for better customers, employees, and community members. Altro, for example, is a startup that allows users to build credit through recurring payments and subscriptions (such as Netflix) in order to build financial health and good credit.[13]

Opportunity #7: Education

You may have heard people say that our current education system is broken. In my opinion, this is not an unfounded claim. The fact that teachers, who do one of the most valuable jobs there is, are barely able to make a living shows us that something is off. However, while education is valuable, the answer is not to simply charge more for it, seeing as accessibility of education is also a major factor in global inequality.

Furthermore, modern research has proven that children learn in very different ways, and a "one-size-fits-all" mode of teaching leaves many intelligent students at a distinct disadvantage. So what to do? While I won't claim to know the answer, there are many startups, working in both high and low tech, seeking to create solutions. As of 2021, the global edtech market size was estimated to be $74.2 billion with an expectation that it would grow over the coming ten-year time period.[14] Three edtech categories with both the opportunity of making a positive social impact and generating profit are the following:

1. Education Inclusivity and Assistive Technology: Children are not machines. They do not grow, develop, and learn in uniform, predictable ways. However, teachers' time, energy, and resources are stretched thin as it is, so making a unique curriculum and learning plan for each student that is customized for each student's abilities and learning styles generally isn't realistic. That's where tools for customized learning and assistive technology can play a role. Technology can help increase learning opportunities through tools for inclusivity and accessibility. Access Ingenuity, for example, develops assistive technology tools such as magnification systems for the visually impaired, Braille displays, screen reading and screen magnification software, scan-and-read solutions, and other software solutions for children with learning differences.[15]

2. Tools to empower educators: It's important to note that the most effective edtech is a supplement, not a replacement, for teachers and in-person learning. However, as mentioned previously, teachers have a lot asked of them, and their success has high stakes, so any tools that can be developed to empower and assist teachers to make their lives easier and give educators more time to focus on students is a win. Startups striving towards this goal include Wonderschool and PowerUp Fitness. Wonderschool provides training, tools, and resources to childcare providers to help them start a sustainable childcare business. The platform also helps parents to find quality childcare and early childhood education options.[16] PowerUp Fitness provides engaging and

educational fitness materials to educators and childcare providers to help children to stay healthy, burn off excess energy, and be engaged in physical learning.[17]

Opportunity #8: Carbon

Carbon has a bad reputation these days, but inherently, it's not a bad thing. Carbon can be found naturally in the earth's crust, in soil, plants, and even our bodies. The problem is, we have too much carbon currently in our atmosphere, and that is wreaking all sorts of havoc. As you've probably heard, excess carbon dioxide and other greenhouse gases are contributing to the steady warming of our planet, which is resulting in unprecedented weather such as droughts, floods, hurricanes, and storms, as well as alarming sea-level rise, which threatens life across our planet. To prevent the most extreme climate scenarios, climate scientists say we must limit global temperature rise to 1.5 degrees Celsius by 2100; however, the planet has already warmed by 1.1 degrees as of 2021.[18] Everyone from nonprofits to governments to individuals is scrambling to figure out ways of limiting the damage done by this persistent temperature rise, and private industry and innovators are no exception. The good news is that this means there are market opportunities for enterprising companies to help fight the global climate disaster, and to make a profit doing so. In fact, despite the fact that venture capital investment as a whole has been slowing down in 2022, climatetech investment has continued to heat up.[19] The global climatetech market in 2022 is valued at $16.9 billion and expected to increase to $147.5 billion by 2032.[20] There are three primary opportunities to build a business within the carbon and climatetech industry:

1. Decreasing carbon: Step one to decreasing the amount of carbon in our atmosphere is to stop emitting so much of it! There are numerous opportunities to decrease carbon emissions across industries, from getting our energy from renewable sources, to making homes and buildings more energy-efficient, to farming in more environmentally friendly ways, to making supply chains more sustainable, to making fewer consumer goods . . . and on and on. Business opportunities exist all along this spectrum. Giant consulting firms like Accenture to small boutique firms

like Strategic Sustainability Consulting are helping businesses to decrease their carbon footprints. Check out the sections on opportunities in agriculture and energy for more examples of companies working in this space.

2. <u>Sequestering carbon</u>: Step two to this conundrum is figuring out what to do with all the excess carbon that is already in our atmosphere. As I mentioned earlier, carbon already exists all throughout the earth, so part of the puzzle is figuring out how to get more carbon out of the air and back into the earth. There are many ways of doing this; some naturally occurring ones are planting trees or keeping soil healthy. Trees and healthy soil naturally take carbon dioxide out of the atmosphere and sequester it. Some innovators have figured out other ways of sucking carbon out of the air. There's actually a whole area of research devoted to this field called Direct Air Capture (DAC).[21] There are several of these machines actively running today, including those made by a company called ClimeWorks. Innovators and researchers are continuing to work to figure out how to make DAC more efficient, less expensive, and more easily scalable.

The trick with any kind of carbon removal, be it from planting trees or running a giant carbon-sucking machine, is figuring out who will pay you to do it. Luckily, there is a growing market for this. The carbon market, mentioned previously on page 120, is used as a way for businesses to "offset" their own carbon emissions by purchasing carbon credits from other companies that are actively working to take carbon out of the atmosphere. While this market is still unregulated and considered a bit of the Wild West, there is no denying that the carbon market is growing, and with it, so are business opportunities. Companies like Gold Standard and Verra are currently the big players in this space, but there are many smaller companies making waves as well, such as Nori and Regen Network.

3. <u>Making things out of carbon</u>: Finally, there are those innovators who take this part of the equation one step further, and think "is there something useful we could do with all this carbon?"

Companies in this camp are discovering ways to make valuable products out of carbon. Interface (company profile on page 93) is one of these companies. This carpet tile company prides itself on seeing carbon as an ally and uses carbon as an ingredient in its carpeting.[22] SkyNano Technologies has developed a method of capturing carbon dioxide and turning it into solid carbon material that can be used in common products such as batteries and tires.[23] Wilder yet, a company called Air Protein takes elements naturally occurring in the air (including carbon dioxide) and turns them into an edible form of protein.[24]

The categories described above are just a sprinkling of the problems (or opportunities, if you're a glass-half-full kind of person) that are open and waiting for social entrepreneurs. I hope this chapter helps provide inspiration for areas in which you could innovate and create a new business venture, and companies you can learn from that are already traveling that path. Notice that many companies appeared multiple times throughout the examples used for different industries. This demonstrates that you do not have to choose just one business model or one problem to focus on. Businesses that can incorporate elements from multiple models and address multiple problems simultaneously often offer the most elegant solutions and solid business models.

Conclusion

Keep your eyes on the stars and your feet on the ground.
—THEODORE ROOSEVELT

By the time you read this book, many of the companies I mentioned or profiled may not be around anymore. The difficult truth of any kind of entrepreneurship is that the failure rate is high. Many accomplished entrepreneurs have at least one failed business under their belt before they achieve success. However, while many of the businesses in this book may no longer exist, many new ones will. There are limitless opportunities out there for the bold, the innovative, and the compassionate. This is the group I hope to inspire and empower with the resources and stories in this book. Hopefully, this book has made it clear that building a social enterprise is not an easy road and is not for everyone; but if you are one of those that feel called to it, being a social entrepreneur can also be one of the most fulfilling and impactful journeys there is.

I also hope that you have gathered from this book that there is no one type of person that is or is not a social entrepreneur. There is no particular type of experience in science or business that qualifies you. There are no required degrees or training. Some people are natural entrepreneurs, born to create, innovate, and sell, while others are called to a particular mission and see social enterprise as the best route to achieve their goal. So whether you are looking to start a business, are already running a business, or are looking to innovate within the company you work for, what matters most is having that spark that calls you to create something that will leave this world better than you found it, and your own willingness to heed that spark. While social enterprise can be more complicated and demanding than traditional business in many ways, belief in the mission behind the work can be a superpower or extra battery pack to see you through the more difficult times of innovating in or building a business.

Finally, never forget that seeking to make a profit and do good at the same time is not shameful or greedy, and it is not overly idealistic. It is part of building an elegant, synergistic solution that aims to simultaneously support and sustain those being served by the business, those running the business, and the world; this concept is described by Ben & Jerry's as the vision of "linked prosperity."

In the introduction of this book, I discussed the concept of *ikigai*, or "reason to get up in the morning," which is the intersection between what you're good at, what you love, what the world needs, and what you can be paid for. What we know without a doubt is that the world needs more people seeking ikigai, and more organizations and workplaces that acknowledge this intersection of needs. Each new social enterprise is an opportunity to build a pathway to ikigai for yourself and for others. I hope that you take the tools and lessons from this book and seek that mission proudly, with your feet on the ground and your eyes on the stars.

NOTES

Introduction

1. Yukari Mitsuhashi, "Ikigai: A Japanese Concept to Improve Work and Life," BBC, August 7, 2017. https://www.bbc.com/worklife /article/20170807-ikigai-a-japanese-concept-to-improve-work-and-life.

2. Lécia Vicente, "The Social Enterprise: A New Form of Enterprise?" *The American Journal of Comparative Law*, 70, Issue Supplement_1, October 2022, i155–i184, https://doi.org/10.1093/ajcl/avac018.

3. Gaurav Lahiri and Jeff Schwartz, "2018 Global Human Capital Trends: The Rise of the Social Enterprise," Deloitte Insights, March 28, 2018, https://www2.deloitte.com/us/en/insights/focus/human-capital -trends/2018/introduction.html.

4. Timothy Carter, "The True Failure Rate of Small Businesses," *Entrepreneur*, January 3, 2021. https://www.entrepreneur.com/article/361350.

1. Business to Consumer (B2C)

1. Grow Appalachia Social Enterprise, Berea College, 2023, https:// growappalachia.berea.edu/socialenterprise/.

2. "What We Do: Our Model," Solar Sister, 2018, https://solarsister.org /what-we-do/our-model/.

3. "The One-For-One Business Model: Avoiding Unintended Consequences," Knowledge@Wharton, February 16, 2015, https://knowledge .wharton.upenn.edu/article/one-one-business-model-social-impact -avoiding-unintended-consequences/.

4. "Buy a Pair, Give a Pair," Warby Parker, accessed June 9, 2023, https://www.warbyparker.com/buy-a-pair-give-a-pair.

5. "About Aravind: Our Story," Aravind Eye Care System, 2023, https:// aravind.org/our-story/.

6. "GreenPrint Survey Finds Consumers Want to Buy Eco-Friendly Products, but Don't Know How to Identify Them," Business Wire, March

22, 2021, https://www.businesswire.com/news/home/20210322005061/en /GreenPrint-Survey-Finds-Consumers-Want-to-Buy-Eco-Friendly-Products -but-Don%E2%80%99t-Know-How-to-Identify-Them.

7. "GreenPrint Survey."

8. "Join Our Citizen-Consumer Community," Equal Exchange, accessed June 9, 2023, https://shop.equalexchange.coop/pages/join.

9. "Our Story," Kreyòl Essence, accessed August 27, 2022, https:// kreyolessence.com/pages/our-story.

10. Ray Ian Ampoloquio, "Shark Tank Kreyòl Essence Oil Update 2022, Season 11," Shark Tank Recap, May 13, 2022, https://sharktankrecap.com /kreyol-essence-oil-update-shark-tank-season-11.

11. "About Us," Kreyòl Essence, accessed August 27, 2022, https:// kreyolessence.com/pages/about-us.

12. "Social Impact," Kreyòl Essence, accessed August 27, 2022, https:// kreyolessence.com/pages/social-impact.

13. Alessandro Suardi, Walter Stefanoni, Francesco Latterini, Roberto Pari, Sandu Lazar, Ana Fernando, and Nadia Palmieri. (2021). "The Economic and Environmental Assessment of Castor Oil Supply Chain." https://www.mdpi.com/2071-1050/12/16/6339.

14. Ray Ian Ampoloquio, "Shark Tank Kreyòl Essence Oil Update."

2. Business to Business (B2B)

1. Latif Peracha, "Carbon Startup Nori Commodifies Carbon Removal," M13, July 27, 2022, https://m13.co/article/investing-in-nori -a-sustainable-solution-against-climate-change.

2. "Founder Spotlight: Tinia Pina (Re-Nuble)," VEGPRENEUR, May 31, 2021, https://www.vegpreneur.org/blog/tinia-pina.

3. "Tinia Pina Wants to End Food Insecurity through Her Company Re-Nuble," Black Enterprise, August 18, 2021. https://www.blackenterprise .com/tinia-pinas-re-nuble-is-working-to-tackle-climate-change-and-food -insecurity/.

4. "About Us," Re-Nuble, 2023, https://www.re-nuble.com/pages /about-us.

5. "2020 ExpoLive Interview with Tinia Pina, CEO of Re-Nuble," 2020, https://youtu.be/1JuS7fz4ZPE.

6. "Food Waste in America in 2020: Statistics & Facts," Recycle Track Systems, 2020, https://www.rts.com/resources/guides/food-waste -america/.

7. "Tinia Pina of Re-Nuble on the Future of Modern American Farming: An Interview with Sean Freeman," *Authority Magazine*, March 24, 2022, https://medium.com/authority-magazine/tinia-pina-of-re-nuble-on -the-future-of-modern-american-farming-2408588c9483.

3. Creative Financing

1. Échale, 2020, https://echale.mx/.

2. Community Development Partners, LLC, accessed July 12, 2023, http://www.cdpllc.com/.

3. Jerome Knyszewski, "Lauren Salz of Sealed: 5 Things I Wish Someone Told Me before I Began Leading My Company," *Authority Magazine*, February 15, 2021, https://medium.com/authority-magazine/lauren-salz -of-sealed-5-things-i-wish-someone-told-me-before-i-began-leading-my -company-aadf2253fa72.

4. Rachel Gordon and Cara Bottorff, "New Analysis: Heat Pumps Slow Climate Change in Every Corner of the Country," Sierra Club, April 23, 2020. https://www.sierraclub.org/articles/2020/04/new-analysis -heat-pumps-slow-climate-change-every-corner-country.

4. Government

1. "How to Sell to the Government," United States General Services Administration, 2023, https://www.gsa.gov/buy-through-us/new-to-gsa -acquisitions/how-to-sell-to-the-government.

2. "Building the Capacity of Drinking Water Systems: The Water Infrastructure Improvements for the Nation Act (WIIN Act) Grant Programs, 2023, https://www.epa.gov/dwcapacity/water-infrastructure -improvements-nation-act-wiin-act-grant-programs.

3. "Local Law 87 of 2009," The Cotocon Group, accessed July 11, 2023, https://www.thecotocongroup.com/nyc-local-law-87/.

4. EnergySage. https://www.energysage.com/solar/solar-101/what-is -community-solar/.

5. Small Business Administration. https://www.sbir.gov/about.

6. "America's Seed Fund," National Science Foundation, accessed July 11, 2023, https://seedfund.nsf.gov/.

7. United States Department of Agriculture Rural Development, Value-Added Producer Grants, accessed July 11, 2023, https://www.rd.usda.gov /programs-services/business-programs/value-added-producer-grants.

8. "Resources for Rural Entrepreneurs a Guide to Planning, Adapting, and Growing Your Business," accessed September 4, 2022, https://www .agmrc.org/media-room/videos/value-added-producer-grant-serenity -acres-farm.

9. Rachel Medina, "Navigating California's Electric Vehicle Incentive Programs," California.com, August 18, 2020, https://www.california.com /navigating-californias-electric-vehicle-incentive-programs/.

10. "Public-Private Partnerships (PPPs): Definition, How They Work, and Examples," Investopedia, April 28, 2022, https://www.investopedia .com/terms/p/public-private-partnerships.asp.

11. https://www.wsj.com/articles/brooklyns-new-lab-is-an-inventors-paradise-1476714981.

12. "TruePani Wins InVenture Prize People's Choice Award," Georgia Tech College of Engineering, March 17, 2016, https://ce.gatech.edu/news/truepani-wins-inventure-prize-people%E2%80%99s-choice-award.

13. Muriel Vega, "How This Water Quality Startup Pivoted to Address the Domestic Market," Hypepotamus, August 30, 2017, https://hypepotamus.com/companies/truepani/.

14. "Drinking Water Sampling," TruePani, accessed November 27, 2022, https://www.truepani.com/drinkingwatersampling.

15. "Sources of Lead Exposure: Lead in Drinking Water," Centers for Disease Control and Prevention, 2023, https://www.cdc.gov/nceh/lead/prevention/sources/water.htm.

16. "Childhood Lead Poisoining Prevention: Health Effects of Lead Exposure," Centers for Disease Control and Prevention, 2022, https://www.cdc.gov/nceh/lead/prevention/health-effects.htm.

5. Nonprofits

1. Troy Segal, "501(c) Organization: What They Are, Types, and Examples," Investopedia, August 3, 2022, https://www.investopedia.com/terms/1/501c.asp.

2. Jonathan Timm, "The Plight of the Overworked Nonprofit Employee," *The Atlantic*, August 24, 2016, https://www.theatlantic.com/business/archive/2016/08/the-plight-of-the-overworked-nonprofit-employee/497081/.

3. "About," Likewise Go & Do, accessed July 11, 2023, https://likewisecoffee.com/about.

4. "Hogar Semilla," Échale, accessed July 11, 2023, https://echale.mx/en/hogar-semilla/.

5. "Financiera," Échale, accessed July 11, 2023, https://echale.mx/en/financiera/.

6. "Study of Social Entrepreneurship and Innovation Ecosystems in the Latin American Pacific Alliance Countries: Case Study: Échale a Tú Casa, Mexico," Inter-American Development Bank, July 2016, https://publications.iadb.org/publications/english/document/Study-of-Social-Entrepreneurship-and-Innovation-Ecosystems-in-the-Latin-American-Pacific-Alliance-Countries-Case-Study-Echale-a-tu-casa-Mexico.pdf.

7. "Fundacíon," Échale, accessed July 11, 2023, https://echale.mx/en/fundacion/.

8. "Ecoblock," Échale, accessed July 11, 2023, https://echale.mx/en/ecoblock/

9. "Study of Social Entrepreneurship . . . Case Study: Échale."

6. Products and Services

1. C. K. Prahalad, *The Fortune at the Bottom of the Pyramid* (Upper Saddle River, N.J.: Wharton School Publishing, 2006).

2. Niall McCarthy, "Food Waste Is Becoming a Billion Tonne Problem," Statista, March 8, 2021, https://www.statista.com/chart/24349/estimated-annual-global-food-waste-by-sector/.

3. Matt Brann, "Darwin Inventor Turning Manure into Fertiliser, with Aim of Solving Global Food Crisis," ABC News, April 2, 2018, https://www.abc.net.au/news/rural/2018-04-03/darwin-inventor-jordan-phasey-turning-manure-into-fertiliser/9598500.

4. Christine Alewell, Bruno Ringeval, Cristiano Ballabio, David A. Robinson, Panos Panagos, and Pasquale Borrelli, "Global Phosphorus Shortage Will Be Aggravated by Soil Erosion," *Nature Communications* 11 (1), September 11, 2020, https://doi.org/10.1038/s41467-020-18326-7.

7. Design

1. "Press Release: Kimberly-Clark Introduces Scott Naturals Tube Free – the First Coreless Bath Tissue for the Home," Kimberly-Clark Corporation, October 28, 2010, https://investor.kimberly-clark.com/news-releases/news-release-details/kimberly-clark-introduces-scott-naturals-tube-free-first.

2. "What Is Biomimicry?," Biomimicry Institute, 2019, https://biomimicry.org/what-is-biomimicry/.

3. Mark Wolverton, "What Termites Can Teach Engineers," ASME, November 21, 2019, https://www.asme.org/topics-resources/content/what-termites-can-teach-engineers.

4. Rachel Hennessey, "Living in Color: The Potential Dangers of Artificial Dyes," *Forbes*, August 27, 2012, https://www.forbes.com/sites/rachelhennessey/2012/08/27/living-in-color-the-potential-dangers-of-artificial-dyes/?sh=2f072fc5107a.

5. "A New Color Paradigm," Cypris Materials, 2022, http://www.cyprismaterials.com/technology.

6. "Projects," Terreform, accessed March 12, 2022, https://www.terreform.org/projects.

7. "How Does Anaerobic Digestion Work?," United States Environmental Protection Agency, March 18, 2019, https://www.epa.gov/agstar/how-does-anaerobic-digestion-work.

8. "AskNature: Innovation Inspired by Nature," AskNature, The Biomimicry Institute, 2016, https://asknature.org/.

9. "Paper Beats Plastic? How to Rethink Environmental Folklore," TED Talk by Leyla Acaroglu, 2013, https://www.ted.com/talks/leyla_acaroglu_paper_beats_plastic_how_to_rethink_environmental_folklore.

10. "Plastics: Material-Specific Data," United States Environmental Protection Agency, July 30, 2018, https://www.epa.gov/facts-and-figures -about-materials-waste-and-recycling/plastics-material-specific-data.

11. Randy Miller, "1, 2, 3, 4, 5, 6, 7: Plastics Recycling by the Numbers," Miller Recycling, February 10, 2019, https://millerrecycling.com/plastics -recycling-numbers/.

12. Starre Vartan, "What Is Cradle to Cradle? Principles, Design, and Certification," Treehugger, October 31, 2021, https://www.treehugger.com /what-is-cradle-to-cradle-5191335.

13. "Certification," BPI, 2023, https://bpiworld.org/certification.

14. Miho Ligare, "Surfrider Foundation Releases New Bioplastic Toolkit," October 19, 2021, Surfrider Foundation, https://www.surfrider.org /coastal-blog/entry/surfrider-foundation-releases-new-bioplastic -toolkit.

15. "Landfills," National Geographic Education, April 16, 2021, https:// www.nationalgeographic.org/encyclopedia/landfills/.

16. "Our History," Interface, 2009, https://www.interface.com/US/en -US/sustainability/our-history-en_US.

17. "i2 Carpet Tiles: Designed by Nature," Interface," 2023, https://www .interface.com/US/en-US/carpet-tile/i2.html.

18. "Carbon FAQs," Interface, accessed July 11, 2023, https:// interfaceinc.scene7.com/is/content/InterfaceInc/Interface/Americas /WebsiteContentAssets/Documents/Sustainability%20Carbon%20Negative %20FAQ/wc_am-carbonnegativefaqfinal.pdf.

19. Jon Gertner, "Has the Carbontech Revolution Begun?," *New York Times Magazine*, June 23, 2021, https://www.nytimes.com/2021/06/23 /magazine/interface-carpet-carbon.html.

20. "ReEntry Reclamation & Recycling Program Guidelines," Interface, February 2021, https://interfaceinc.scene7.com/is/content/InterfaceInc /Interface/Americas/WebsiteContentAssets/Documents/ReEntry/ReEntry %20Guidelines/wc_am-reentryguidelines-us-22021-final.pdf.

21. "Carbon Negative: Going Beyond Carbon Neutral," Interface, 2023, https://www.interface.com/US/en-US/sustainability/carbon-negative -en_US.

22. *The Guardian*, https://www.theguardian.com/sustainable-business /creating-sustainable-livelihoods-recycling.

23. Green, Jared. 2016. "The Factory as Forest." THE DIRT. October 18, 2016. https://blog.interface.com/revisiting-our-factory-as-a-forest -thinking/.

24. Jon Gertner, "Has the Carbontech Revolution Begun?"

25. "Design with the Climate in Mind," Interface, accessed March 26, 2022, https://interfaceinc.scene7.com/is/content/InterfaceInc/Interface

/Americas/WebsiteContentAssets/Documents/CNF%20Certification /wc_am-carbonneutralfloors-offsetprojects2019.pdf.

26. "Reuse and Recycling," Interface, 2023, https://www.interface.com /US/en-US/sustainability/recycling/recycling-en_US.

27. Ken Ryan, "California Recycling Bill Signed into Law," Floor Covering News, October 27, 2017, https://www.fcnews.net/2017/10/california -recycling-bill-signed-into-law/.

8. Material Sourcing

1. Forest Stewardship Council International, accessed July 11, 2023, https://fsc.org/en.

2. Leather Working Group, 2023, https://www.leatherworkinggroup .com/.

3. "About B Lab | Certified B Corporation." 2018. Bcorporation.net. 2018. https://bcorporation.net/about-b-lab.

4. "Forge: Forging Innovation from Prototype to Impact," Forge Impact, accessed July 11, 2023, https://forgeimpact.org/.

5. "The Moment thredUP CEO James Reinhart Knew He Wanted to Inspire Others," HuffPost, February 7, 2014, https://www.huffpost.com /entry/thredup-james-rienhart-_n_4746830.

6. "thredUP," Cleverism, October 25, 2016, https://www.cleverism.com /company/thredup/.

7. "Press Release: thredUP Announces Second Quarter 2021 Results, thredUP, August 10, 2021, https://ir.thredup.com/news-releases/news -release-details/thredup-announces-second-quarter-2021-results.

8. "ThredUP Resale-As-a-Service." Raas.thredup.com. Accessed June 11, 2022. https://raas.thredup.com/p/2.

9. "Shop Their Closets: Scoop up Goodies from Your Style Crushes!," thredUP Blog, June 3, 2021, https://www.thredup.com/bg/p/shop-their -closets.

10. "Impact at thredUP," accessed June 11, 2022, https://www.thredup .com/impact#educate.

11. Rachael Dottle and Jackie Gu, "The Global Glut of Clothing Is an Environmental Crisis," Bloomberg, February 23, 2022,https://www .bloomberg.com/graphics/2022-fashion-industry-environmental-impact/.

12. "What Is Bundled Shipping?" thredUP, accessed June 11, 2022, https://help.thredup.com/en_us/what-is-buy-and-bundle-H1EAJI4p4.

9. Manufacturing

1. "The Story of Stuff," The Story of Stuff Project, April 22, 2009, https://www.youtube.com/watch?v=9GorqroigqM.

2. "Mechanical and Molecular Recycling: Some Things Are Just Better Together," Eastman, accessed May 1, 2022, https://www.eastman.com /Company/Circular-Economy/Solutions/Pages/Mechanical-Molecular .aspx.

3. Suzanne Downing, "Using Spent Grain for Livestock Feed and Lessons Learned from Farmer John," AGDAILY, March 25, 2020. https://www.agdaily.com/features/brewery-to-farm-using-spent-grain -livestock-feed-farmer-john/.

4. Geert Peeters,"Levi's: Making Water Less Jeans," *The Guardian*, December 20, 2010, https://www.theguardian.com/sustainable-business /levis-water-less-jeans.

5. "Industrial Effluent Guidelines," United States Environmental Protection Agency, July 16, 2015, https://www.epa.gov/eg/industrial -effluent-guidelines.

6. Kevin T. Higgins, "Sustainable Plant of the Year: New Belgium Brewing Co. Hits the Spot," Food Engineering, September 1, 2010, https:// www.foodengineeringmag.com/articles/88202-sustainable-plant-of-the -year-new-belgium-brewing-co-hits-the-spot.

7. "Sources of Greenhouse Gas Emissions," United States Environmental Protection Agency, October 9, 2018, https://www.epa.gov/ghgemissions/ sources-greenhouse-gas-emissions.

8. "Method - Our Soap Factory," Method Products, accessed July 11, 2023, https://methodhome.com/beyond-the-bottle/soap-factory/.

9. "Community Solar Basics," Office of Energy Efficiency & Renewable Energy, United States Department of Energy, accessed July 11, 2023, https:// www.energy.gov/eere/solar/community-solar-basics.

10. "Method Soap Factory (People against Dirty)," U.S. Green Building Council, accessed May 13, 2022, https://leed.usgbc.org/methods-products -factory.

11. "Carbon Offsets," MIT Climate Portal, November 8, 2022, https:// climate.mit.edu/explainers/carbon-offsets.

12. "Air Conditioned Stadiums. Cruise Ships. New Hotels. Can the World Cup in Qatar Really Be Carbon Neutral?," How to Save a Planet podcast, produced by Lonnie Ro, July 7, 2022, https://open.spotify.com /episode/6Msfjvo21Y6S3Usa1ZupZW.

13. "Transparent Scores for Carbon Credit Quality," The Carbon Credit Quality Initiative, 2022, https://carboncreditquality.org/.

14. "TRI Toxics Tracker," United States Environmental Protection Agency, 2023, https://edap.epa.gov/public/extensions/TRIToxicsTracker /TRIToxicsTracker.html.

15. "TRI Toxics Tracker."

16. If you don't get this reference, search for it online and you'll see what I mean. Hexxus is a pollution monster from the 1992 animated movie *FernGully*.

17. "Safer Chemicals," Supply Chain Solutions Center, Environmental Defense Fund, accessed May 13, 2022, https://supplychain.edf.org/category /safer-chemicals/.

18. Keith Loria, "Fashion Tech Startup Stony Creek Colors Secures $9m Series B for Plant-Based Dye," Lewis & Clark Agrifood, March 3, 2021, https://lewisandclarkagrifood.com/2021/03/03/fashion-tech-startup-stony -creek-colors-secures-9m-series-b-for-plant-based-dye/.

19. Loria, "Fashion Tech Startup Stony Creek Colors."

20. "Our Partnerships," Stony Creek Colors, accessed May 13, 2022, https://www.stonycreekcolors.com/pages/partnerships.

21. "OECD Substitution and Alternatives Toolbox," Organisation for Economic Co-Operation and Development, accessed May 13, 2022, http:// www.oecdsaatoolbox.org/.

22. Amplytica, accessed May 13, 2022, https://amplytica.io/.

23. "New Belgium Brewing's Asheville Brewery: An Exemplary Model of Brownfields to Brewfields," Center for Creative Land Recycling, December 9, 2018, https://www.cclr.org/project-highlights/new-belgium-brewings -asheville-brewery-an-exemplary-model-of-brownfields-to-brewfields.

24. "Method - Our Soap Factory."

25. "LEED | LEED Lookbook." n.d. Leed.usgbc.org. https://leed.usgbc .org/leed.

26. "Living Building Challenge," International Living Future Institute, May 2, 2019, https://living-future.org/lbc/.

27. https://www.epa.gov/ems/learn-about-environmental-management -systems.

28. "Lean Thinking and Methods – Kaizen," United States Environmental Protection Agency, November 16, 2016, https://www.epa.gov /sustainability/lean-thinking-and-methods-kaizen.

29. "Lean Thinking and Methods - 5S," United States Environmental Protection Agency, November 16, 2016, https://www.epa.gov/sustainability /lean-thinking-and-methods-5s.

30. "Lean Thinking and Methods - Cellular Manufacturing." United States Environmental Protection Agency, November 16, 2016, https://www.epa.gov/sustainability/lean-thinking-and-methods -cellular-manufacturing.

31. "Lean Thinking and Methods - JIT/Kanban," United States Environmental Protection Agency, November 17, 2016, https://www.epa.gov /sustainability/lean-thinking-and-methods-jitkanban.

32. "Lean Thinking and Methods – TPM," United States Environmental Protection Agency, November 17, 2016, https://www.epa.gov/sustainability/lean-thinking-and-methods-tpm.

33. "Lean Thinking and Methods - Six Sigma," United States Environmental Protection Agency, November 17, 2016, https://www.epa.gov/sustainability/lean-thinking-and-methods-six-sigma.

34. "Lean Thinking and Methods - 3P," United States Environmental Protection Agency, November 17, 2016, https://www.epa.gov/sustainability/lean-thinking-and-methods-3p.

35. "2018 Force for Good Report," New Belgium Brewing, https://www.newbelgium.com/siteassets/mission/force-for-good-digital-report.pdf.

36. "Live Episode! New Belgium Brewing Company: Kim Jordan," *How I Built This with Guy Raz*, podcast, September 10, 2018, https://www.npr.org/2018/09/07/645620049/live-episode-new-belgium-brewing-company-kim-jordan.

37. "2018 Force for Good Report," New Belgium Brewing.

38. "New Belgium Brewing Company Project Highlights," Integral Group, accessed July 11, 2023, https://www.integralgroup.com/projects/new-belgium-brewing-company/.

39. "A Day in the Life of Sustainable Beer: New Belgium Brewery," The Rational Middle, December 9, 2013, https://www.youtube.com/watch?v=Qv8gMuSVhvI&ab.

40. "Scope 1, 2 and 3 Emissions," Deloitte, 2023, https://www2.deloitte.com/uk/en/focus/climate-change/zero-in-on-scope-1-2-and-3-emissions.html.

41. "2018 Force for Good Report," New Belgium Brewing.

42. "New Belgium Brewing Company Project Highlights," Integral Group.

43. "Brewed for All," New Belgium Brewing, accessed July 11, 2023, https://www.newbelgium.com/company/mission/diversity-and-inclusion/.

44. "Giving Back: Do Good & Feel Good," New Belgium Brewing, accessed July 11, 2023, https://www.newbelgium.com/company/mission/giving-back/.

45. Darren Dahl, "How New Belgium Brewing Has Found Sustainable Success," *Forbes*, January 27, 2016, https://www.forbes.com/sites/darrendahl/2016/01/27/how-new-belgium-brewing-has-found-sustainable-success/?sh=c85a4f086a61.

46. Darren Dahl, "How New Belgium Brewing Has Found Sustainable Success."

47. "The End of Employee Ownership at New Belgium Brewing," National Center for Employee Ownership Newsletter, March 2020, https://www.nceo.org/article/end-employee-ownership-new-belgium-brewing.

48. "Giving Back," New Belgium Brewing."

49. "Ceres Policy Network." n.d. Ceres. https://www.ceres.org/networks/ceres-policy-network.

50. "2018 Force for Good Report," New Belgium Brewing.

51. "Drink Sustainably," New Belgium Brewing, accessed July 11, 2023, https://www.drinksustainably.com/.

52. Darren Dahl, "How New Belgium Brewing Has Found Sustainable Success."

10. Packaging and Shipping

1. Laura Parker, "The World's Plastic Pollution Crisis Explained," *National Geographic*, June 7, 2019, https://www.nationalgeographic.com/environment/article/plastic-pollution.

2. Damian Carrington, "Microplastics Found in Human Blood for First Time," *The Guardian*, March 24, 2022, https://www.theguardian.com/environment/2022/mar/24/microplastics-found-in-human-blood-for-first-time.

3. Forest Stewardship Council, accessed July 11, 2023, https://fsc.org/.

4. Miho Ligare, "Surfrider Foundation Releases New Bioplastic Toolkit," October 19, 2021, Surfrider Foundation, https://www.surfrider.org/coastal-blog/entry/surfrider-foundation-releases-new-bioplastic-toolkit.

5. Keith Laidler, "The bear's necessity." *The Guardian*, March 20, 2003, https://www.theguardian.com/environment/2003/mar/20/research.science#.

6. Walé Azeez, "These 4 Start-Ups Are Using Seaweed to Help Save the Planet," Virtual Ocean Dialogues, World Economic Forum, May 25, 2021. https://www.weforum.org/agenda/2021/05/startups-seaweed-farming-ocean-planet-climate/.

7. "Searo - Technology." n.d. Searo.co. https://searo.co/technology.

8. "Notpla: Products," accessed July 11, 2023, https://www.notpla.com/products/.

9. "Packaging," Ecovative, accessed May 29, 2022, https://www.ecovative.com/pages/packaging.

10. Carly Ledbetter, "KFC's 'Scoff-ee Cup' Is an Edible Coffee Cup that Smells like Grass and Sunscreen," HuffPost, February 25, 2015, https://www.huffpost.com/entry/kfc-edible-coffee-cup_n_6752366.

11. Aashmita Nayar, "KFC to Debut Edible, Tortilla Rice Bowls in India to Curb Plastic Use," HuffPost, April 28, 2016, https://www.huffpost.com/archive/in/entry/kfc-rice-bowlz-edible_n_9792262.

12. *Not Past It*. Gimlet Media. "The Crying Indian Ad." 2022. https://open.spotify.com/episode/6Qe37WTHCNB9FngNsJbImA.

13. "Guidance for Reusable Packaging," Sustainable Packaging Coalition, 2022, https://sustainablepackaging.org/wp-content/uploads/2022/04/Guidance-for-Reusable-Packaging.pdf.

14. Rebecca Byers, "This H&M Packaging Concept Transforms into a Clothing Hanger," TrendHunter, February 3, 2016, https://www.trendhunter.com/trends/hm-packaging-concept.

15. "Loop: A Global Platform for Reuse," 2023, https://exploreloop.com/.

16. "Carbon Pollution from Transportation," United States Environmental Protection Agency, June 8, 2018, https://www.epa.gov/transportation-air-pollution-and-climate-change/carbon-pollution-transportation.

17. "Smog, Soot, and Other Air Pollution from Transportation," United States Environmental Protection Agency, May 11, 2023, https://www.epa.gov/transportation-air-pollution-and-climate-change/smog-soot-and-other-air-pollution-transportation.

18. Anna Nagurney, "Our Economy Relies on Shipping Containers. This Is What Happens When They're 'Stuck in the Mud,'" World Economic Forum, October 1, 2021, https://www.weforum.org/agenda/2021/10/global-shortagof-shipping-containers/.

19. "SmartWay," United States Environmental Protection Agency, August 19, 2019, https://www.epa.gov/smartway.

20. Camila Domonoske, "From Amazon to FedEx, the Delivery Truck Is Going Electric," National Public Radio, March 17, 2021, https://www.npr.org/2021/03/17/976152350/from-amazon-to-fedex-the-delivery-truck-is-going-electric.

21. "Fleet Electrification Solution Center," Environmental Defense Fund, accessed June 4, 2022, https://www.electricfleet.org/.

22. Dave Burdick, "Brewer to Turn Beer Waste into Fuel for Its Trucks," HuffPost, March 8, 2009, https://www.huffpost.com/entry/brewer-to-turn-beer-waste_n_164167.

23. Vishal Paul, P. S. Chandra Shekharaiah, Shivbachan Kushwaha, Ajit Sapre, Santanu Dasgupta, and Debanjan Sanyal, "Role of Algae in CO_2 Sequestration Addressing Climate Change: A Review," *Renewable Energy and Climate Change*, September 4, 2019, 257–65. https://doi.org/10.1007/978-981-32-9578-0_23.

24. Katherine Gallagher, "Algae Biofuel as an Alternative Energy Source," Treehugger, February 7, 2022, https://www.treehugger.com/making-biodiesel-from-algae-85138.

25. "Hydrogen Fuel Cell Vehicles," United States Environmental Protection Agency, September 22, 2015, https://www.epa.gov/greenvehicles/hydrogen-fuel-cell-vehicles.

26. "Hydrogen Fuel Basics," Office of Energy Efficiency & Renewable Energy, United States Department of Energy, 2019, https://www.energy.gov/eere/fuelcells/hydrogen-fuel-basics.

27. "Exploring Life & Business with Michaela Barnett of KnoxFill," Local Stories, *Knoxville Voyager*, October 28, 2021, https://knoxvillevoyager.com/interview/exploring-life-business-with-michaela-barnett-of-knoxfill/.

28. Katie Inman, "Zero-Waste Business KnoxFill Aims to Make Knoxville 'the Sustainable City,'" WBIR, September 22, 2021, https://www.wbir.com/article/news/local/five-at-four/new-zero-waste-business-knoxfill-aims-to-make-knoxville-the-sustainable-city/51-3c40dd25-1d99-483a-be78-39de61bfb649.

29. "How Does It Work?" KnoxFill, accessed June 12, 2022, https://knoxfill.com/pages/how-does-it-work-1.

30. Amna Nawaz, "The Plastic Problem," PBS NewsHour, November 28, 2019, https://www.pbs.org/newshour/show/the-plastic-problem.

31. "FAQs," KnoxFill, accessed June 12, 2022, https://knoxfill.com/pages/faqs.

11. Hiring and Labor

1. Gianna Melillo, "US Wealth Gap between Races Widening over Last 160 Years," The Hill, June 7, 2022, https://thehill.com/changing-america/respect/equality/3514799-us-wealth-gap-between-races-widening-over-last-160-years/.

2. Eileen Patten, "Racial, Gender Wage Gaps Persist in U.S. Despite Some Progress," Pew Research Center, July 1, 2016, https://www.pewresearch.org/fact-tank/2016/07/01/racial-gender-wage-gaps-persist-in-u-s-despite-some-progress/.

3. "How Systemic Racism Infiltrates Education," Ben & Jerry's, 2017, https://www.benjerry.com/whats-new/2017/11/systemic-racism-education.

4. David Brancaccio, Rose Conlon, and Daniel Shin, "New Research Shows Racial Discrimination in Hiring Is Still Happening at the Earliest Stages," Marketplace Morning Report, August 3, 2021, https://www.marketplace.org/2021/08/03/new-research-shows-racial-discrimination-in-hiring-is-still-happening-at-the-earliest-stages/.

5. David Atkin, Antoinette Schoar, and Kiara Wahnschat, "Evaluating Sama's Training and Job Programs in Nairobi, Kenya," Sama, April 6, 2021, http://www.sama.com/wp-content/uploads/2022/04/Samasource-Evaluation-Final.pdf.

6. "One Third of Your Life Is Spent at Work," Gettysburg College, 2021. https://www.gettysburg.edu/news/stories?id=79db7b34-630c-4f49-ad32-4ab9ea48e72b.

7. Global Living Wage Coalition, accessed July 11, 2023, https://www
.globallivingwage.org/.

8. Sarah Anderson and Sam Pizzigati, "No CEO Should Earn 1,000 Times More than a Regular Employee," *The Guardian*, March 18, 2018, https://www.theguardian.com/business/2018/mar/18/america-ceo-worker-pay-gap-new-data-what-can-we-do.

9. Ana Hernández Kent and Lowell Ricketts, "Wealth Inequality in America over Time: Key Statistics," Open Vault Blog, Federal Reserve Bank of St. Louis, December 2, 2020, https://www.stlouisfed.org/open-vault/2020/december/has-wealth-inequality-changed-over-time-key-statistics.

10. "About Us," Equal Exchange, accessed June 20, 2022, https://shop
.equalexchange.coop/pages/about-us#mission.

11. "Does More Money Make You Work Harder?" BBC Ideas, accessed June 19, 2022, https://www.bbc.com/worklife/article/20180320-does-being-paid-more-make-you-perform-better.

12. Dan Ariely, "What Makes Us Feel Good about Our Work?" TED Talk filmed at TEDx Río de la Plata, TEDEd, 2013, https://ed.ted.com/lessons/what-makes-us-feel-good-about-our-work-dan-ariely.

13. Sara Horowitz, "94 Percent of Millennials Want to Use Their Skills for Good," HuffPost, July 24, 2014, https://www.huffpost.com/entry/94-of-millennials-want-to_b_5618309.

14. Margaret Heffernan, "Forget the Pecking Order at Work,'" Ted.com. TED Talks. 2015. https://www.ted.com/talks/margaret_heffernan_forget_the_pecking_order_at_work/transcript.

15. Michael O'Malley, "What the 'Best Companies to Work For' Do Differently," *Harvard Business Review*, December 12, 2019, https://hbr.org/2019/12/what-the-best-companies-to-work-for-do-differently.

16. "What Is Employee Ownership?" National Center for Employee Ownership, accessed July 11, 2023, https://www.nceo.org/what-is-employee-ownership.

17. "Research on Employee Ownership," National Center for Employee Ownership, accessed July 11, 2023, https://www.nceo.org/article/research-employee-ownership.

18. Adam Gopnik, "Livelihood," *The New Yorker*, May 15, 1989, https://www.newyorker.com/magazine/1989/05/22/livelihood.

19. "The Bakery & History," Greyston Bakery, accessed June 20, 2022, https://shop.greyston.org/pages/the-bakery-history.

20. "Greyston Foundation for Employers," Greyston Bakery, accessed June 22, 2022, https://www.greyston.org/employers/.

21. Greyston Bakery, accessed June 22, 2022, https://shop.greyston.org/collections/frontpage.

22. Greyston Bakery.

23. "Greyston Foundation for Employers," Greyston Bakery, accessed June 22, 2022, https://www.greyston.org/employers/.

24. "Job Seekers," Greyston Bakery, accessed June 27, 2022, https://www.greyston.org/job-seekers/#transitionalemployment.

12. Community

1. J. David Goodman, "Amazon Pulls out of Planned New York City Headquarters," *The New York Times*, February 14, 2019, https://www.nytimes.com/2019/02/14/nyregion/amazon-hq2-queens.html.

2. Charles Baer and Terry Brown, "Location Quotients: A Tool for Comparing Regional Industry Compositions," IN Context, Indiana Business Research Center, Kelley School of Business, Indiana University, accessed June 27, 2022, https://incontext.indiana.edu/2006/march/1.asp.

3. "Local Multiplier 3 (LM3)," NEF Consulting, 2023, https://www.nefconsulting.com/training-capacity-building/resources-and-tools/local-multiplier-3/.

4. "'Build Authenticity of Place' - Judy Wicks, Founder, White Dog Cafe," American Sustainable Business Network, January 15, 2015, https://www.youtube.com/watch?v=M5WItDonqoM.

5. "Method Soap Factory (People against Dirty)," U.S. Green Building Council, accessed May 13, 2022. https://leed.usgbc.org/methods-products-factory.

6. Enrico Colla, Catherine Chastenet de Géry, Laurence-Claire Lemmet, Martine Deparis, Maryline Schultz, and Maria Ruiz-Molina, "Franchisee autonomy: a key to a successful franchising?"

7. "Business Meets Goodness: The Goodwill Model," Adelphi University, June 22, 2018, https://www.adelphi.edu/news/business-meets-goodness-the-goodwill-model/.

8. Amie Vaccaro, "The White Dog Cafe: A Study of Social Business and Mission-Aligned Exit," Greenbiz, April 24, 2009, https://www.greenbiz.com/article/white-dog-cafe-study-social-business-and-mission-aligned-exit.

9. AgLaunch, accessed July 11, 2023, https://www.aglaunch.com.

10. CleanTech Open, accessed July 11, 2023, https://www.cleantechopen.org.

11. Common Future, accessed July 11, 2023, https://www.commonfuture.co.

12. "Allies of the Regenerative Organic Alliance," Regenerative Organic Alliance, accessed July 11, 2023, https://regenorganic.org/allies/.

13. "Drink Sustainably," New Belgium Brewing, accessed July 11, 2023, https://www.drinksustainably.com/.

14. "About," WeSolar, accessed July 11, 2023, https://wesolar.energy/about/.

15. Saijel Kishan, "Solving America's Solar Inequality Starts in the Neighborhood," Bloomberg, January 26, 2021, https://www.bloomberg .com/news/features/2021-01-26/solving-america-s-solar-inequality -starts-in-the-neighborhood.

16. Benjamin Goldstein, Dimitrios Gounaridis, and Joshua P. Newell, "The Carbon Footprint of Household Energy Use in the United States," *Proceedings of the National Academy of Sciences* 117 (32), https://doi.org /10.1073/pnas.1922205117.

17. Yessenia Funes, "'Born for This': Meet the First Black Woman to Launch a Community Solar Company," *Vogue*, October 27, 2020, https:// www.vogue.com/article/meet-kristal-hansley-wesolar-ceo.

13. Operations

1. Ovul Sezer, Kelly Nault, and Nadav Klein, "Don't Underestimate the Power of Kindness at Work," *Harvard Business Review*, May 7, 2021, https://hbr.org/2021/05/dont-underestimate-the-power-of-kindness-at -work.

2. N. P. Podsakoff, S. W. Whiting, P. M. Podsakoff, and B.D. Blume, "Individual- and organizational-level consequences of organizational citizenship behaviors: A meta-analysis," *Journal of Applied Psychology*, 94(1), 122–141, https://doi.org/10.1037/a0013079.

3. "The Fundamentals of Open-Book Management," The Great Game of Business, accessed July 11, 2023, https://www.greatgame.com/faq/open -book-management.

4. "2019 Edelman Trust Barometer Global Report," https://www.edelman .com/sites/g/files/aatuss191/files/2019-02/2019_Edelman_Trust_Barometer _Global_Report.pdf.

5. News, A. B. C. n.d. "52 Dead in Bangladesh Factory Fire as Workers Locked Inside." ABC News. https://apnews.com/article/business-fires -bangladesh-19a033b8302726a5ff018edbbd5b5a2b.

6. Elle Morris, "Council Post: Why Consumer Trust in Direct-To-Consumer Brands Is on the Rise," *Forbes*, September 24, 2019, https://www .forbes.com/sites/forbesagencycouncil/2019/09/24/why-consumer-trust-in -direct-to-consumer-brands-is-on-the-rise/?sh=632d9607134d.

7. Emy Demkes, "The More Patagonia Rejects Consumerism, the More the Brand Sells," The Correspondent, April 28, 2020, https://thecorrespondent .com/424/the-more-patagonia-rejects-consumerism-the-more-the-brand -sells.

8. Craft. "Patagonia Revenue." Accessed June 25, 2020. https://www .statista.com/chart/28257/patagonia-inc-revenue-company-db/.

9. David Gelles, "Billionaire No More: Patagonia Founder Gives Away the Company," *The New York Times*, September 14, 2022, https://www

.nytimes.com/2022/09/14/climate/patagonia-climate-philanthropy
-chouinard.html.

10. "Why Regenerative Organic?," Patagonia, accessed July 11, 2023,
https://www.patagonia.com/regenerative-organic/.

11. "Recycled Down," Patagonia, accessed July 11, 2023, https://www
.patagonia.com/our-footprint/recycled-down.html.

12. "Advanced Global Traceable Down Standard," Patagonia, accessed
July 11, 2023, https://www.patagonia.com/our-footprint/traceable-down
-standard.html.

13. "Recycled Nylon Fabric," Patagonia, accessed July 11, 2023, https://
www.patagonia.com/our-footprint/recycled-nylon.html.

14. "Fair Trade," –Patagonia, accessed July 11, 2023, https://www
.patagonia.com/our-footprint/fair-trade.html.

15. "Owned and Operated," Patagonia, accessed July 11, 2023, https://
www.patagonia.com/where-we-do-business/owned-and-operated.html.

16. "Family Business," Patagonia, accessed July 11, 2023, https://www
.patagonia.com/family-business/.

17. "Worn Wear," Patagonia, accessed July 11, 2023, https://wornwear
.patagonia.com/.

18. "Living Wage," Patagonia, Accessed July 11, 2023, https://www
.patagonia.com/our-footprint/living-wage.html.

19. Corey Simpson, "Broad Coalition Sues to Stop Trump Administration's Unlawful Dismemberment of the Bears Ears National Monument,"
Patagonia Works, December 6, 2017, https://www.patagoniaworks.com
/press/2017/12/11/broad-coalition-sues-to-stop-trump-administrations
-unlawful-dismemberment-of-the-bears-ears-national-monument.

14. Giving Back

1. "Champion for All," Champion, Hanes Brands, 2023, https://www
.champion.com/championforall.

2. "Our Mission," Soapbox Soaps, 2023, https://www.soapboxsoaps
.com/pages/ourmission.

3. "Pro Bono," Chapman, 2023, https://www.chapman.com/probono.

4. "About," Likewise Go & Do, accessed July 11, 2023, https://
likewisecoffee.com/about.

5. "How We Fund," Patagonia, accessed July 11, 2023, https://www
.patagonia.com/how-we-fund/.

6. Tin Shed Ventures, Patagonia, accessed July 11, 2023, https://www
.tinshedventures.com/.

7. One Percent for the Planet, 2023, https://onepercentfortheplanet.org/.

8. "Portfolio," Tin Shed Ventures, accessed July 31, 2022, https://www
.tinshedventures.com/#partners.

9. "Cleaning up Electronic Waste (E-Waste)," United States Environmental Protection Agency, December 3, 2018, https://www.epa.gov/international-cooperation/cleaning-electronic-waste-e-waste.

10. "Explore a World of Repair," iFixit, accessed July 11, 2023, https://www.ifixit.com/.

15. Voice

1. Larissa Faw, "Millennials Expect More than Good Products, Services to Win Their Loyalty," *Forbes*, May 22, 2014, https://www.forbes.com/sites/larissafaw/2014/05/22/millennials-expect-more-than-good-products-services-to-win-their-loyalty/.

2. Aryn Fields, "60+ Major Companies Join HRC Urge Texas Governor Abbott & Elected Leaders across the Country to Abandon Anti-Transgender Efforts," Human Rights Campaign, 2022, https://www.hrc.org/press-releases/60-major-companies-join-hrc-urge-texas-governor-abbott-elected-leaders-across-the-country-to-abandon-anti-transgender-efforts.

3. "Businesses for the Ban on Styrofoam Containers in NYC!" petition, Change.org, July 10, 2017, https://www.change.org/p/ban-styrofoam-a-petition-to-the-nyc-city-council-speaker-from-nyc-businesses.

4. Rachel Barton, Masataka Isikawa, Kevin Quiring, and Bill Theofilou, "To Affinity and Beyond: From Me to We, the Rise of the Purpose-Led Brand," Accenture Strategy, 2018, https://www.accenture.com/_acnmedia/thought-leadership-assets/pdf/accenture-competitiveagility-gcpr-pov.pdf.

5. "We Are Still In," accessed July 11, 2023, https://www.wearestillin.com.

6. Dan Avery, "LGBTQ Rights Fight Reignited 4 Years after N.C.'S 'Bathroom Bill' Controversy," NBC News, December 8, 2020, https://www.nbcnews.com/feature/nbc-out/lgbtq-rights-fight-reignited-4-years-after-n-c-s-n1250390.

7. "Socially Responsible Causes Ben & Jerry's Has Advocated For," Ben & Jerry's, accessed July 11, 2023, https://www.benjerry.com/whats-new/2014/corporate-social-responsibility-history.

8. "5 Ben & Jerry's Flavors on a Mission," Ben & Jerry's, February 22, 2018, https://www.benjerry.com. https://www.benjerry.com/whats-new/2018/02/social-mission-flavors.

9. "Environmental Internship Program," Patagonia, accessed July 11, 2023, https://www.patagonia.com/environmental-internship-program.html

10. Finis Dunaway, "The 'Crying Indian' Ad that Fooled the Environmental Movement," November 21, 2017, https://www.chicagotribune.com/opinion/commentary/ct-perspec-indian-crying-environment-ads-pollution-1123-20171113-story.html.

11. Mary Papenfuss, "Nike's Online Sales Soar after Colin Kaepernick Ad Campaign Launches," HuffPost, September 7, 2018. https://www .huffpost.com/entry/nike-online-sales-soar-in-wake-of-kaepernick-ad -campaign_n_5b92f887e4b0511db3e24df2.

12. Gijs Corstens, "Corporate Activism: Why Is This a Thing, and What Does It Mean for Us?" Medium, August 12, 2019, https://medium.com /@gijscorstens/corporate-activism-why-is-this-a-thing-and-what-does-it -mean-for-us-b9216cc9d9eb.

13. Alex Goldmark, "Ben and Jerry's Becomes a B Corporation," *Fast Company*, October 22, 2012, https://www.fastcompany.com/2680771/ben -and-jerry-s-becomes-a-b-corporation.

14. "About Us," Ben & Jerry's, accessed July 11, 2023, https://www .benjerry.com/about-us.

15. "Brands: Ben & Jerry's," Unilever, accessed July 11, 2023, https:// www.unileverusa.com/brands/ice-cream/ben-jerrys/.

16. "Our Caring Dairy Standards," Ben & Jerry's," https://www.benjerry .com/whats-new/2020/08/caring-dairy-standards.

17. "Cage Free Eggs," Ben & Jerry's, accessed July 11, 2023, https://www .benjerry.com/values/how-we-do-business/cage-free-eggs.

18. "Sustainable Packaging," Ben & Jerry's, accessed 11, 2023, https:// www.benjerry.com/values/how-we-do-business/sustainable-packaging.

19. "About the Milk with Dignity Program," Migrant Justice, accessed July 11, 2023, https://migrantjustice.net/about-the-milk-with-dignity -program.

20. Marie Solis, "Ben & Jerry's Showed America What Real Corporate Activism Looks Like" HuffPost, July 31, 2020, https://www.huffpost.com /entry/ben-jerry-ice-cream-corporate-activism_n_5f1b11dec5b6296 fbf423019.

21. "2020 Social and Environmental Assessment Report," Ben & Jerry's, https://www.benjerry.com/about-us/sear-reports/2020-sear-report.

22. "2020 Social and Environmental Assessment Report," Ben & Jerry's.

23. https://www.huffpost.com/entry/ben-jerry-ice-cream-corporate -activism_n_5f1b11dec5b6296fbf423019

24. Ariel Knoebel, "Ben & Jerry's and the Business of Brands Getting Political," *Forbes*, November 5, 2018, https://www.forbes.com/sites /arielknoebel/2018/11/05/ben-jerrys-and-the-business-of-brands -getting-political/.

25. Jessica DiNapoli and Jonathan Stempel, U.S. Judge Weighs Ben & Jerry's Claims against Owner over Israeli Business, *U.S. News & World Report*, August 8, 2022, https://money.usnews.com/investing/news /articles/2022-08-08/u-s-judge-weighs-ben-jerrys-claims-against-owner -over-israeli-business.

18. Measuring Impact

1. "How to Measure Social Impact," Brightest, accessed July 11, 2023, https://www.brightest.io/social-impact-measurement.

2. "B Impact Assessment," B Lab, 2023, https://www.bcorporation.net /en-us/programs-and-tools/b-impact-assessment.

3. "IRIS+," Global Impact Investing Network, 2023, https://iris.thegiin .org/.

4. "SASB Standards," IFRS Foundation, 2023, https://www.sasb.org/.

5. "ISO: International Organization for Standardization," January 22, 2019, https://www.iso.org/home.html.

6. "Learn about Environmental Management Systems," United States Environmental Protection Agency, November 5, 2014, https://www.epa .gov/ems/learn-about-environmental-management-systems.

7. "GRI Standards Download Homepage." 2019. Globalreporting.org. 2019. https://www.globalreporting.org/standards.

19. Lessons Learned

1. Urban metabolism is a theory defined by C. Kennedy as "the sum total of the technical and socio-economic process that occurs in cities, resulting in growth, production of energy and elimination of waste." *Source*: Kennedy, C., J. Cuddihy, and J. Engel-Yan. 2007. "The Changing Metabolism of Cities." *Journal of Industrial Ecology*, 11(2), 43–59.

20. Opportunities Unique to Social Enterprise

1. Witold Henisz, Tim Koller, and Robin Nuttall, "Five Ways that ESG Creates Value," *McKinsey Quarterly*, November 14, 2019, https://www .mckinsey.com/capabilities/strategy-and-corporate-finance/our-insights /five-ways-that-esg-creates-value.

2. "2022 Sustainable Investment Survey," PitchBook," October 4, 2022, https://pitchbook.com/news/reports/2022-sustainable-investment -survey.

3. Rachel Barton, Masataka Isikawa, Kevin Quiring, and Bill Theofilou, "To Affinity and Beyond: From Me to We, the Rise of the Purpose-Led Brand," Accenture Strategy, 2018, https://www.accenture.com/_acnmedia /thought-leadership-assets/pdf/accenture-competitiveagility-gcpr-pov.pdf.

4. Sara Horowitz, "94 Percent of Millennials Want to Use Their Skills for Good," HuffPost, July 25, 2014, https://www.huffpost.com/entry/94-of -millennials-want-to_b_5618309.

5. Gaurav Lahiri and Jeff Schwartz, "2018 Global Human Capital Trends: The Rise of the Social Enterprise," Deloitte Insights, March 28,

2018, https://www2.deloitte.com/us/en/insights/focus/human-capital-trends/2018/introduction.html.

6. "Rural Energy for America Program Renewable Energy Systems & Energy Efficiency Improvement Guaranteed Loans & Grants, Rural Development, United States Department of Agriculture, 2023, https://www.rd.usda.gov/programs-services/energy-programs/rural-energy-america-program-renewable-energy-systems-energy-efficiency-improvement-guaranteed-loans.

7. "Grant Programs for Pollution Prevention," United States Environmental Protection Agency, June 3, 2013, https://www.epa.gov/p2/grant-programs-pollution-prevention.

8. "Funding Database," Social Enterprise Alliance, accessed July 10, 2023, https://socialenterprise.us/funding.

9. "Loans," United States Small Business Administration, accessed July 10, 2023, https://www.sba.gov/funding-programs/loans.

10. "Lender Match Connects You to Lenders," United States Small Business Administration, accessed July 10, 2023, https://www.sba.gov/funding-programs/loans/lender-match.

11. "About CDFIs," CDFI Coalition, May 19, 2021, https://cdfi.org/about-cdfis/.

12. "Lending," Mountain Association, accessed December 6, 2022, https://mtassociation.org/lending/.

13. GroFin, 2023, https://www.grofin.com/.

14. "How IA Works," Invest Appalachia, accessed July 10, 2023, https://www.investappalachia.org/how-ia-works.

15. "Invest," RSF Social Finance, accessed July 10, 2023, https://rsfsocialfinance.org/invest/social-investment-fund/.

16. James Chen, "Impact Investing Explained: Definition, Types, and Examples," Investopedia, July 20, 2022, https://www.investopedia.com/terms/i/impact-investing.asp.

17. "Our Work in Action: Fund," Common Future, accessed December 7, 2022, https://www.commonfuture.co/initiatives/capital-strategies/.

18. A cap table, or capitalization table, is a document that lists all of a company's investors and security holders and the amount of the company each party owns.

19. "Invest in Founders Building the Future," Wefunder, accessed July 10, 2023, https://wefunder.com/.

20. Raise Green, accessed July 10, 2023, www.raisegreen.com.

21. Kiva, accessed July 10, 2023, https://www.kiva.org/borrow.

22. "The Ashoka Fellowship," Ashoka, accessed December 4, 2022. https://www.ashoka.org/en-us/program/ashoka-fellowship.

21. Eight Industries Ripe for Social Innovation

1. "Average Age of U.S. Farmer Climbs to 57.5 Years," Farm Progress, April 11, 2019, https://www.farmprogress.com/farm-life/average-age-us-farmer-climbs-575-years.

2. "Q1 2022 Agtech Report," | PitchBook," June 17, 2022, https://pitchbook.com/news/reports/q1-2022-agtech-report.

3. "Technology Solutions for a Safer Global Food Supply," Secure Food Solutions, accessed July 10, 2023, http://www.secure-food-solutions.com/.

4. Goodr, accessed July 10, 2023, https://goodr.co/.

5. Re-nuble, accessed July 10, 2023, https://www.re-nuble.com/.

6. Phinite, accessed July 10 2023, https://www.phinite-us.com/.

7. Nori, accessed July 10, 2023, https://nori.com/.

8. CQ Insights. https://www.cq-insights.com/what-we-do.

9. "About Mae," Mae, accessed July 10, 2023, https://www.meetmae.com/aboutus.

10. Farm to Flame Energy. https://ftfenergy.com/.

11. EarthEn. https://www.earthen.energy/.

12. Zoe Bulger and Ethan Rouen, "How Fintech Can Deliver on Its Social Impact Promises," *Harvard Business Review*, July 15, 2022, https://hbr.org/2022/07/how-fintech-can-deliver-on-its-social-impact-promises.

13. Altro, accessed July 10, 2023, https://www.altro.io/.

14. "Edtech Market," Future Market Insights, May 2022, https://www.futuremarketinsights.com/reports/edutech-market.

15. Access Ingenuity, accessed July 10, 2023, https://www.accessingenuity.com/our-products/.

16. Wonderschool, accessed July 10, 2023, https://corp.wonderschool.com/.

17. PowerUp Fitness, accessed July 10, 2023, https://www.powerupfitness.net/.

18. NPR. https://www.npr.org/2021/11/08/1052198840/1-5-degrees-warming-climate-change.

19. "Q3 2022 Carbon & Emissions Tech Report," PitchBook,November 9, 2022, https://pitchbook.com/news/reports/q3-2022-carbon-emissions-tech-report.

20. "Climate Tech Market," Future Market Insights, June 2023, https://www.futuremarketinsights.com/reports/climate-tech-market.

21. Jackson Ryan, "Machines That Suck CO2 out of the Air Promise to Reverse Emissions. Will They Work?" CNET, November 9, 2021, https://www.cnet.com/science/machines-that-suck-co2-out-of-the-air-promise-to-reverse-emissions-will-they-work/.

22. "Carbon Overview," Interface, accessed July 10, 2023, https://www
.interface.com/US/en-US/sustainability/carbon-overview.html.

23. SkyNano Technologies, accessed July 10, 2023, https://www
.skynanotechnologies.com/.

24. Air Protein, accessed July 10, 2023, https://www.airprotein.com/.

INDEX

Lilly Tench believes in using innovation and entrepreneurship to address the world's most pressing problems. Over the past ten years, she has worked with hundreds of social entrepreneurs in industries from energy to agriculture and gained crucial insight into the opportunities and complexities of mixing mission and money. Early in her career, Lilly worked alongside No Impact Man to design sustainability education and engagement programs around the world and also helped manufacturers to improve their environmental impact through an organization called ITAC. She later joined the NewLab team and helped to start an innovation center for entrepreneurs in an abandoned shipbuilding facility that is now home to over 800 entrepreneurs. Lilly went on to support cleantech researchers at Columbia University Technology Ventures and agtech innovators at the non-profit AgLaunch, and she currently works as director of the Spark Cleantech Accelerator at the University of Tennessee Research Park. Lilly has a BA in Peace and Social Justice from Berea College and an MBA and MS in Agricultural and Natural Resource Economics from the University of Tennessee.

Valentina Kalashnikova (@segoshvishna) is an illustrator who specializes in creating beautiful, hand-drawn pieces in a playful, whimsical style. With a passion for traditional art techniques, she has honed her skills in sketching, inking, and coloring to bring her imaginative ideas to life. She started her journey as an artist at a young age, constantly doodling and experimenting with different mediums. As she grew older, she discovered a love for storytelling through illustration and decided to pursue it as a career. Eventually she launched her own business as a freelance illustrator, working on a variety of projects, ranging from website graphics to book illustrations.

For Indiana University Press

Brian Carroll, Rights Manager

Dan Crissman, Trade and Regional Acquisitions Editor

Samantha Heffner, Trade Acquisitions Assistant

Brenna Hosman, Production Coordinator

Katie Huggins, Production Manager

Darja Malcolm-Clarke, Project Manager/Editor

Dan Pyle, Online Publishing Manager

Pamela Rude, Senior Artist and Book Designer

Stephen Williams, Marketing and Publicity Manager